Light for the Way

LIGHT FOR THE WAY

Seeking Simplicity, Connection, and Repair in a Broken World

THE EDITORS OF *SOJOURNERS*

Broadleaf Books
Minneapolis

LIGHT FOR THE WAY
Seeking Simplicity, Connection, and Repair in a Broken World

31 30 29 28 27 26 25 1 2 3 4 5 6 7 8 9

Library of Congress Control Number: 2025938996 (print)

Cover design: Studio Gearbox
Cover art by David Carlson, Studio Gearbox

Print ISBN: 979-8-8898-3541-7
eBook ISBN: 979-8-8898-3542-4

Printed in India.

Compiled and edited by Rose Marie Berger for Sojourners.

The mission of *Sojourners* magazine is to articulate the biblical call to social justice, inspiring hope and faith-rooted action.

Rose Marie Berger is senior editor for *Sojourners* magazine. The editorial team at *Sojourners* includes Mitchell Atencio, Jenna Barnett, Josiah R. Daniels, Mariela Esparza, Josina Guess, Tyler Huckabee, Hojung Lee, Darren Saint-Ulysse, Julie Polter, and Betsy Shirley.

The Life-Light blazed out of the darkness;
the darkness couldn't put it out.

—John 1:5

Contents

Chapter 2
Lay Me Down
Rest and Sabbath

Chapter 3
When Enough Is Enough
Simplified Life

Chapter 5
Green Confessions
Creatureliness

Chapter 6
"Led Out in Joy"
Communal Resilience

Acknowledgments

Sojourners owes a debt of gratitude to all the writers of faith and social witness who have contributed to our magazine in print and online for more than fifty years. We are honored to share a few of them in this anthology.

Introduction

Welcome. We're glad you are here.

If you have picked up this book or opened it on your reader, there is a reason. Something in you is seeking an authentic spirituality—something deeper, wider, more truthful, and more generous than what you may have grown up with or are experiencing in the surrounding culture. Maybe you are worn out by grief, exhausted by work, or sick of the politics of hate and division. Or maybe you have decided that no one is going to steal your joy, hijack your happiness, or trivialize your truth. Welcome. You are in the right place. This is the right book.

More than fifty years ago, a group of students at a Christian seminary were having an experience similar to yours. They were studying the Bible, reading the newspaper, and throwing house parties. Many of them were from conservative Christian families, but the lessons learned there didn't prepare them for a world that was changing rapidly. When they read their Bibles, they paused on certain passages. From the prophet Micah: "Do what is fair and just to your neighbor, be compassionate and loyal in your love, and don't take yourself too seriously—take God seriously." From Jesus: "I was hungry and you fed me, I was thirsty and you gave me a drink, I was homeless and you gave me a room . . ." and "You cannot serve God and wealth." From the father of a sick child: "I believe; help my unbelief!"

Those seminary students wanted to expand the conversation. They put their questions into a magazine that eventually took the name *Sojourners*. They landed on this name because they felt like strangers in their own country. The questions they asked about war and peace, white supremacy, economics, care for the earth, the dignity of women, the joy of children, and what daily habits *actually* bring us closer to God were spread across the magazine pages—sparking a conversation that goes on today in our print and online publications. *Sojourners* is less interested in "sin management" and more interested in prompting conversations that help us become more who God made us to be.

Today, Sojourners is a place where we put faith into action for social justice. We cherish the perspective of the marginalized—whether from communities that are economically poor, or communities made vulnerable because of gender or sexuality or immigration status, or those suffering from state or social violence, or the marginalized earth community itself. It is in these communities that one can find the front lines of liberation. Liberation of the mind, body, and spirit. But liberation and finding one's true self are not for the self alone. Liberation is always for the service and mutual aid of others.

Sojourners are ordinary people trying to follow Jesus in a complex and changing world. We have one foot in the church and one foot in social movements—so we are constantly tripping over our own feet! But we try to own our mistakes, make amends, and pick ourselves up when we fall. We are constantly changing, while holding fast to our faith and our practices. This book is one way of sharing our conversations with you.

The essays in this collection—some very short and some more in-depth—are the fruit of generations of "question askers." Is it possible to be truly, deeply quiet in this world? Is holy rest even an option in a culture that works us to exhaustion? Does the way I live really matter as long as I try to be an honest person? Do churches do any good? What do trees know that people have yet to learn? Can different religions work together? Why might an agnostic go back to church?

What are your questions? If you are ready to step onto a road that started before you and will go on after you, then read on. Enjoy the stories. Laugh at the humor. Mark up what makes you angry or afraid. Underline what makes your soul sing and share it with a friend. Trust your own wisdom and be curious about the experiences of others.

Welcome. There *is* a light blazing in the darkness. Let's step toward it together.

—Rose Marie Berger
Senior Editor, *Sojourners*

Chapter 1

How to Be Alone

Contemplative Practices

In an era of epidemic-level loneliness, why is it a good thing to spend time alone? To be alone with God is very different from the loneliness of not being known, seen, or recognized. Growing our souls depends on practicing spiritual openness to the Mystery that created us. Whether fumbling through centering prayer, as Julia Alvarez describes in this chapter, living deeply into fifteen-hundred-year-old Benedictine practices, or teaching contemplation in prisons, hospitals, and shelters, we must constantly be refreshed by the divine. But is a contemplative life still possible?, asks Jonathan Wilson-Hartgrove. At Sojourners, we continually experiment with new ways to grow our souls.

(Mis)understanding the Spiritual Practice of Centering Prayer

Julia Alvarez

I was going through a period of grieving when a friend in my St. Stephens' family told me about a centering prayer/meditation group that met Thursday afternoons at the church. I had never heard the term "centering prayer," but I had tried meditation a number of times. "I'm no good at that," I explained, but her quiet kindness was persuasive. Hey, maybe there was something in it for me, too. I thought I'd give it a try.

As I attended more sessions and read more and more about centering prayer, I realized that my initial reaction revealed what was impeding growth. Being good at something, succeeding at it, was how the hardworking, achievement-oriented me had (mis)understood this spiritual practice. That hardy, eager little self—going also by the name of ego—had served me well to get to where I had gotten, but it was often a handicap in the territory I was beginning (cautiously) to enter with my Thursday afternoon group.

I recall at one point complaining, as little selves are wont to do, that I felt like a too-large Alice crammed into a small box when I meditated. I was right. My robust ego, with whom I was overly identified, would never make it through the narrow meditation door and into the beautiful garden. No wonder I had been baffled by phrases such as "Blessed are the poor in spirit." Really? Wouldn't Jesus want us to be rich in spirit? Poverty empties us for the hugeness of God. I had to let go.

At one point we went around the circle, sharing what had brought each one here. When my turn came, I blurted out that I had come to learn to die. I thought the group would sigh and single me out as a soul in need of some serious work—they wouldn't have been far off the mark there. Nevertheless, everyone nodded. We're all here to learn how to die.

I know, it sounds unappealing. But that's only if we forget the second part of the story: resurrection, new life. Unfortunately, the way there leads through Golgotha, no shortcuts.

It's not an easy task: the continual putting aside of that eager little self and returning to a prayer phrase (hundreds of little deaths in the half hour). Feelings, thoughts, prizeworthy lines of poetry, amazing insights, mounting to-do lists blow in like weather. We sit quietly until that front blows through, knowing that, inevitably, another front follows. (Did I say hundreds? Make that thousands!) Doing so is a lesson in humility, in letting go, in not succeeding, dying to perfection. "Letting go, letting God," the popular phrase goes.

There's a poem by Czeslaw Milosz, "Love," that summarizes what I've experienced on this journey. Milosz writes that love means learning to look at ourselves the way we look at distant things. He adds that this practice will heal our hearts. Birds and trees will call us "friend."

I like to think of centering prayer as the discipline by which we put ourselves in perspective, breath by breath, moment by moment, so that love in all its forms can enter us, befriend us.

Ultimately, the work is not really done by us. Transformation happens without our knowing or controlling it, even without our understanding it. But, friend, the good news is that healing happens, the door opens a crack, we catch a glimpse of the garden.

Julia Alvarez was the author of many books, including *Afterlife*, *How the García Girls Lost Their Accents*, and a picture book for young readers, *Already a Butterfly: A Meditation Story* when this appeared in the June 2020 issue of *Sojourners*.

How a Week with Benedictine Sisters Made Me a Better Radical

Hannah Keziah Agustin

In the quiet oratory of Holy Wisdom Monastery in Middleton, Wisconsin, I spent my mornings gazing at the face of Jesus. On the far wall of the room where we prayed, hung an icon of Jesus holding a tablet that read, "Behold, I make all things new." Outside, the prairie was a technicolor parade of coneflowers, whorled milkweed, and purple loosestrife, while robins, cardinals, and song sparrows continued their song; but it was hard for me to believe that Christ was making things new in the present.

It was July 2023, and the smog from the wildfires in Canada covered much of Wisconsin, including the grounds of the monastery. Israel had just launched the largest military operations in the West Bank city of Jenin since 2002. Typhoon Egay had caused landslides and flooding in the northern part of the Philippines, where many of my friends and family members resided. All creation groaned, and even in the monastery, I could hear the cry so clearly.

I was sure the Benedictine sisters heard it too, because part of the liturgy was dedicated to praying for the prisoners on death row, the hungry who did not have food, and the unhoused who didn't have shelter during the smog and the heat wave. I was there for a week as a summer steward, a program of the monastery to teach young single women about Benedictine spirituality, creation care, and monastic rhythms. While the world burned around us, we sat in stillness, praying three times a day, speaking the words of a forthcoming kingdom in the Magnificat, "He has cast down the mighty from their thrones, and has lifted up the lowly."

Sister Lynne Smith, prioress of Holy Wisdom, said that her love for justice began with reading the Psalms. During the Gulf War in 1990, Psalm 79 struck her, particularly verse 3: "They have poured out blood like water all around Jerusalem, and there is no one to bury the dead." More than three decades later, this passage still resonates with her, especially as she has seen Palestinian blood pouring out in Gaza. Because she is pained by seeing people suffer, she believes that God, too, is pained by seeing people suffer.

"These were not just words. People experienced it," Smith said, hit with the daunting realization that the Psalms, too, were prayers for people who were suffering. It is a book about Hebrew people on the margins who are exiled, oppressed, and affected deeply by war, which then gives us a picture of a people cared for by God. "[Justice] is a central concern of God, hence it should be a central concern for us," she said.

This is why Smith finds it important to pray specifically for those who sigh under the heavy hand of injustice. She learned to trust that even though she is not directly involved in providing aid for a war on the other side of the world, she can still pray in solidarity with people. Prayer, too, is necessary in the work of restoration.

The Benedictines live this restoration out by seeing the image of God in everyone. Praying for people in marginalized communities broadens the world of Benedictine brothers and sisters who have vowed to be rooted in their community and may not interact regularly with the people for whom they are praying.

"In the Benedictine life, prayer is at the center," Smith said. "But that does not absolve [us] from action."

This action shows in works of mercy, which requires a faith that is neither bound by time nor geography. God carries out justice through all of those who have been called—whether we are in the monastery or in the world.

The God Who Finishes Justice

In the Benedictine tradition, there is a belief that God is the one who finishes the good work of justice.

"[W]hen thou dost begin any good thing that is to be done, with most insistent prayer beg that it may be carried through by Him to its conclusion," writes Benedict of Nursia in the Prologue to his Rule.

Humankind is simply invited to offer the work of our hands to be used as God wills. Having developed a deep center in Christ, what we do flows not from our own strength, which can cause burnout and make our hearts callous. Instead, God's grace gives us the capacity to be tender to the sufferings of the world, just as Christ was tender. It gives us the ability to be firmly anchored in the knowledge that God will not tarry in carrying out justice.

In the week I spent at the monastery, faithfulness was cultivated in me. Every day, after morning prayer, we went out to work. In the sisters' garden, we harvested bok choy, Swiss chard, and zucchini. In the prairie, we weeded invasive species and collected seeds for the Dane County Park System. The monastic life taught me to return to the ground with patience and expectant hope, just as I would in prayer. Every day, we returned to the field to get dirt under our fingernails and do the same thing over again. Through this, I learned that the life of work and prayer are not separate. They both draw from the well of Christ's love.

It was with the Benedictines that I learned that the work of justice and prayer for it to come to earth are rooted in the same hope and spoken in the same breath. While tilling the ground, I realized I was harvesting the fruits of centuries of impassioned work and prayer of monastics, and I, too, was partaking in it by being devoted to work the patch of land that was in front of me. And when I failed, I was liberated to try again because my flailing attempts at obedience were not in vain.

In the monastery, I was radicalized to believe again—that mercy abounds for the hurting, that faith is available to the unbelieving, and that justice is coming. I needed God to give me the eyes to see it and the hands to work for it. As a radical, it is my job to work and pray but it is not my job to bring justice to this world. I remember the gentle gaze of Jesus in the oratory. During centering prayer, when my mind would wander to the thick haze of smog outside the window, his face grounded me. I remember how revelatory it was to realize that it is Jesus who I am called to behold, not injustice. For even the dark is not dark to him who is light.

Hannah Keziah Agustin was an opinion writer for the Spring 2024 Sojourners Journalism Cohort when this article appeared on sojo.net on July 30, 2024.

A Sign and a Choice
An Interview with Joan Chittister

Joyce Hollyday

The Benedictine sisters in Erie, Pennsylvania, share a rich community life centered in prayer and ministry and, under Joan Chittister's leadership, have become well known for their commitment to feminism and peacemaking. Joyce Hollyday interviewed Chittister while enjoying their hospitality.—The Editors

SOJOURNERS: You are part of a tradition that goes back more than fifteen hundred years, and one of the major aspects of that tradition is the importance of community. Religious life has always taken the shape of community. Could you talk a little about why that is so?

JOAN CHITTISTER: It's Basil, a Father of the Church, who says, "Whose feet shall the hermit wash?" That question is the basis of the spirituality of community.

The function of the Christian community in sharing the bedrock of Christian spirituality is the upbuilding, the co-creation of the kingdom; the bringing of the kingdom now, the bringing of now for the kingdom. So, like the community recorded in the book of Acts, the major witness of the new Christian community is the creation of an alternative way of life.

Benedict of Nursia, founder of the Benedictines, deepened his own spirituality to the point that he had a new vision of the

Christian life. He looked around post-Constantinian Rome and saw a well-established, politicized church. It was a church that had been made church by virtue of the baptism of the emperor and his decree that all his subjects would likewise be baptized.

An analogy would be an emperor who was a basketball player decreeing that basketball should be the only sport in the empire. So everybody plays it; but that doesn't make everybody a basketball player. So the emperor decreed that everybody was Christian, but that didn't make everybody a Christian. Benedict was immersed therefore in a "pagan Christian" culture.

Although the Edict of Constantine in 313 liberated Christianity in Europe, it also began the murky merger of the sacred and the secular. And that's been as much a burden as it has been a blessing.

That's the environment that young Benedict of Nursia saw 150 years later in the late fifth century in Rome. He didn't attempt to convert Rome. We have no history of Benedict of Nursia preaching in the streets, approaching the government, or going to church figures; he simply left Rome to begin an alternative way of living.

He provided a sign and a choice—not an argument or a program. And that sign and choice is the Christian community at the level of a radical dimension of love.

What is the radical dimension of love? It is the sign that strangers can become sisters and brothers in Christ. And what's the power of this community in 1987? We've never had a more fragmented world, or a more pseudo-nationalistic world, or a more chauvinistic world. And so, if monasteries and convents and intentional religious communities are a sign of anything, they're a sign that you can transcend all the differences, all the barriers, all the impossibilities, all the things that people say can't come together.

Monasteries are a collection of all the differences of the world made one in Christ. And that's the nature of communal spirituality. It's reflecting in the contemporary community, in the ongoing Christian community, what was the sign and model of the community of Acts.

SOJOURNERS: Could you say a little more about how communities continue to be signs and models in contemporary society?

CHITTISTER: Any Christian community has within itself the possibility of transcending every institutionalized division against which the world is presently struggling. Economic divisions are transcended in communities with a common purse. Personal differences, meaning ethnic differences, are transcended in common living. Hierarchical differences, differences in power and wealth, are transcended by the creation of a community of equals.

Political differences are transcended in the gospels. We carry one banner, we follow one Christ, we develop one kingdom. And those are precisely the enigmas and the conundrums with which the present world is dealing. Those who say that Christian community life is irrelevant or out of date may well themselves be irrelevant and out of date. It has never been more contemporary, except maybe when it all started!

Prayer

SOJOURNERS: Could you comment on the role of prayer in your community specifically, and in the life of any community? How have you developed a spirituality of community?

CHITTISTER: We all, I believe, accept the notion that the function of prayer is not to cajole God into saving us from ourselves. The function of prayer is not magic. The function of prayer is not bribery of the Infinite. The function of prayer is not to change the mind of God.

The function of prayer is to change my own mind, to put on the mind of Christ, to enable grace to break into me. So, if you're going to have a communal spirituality and witness, then you must have a praying community.

The monastic community has a prayer life, developed around what St. Benedict called the *opus dei* and what the churches traditionally called the "divine office," what we now call the "liturgy of the hours." It's the speaking of the psalm life of the people of God for our own time.

The psalm life has three dimensions: personal, national, and global. The psalmist prays out of the struggles of the psalmist, out of the struggles of the people, and out of the consciousness of the cosmic, of the universal: "All nations shall stream to you"; "You shall see the poor"; "In you are all things." So, this prayer life of a Benedictine monastic community is equally conscious on all three levels.

I'm here as an individual intent on contemplative conversion, intent on developing in my life over a period and process of time the ability to see with the eyes of Christ, and to put on the mind of Christ. I'm here as part of a community that claims to be a Christian community, and therefore has to struggle with its interpersonal agendas, with the life needs of one another, with being something other than itself. In order to do something, I have to be something. In order to be for someone else, I have to be part of a group. And then finally, we're here praying out of consciousness for the whole global community, for all the people of God.

To some the notion of monastic life is a phenomenally well-institutionalized narcissism. It is precisely the opposite. If and when it ever becomes that, it's at its most decadent. When monastic life is life only for the monastics, then it ceases to be monastic life. That's the paradox of it. When prayer is privatized religion on a spree, it's not prayer.

What is the contemplative life? In the first place, "contemplation" and "enclosure" are not synonyms. Enclosed communities are not necessarily called to be any more contemplative than my own community. Enclosure is a vehicle for contemplation. But so is stopping by the beaten person on the roadside.

The oldest mystics that we have in organized religious expression—the fathers and mothers from the desert, the gurus of the Sufi tradition, the masters among the Hasidim—all have similar parabolic insights into contemplation. There is a story about the master saying to the disciples, "Tell me how you know when it is dawn." And one disciple says, "Master, is it when we can tell the fig tree from the lemon tree at a hundred paces?" And the master says to the disciple, "No, that is not how you will know it is dawn."

So a second disciple says, "Well then, master, is it when you can tell the sheep from the goats at fifty paces?" And the master says, "No, that is not how we shall know when it is dawn." Then the third disciple says, "Well then, master, how do we know that we have seen the dawn?" And the master says, "We will know that we have seen the dawn when we can see the face of Christ in the face of any brother or sister, no matter how near or how far."

That's contemplation. That's the fruit of the contemplative life. And unless you're putting on the mind of Christ, I don't know if you'll ever see the face of the Christ in the other, or the face of the cosmic, or the face of the people of God in the other. You may be a highly efficient social worker or a marvelously compassionate do-gooder, but you will not necessarily be a Christian contemplative.

SOJOURNERS: Given all that you've said about the different ways contemplation happens, how important are discipline and ritual as part of contemplation, particularly in the life of a community?

CHITTISTER: I happen to think it is of the essence. It's profoundly important. Obviously, we don't think a discipline of prayer can be dispensed with; we do it three times a day as a community. That's the essence of the monastic vocation.

I wouldn't argue that every community has to do it as a community. But I would argue that every community has to have a community spirituality, and that it must be regularly ritualized, so that in prayer and liturgy and ritual we are as able to express ourselves as a community as we would at supper, at Christmas, or in work. Because the spirituality is the bedrock of the community. We have to be formed in a common spirituality not just for the sake of communication but for the sake of common energy, common values.

In a monastic community it's imperative for us that as a whole group we call ourselves to spiritual development at least twice, and usually three times, a day; and that we be a place where others can come, knowing at certain times the community will always be in prayer together, and that they have a praying community to relate to as their own life requires it. I can't honestly think that you could have a community spirituality unless that spirituality were communal.

SOJOURNERS: But I've also heard here a great deal of emphasis put on individual spirituality and the recognition that the communal spirituality is made up of individual spiritualities.

CHITTISTER: Absolutely. By communal spirituality and common values, I never mean a "marshmallow mind."

Religious communities, and monastic communities in a special way, are probably the only institutions left in the United States in which every generation lives under the same roof.

We have sisters upstairs in their eighties who have been in this community for more than sixty years! There is no way that the spiritual life of a twenty-five-year-old can match the spiritual life of an eighty-year-old. It doesn't make the eighty-year-old's spiritual life better, necessarily. It isn't any more sincere or any more real than the spiritual life of our twenty-five-year-olds.

But a twenty-five-year-old can only have a spiritual life that comes out of twenty-five years of experience. So she comes in with her own agendas, her own angels to wrestle with, her own ideals, her own questions; and the eighty-year-old has long since put those questions down. She has another full set of questions.

We each bring our own questions, our own angels, our own internal wrestlings, and our own special gifts to community prayer and out of community prayer to be lived in very special ways. We're not talking about a "common mind," we're talking about a "communal mind." And they're not the same thing.

In addition to that, in the Benedictine monastic tradition, preceding and succeeding the communal prayer is also the concept of Lectio Divina, the meditative personal reading of scripture. What is this scripture about? And what is it saying to my life? And the development of the private contemplative mentality comes out of all that. Communal spirituality guarantees the provision of an environment together for growth alone.

SOJOURNERS: One of the things that has most touched me here is the sense of community that exists not only among those of you who are here, and not only among contemporaries in other places, but also with those sisters who preceded you. During the daily prayer, you often pray for the sister who died on this day in 1970, or 1906, or 1862. Being a member of a community with fifteen years rather than fifteen-hundred years of tradition, I sometimes envy that sense of history. What does it mean to have the strength of that tradition, what do you feel you draw from it, and what responsibility do you feel toward the generations that will come after you?

CHITTISTER: Well, you've put your finger very, very sensitively on what, for me, and I think for most of the members of this community, is one of the gems of the tradition and a piece of glue in the house. That is, we pray for two people every single day, and they will be prayed for from now for as long as this community lasts.

In the morning we pray for the sister who died on this date in any year since our community's foundation in 1856; and in the evening we pray for the sister next to die. So here you have a custom that very consciously links the great moment of community, the past and the future.

When people ask, "How many are there in your community?" I always say, "A little over three hundred—about one hundred and fifty of us are in the cemetery, and about one hundred and fifty of us are at home." Our older sisters have lived with almost all those people, except our earliest founders; but they lived with people who lived with our earliest founders.

So all of that history is very much alive in the house. Why? Because we know who built the buildings that we all live in. And we know who's going to build the next set of buildings that we're going to minister in.

The irony is that this notion of the continuing community through time to the end of time becomes a very strong foundation for change. Because you are continuous, you can change.

Because so many went before you, on such a different path, you are freed to make your own path. Because if they did it, so can you. They survived, so can you. If they were made holy by it, so can you. It's a chain of memories that makes the future possible.

When we were facing renewal in 1970, after Vatican II, we remembered that in 1850 three young women left a monastery in Bavaria that was already seven hundred years old and came here to start over again. So, that prayer is a prayer of possibility and a prayer of support. Since it's happened to those before us, we will be with those for whom the great light is now. And some day our own great light will come and be appended to that list.

For instance, I entered the community when I was sixteen, and I've been here now more than thirty years. So in the chapel when we pray for Sr. Pierre, that first sweet old wonderful woman who showed us how to do dishes here, she's right there. I remember her.

Sr. Pierre was already a little sunken gnome of a woman by the time I got here, but very bustling, very quick, obviously the cornerstone of the house. She was what in those days was called a "domestic sister." She was a cook, and she did laundry and things of that nature. And she always had a wonderful word for the youngsters in the house.

In those days, the mother superior always put out the assignment book—we called it just "The Book"—on Friday nights. And you rushed home from school on Fridays to check the book on the chapel window to see what you were assigned to do the next week. Was it to wait tables, or to read the scripture, or to answer the door? I can remember standing at the book on a Friday afternoon, and I obviously was not pleased with my assignment. Sr. Pierre came by and put her little gnarled arm around me and said, "Now darlin', you be rememberin' this. When you come to the book and ya get what you like then Jesus give ya a hug. But if ya come to the book and ya get what ya don't like, then Jesus bends right down and kisses ya." When we pray for her in chapel, I say to myself, "Okay, Pierre, I'll try to remember."

SOJOURNERS: It is often said that one of the signs of the health of a community is its sense of hospitality toward others who are not part of a community, and certainly the many times I've visited here I've been overwhelmed by this community's sense of hospitality. I would say that among your many gifts, hospitality is one of the strongest. How does that sense of hospitality relate to your sense of community and spirituality?

CHITTISTER: Well, it's definitely basic to the Benedictine Rule. One of the most widely quoted phrases from the Rule is the chapter on the reception of guests. It's a very interesting chapter when you consider that, at least in modern minds, the Benedictine life is seen as a basically ascetic, withdrawn, otherworldly mode.

But you cannot find the foundation for that mode in the Rule, which contains an entire chapter on the reception of guests. The chapter begins, "Let all guests who arrive be received as Christ, because Christ will say 'I was a stranger and you took me in.' And let due honor be shown to all, especially to those of the household of the faith and to wayfarers."

Now that's a key line in a fifth-century rule. Nothing was more dangerous than crossing Europe. Benedictine monasteries were the first Holiday Inns of the Western world. [They were some] of the few places where people could come and sleep well and not have to worry about being mugged, rolled, or knifed in their sleep.

It was a tremendous contribution to the western Europe of the time. You could cross Europe and stay in a monastery of your own tradition every single night, because they were spaced a day's journey apart. So, for a Benedictine not to practice hospitality is for a Benedictine not to practice Benedictinism.

It's a very special gift, and I think it has an awful lot to say to our own time. The Benedictine monasteries were among the first to take the sick and the dying into their own infirmaries. Because death in a pagan world was a punishment, there were all sorts of taboos surrounding death. Barbarian peoples left the dying on the sides of the roads. And the monasteries were very, very quick to begin the first hospices, so that these people could die in clean beds in a Christian environment.

The chapter goes on to say, "When therefore a guest is announced, let them be met by the superior and the community with every mark of charity."

Now, what's the implication? They're not pests. You don't throw them in a room and ignore them. You make them welcome: "It is good for us that you have come."

The Rule says, "And let them first pray together." This is the Christian community that you've come to. And our first gift is to come down into this consciousness of God with us, so that we can get the most from one another. It's a contemplative encounter, an encounter blessed by the presence of God.

"And then let them associate with one another in peace." We're not here to contend. You did not come to be converted. There'll be no Catholic magic. No attempt to evangelize. No proselytizing. You will simply come as a creature of God, and therefore you must be [a] gift.

"The kiss of peace should not be given before a prayer hath been said on account of satanic deception." That's not necessarily a reference to chastity. It's a reference to the notion of why you are about what you are about. This is not a human act. You're not here because you're friend or lover. This is the reception of the people of God to the place of God, in a godly way.

And then the chapter says, "In the greeting let all humility be shown to the guest, whether coming or going." In other words, no arrogance, no status, no display of pomp. "Welcome to my house." This is hospitality almost in the biblical Middle Eastern sense, meaning you are doing me the favor. I get to give something away. I've been given a great abundance. Now how shall I possibly distribute it, unless you come?

So the function of community is to make community for the other. For those who don't have the opportunity, perhaps, for community. Or for those who are without their own community at this moment. Or for those who think that no community would have them at this moment.

There's another great chapter in the Rule on the abbot's table. It reads, "Let the abbot's table always be with the guests and the travelers." When I was a kid in this community, we weren't allowed to eat with anybody, and we weren't allowed to eat out. When we read this, I would think, "Huh, Mother gets to go to all the parties."

When I got older, I discovered what they were really asking of the Superior. If you are the sign and symbol of the center of this community, of its environment and its character, its ministry and its fidelity to the gospel, then you, my friend, shall be the sign of hospitality and community to every person who walks into this house.

And they shall all eat with you. Not in the kitchen, not with the help, not with the novices. They shall be received at your table. You are going to take them right into the heart of the community—the abbot who is the house, the abbot who breaks bread, the abbot who gives away what the community has to give away. The abbot who says there's no separation here, we don't receive you here as an inconvenience or a stranger. You are here as gift so that we can give.

SOJOURNERS: I think younger communities can learn from your tradition of hospitality. When you're involved in so many activities, as we are at Sojourners, sometimes you want to come home and have home just be home. And welcoming people isn't always easy. But when I come here, I always experience the richness of that tradition and the fact that hospitality is indeed a commitment of every member of this community.

CHITTISTER: There must be some truth in what you're saying, because I've heard it from so many people. One guest summed it up with exquisite artistry. She said, "I always get the feeling when I come to this community that I am everybody's guest. You can't pass anybody in the hall who doesn't say, 'Can I help you?' or 'Do you know where the coffee is? I'll take you there.'"

As I listened to her, I couldn't understand why this was surprising to her. I would just take that for granted. Then I discovered that she is a businesswoman and a single parent; she's always doing for somebody else. And she is basically ignored in the apartment complex in which she lives. She carries the kids and the groceries up and down the stairs without any help. She does all those things that people have to do to struggle through life and expects to be ignored.

And then she comes to a place where everybody is expressing concern about her comfort. It seems to me, God willing, it does exist here; but if it does, it's because it should.

SOJOURNERS: I think it exists because you don't just receive the guest, you receive each other in a way that says "I care about your comfort. I'm concerned about you."

CHITTISTER: I'm completely convinced that you cannot have hospitality in the community unless the level of the community cohesion and concern is high at all times. I have always maintained that the level of your hospitality will be measured by the depth of your prayer. And the depth of your prayer will be measured by your degree of hospitality. These three things are sides of a triangle—the members' genuine human concern and affection for one another; their opening [of] that concern to take in the others who come; and the prayer and the gospel, which are the reason we're doing this.

SOJOURNERS: On one hand, you've said community can't exist only for itself, because it needs to exist for people beyond itself. On the other hand, I think there is sometimes the temptation among those of us who live in community to see community only as a base out of which we offer our ministry to the rest of the world. Could you discuss that kind of tension?

CHITTISTER: That's an important question, and not easily answered. It touches on a much broader and much more clarifying question of communal spirituality. Let me look first of all at what I clearly know best, which is the history of Roman Catholic communities and spirituality.

In the history of community life in the Roman tradition, we have two types of community spirituality: monastic spirituality and apostolic spirituality. Everything I have said to this point, I would argue, applies to both traditions, but monastic spirituality institutionalizes some of those qualities quite differently than apostolic spirituality.

Monastic life is communal life, and so is apostolic life, to a certain extent. But to the monastic, community is primary, and out of community comes the expression of prayer and ministry. In apostolic communities, ministry is primary. And ministry leads to the formation of community and the development of the prayer life.

Benedictine tradition says that the Benedictine charism is to seek God in community and to respond in prayer and ministry. The apostolic tradition says, "Our function as Christian communities of faith is to serve the people of God in ministry for the upbuilding of the kingdom." I think that is an accurate rendering of how most apostolic communities would state their mission. If you are a monastic, you certainly have ministries. And if you are in the apostolic tradition, you certainly have faith communities, so they're going to erupt in prayer. But the styles of community, the expressions of community in prayer, and even the ministry, may well differ, in order to focus on the basic element.

Community life as it's structured or expressed by a monastic community may not be at all the same as in an apostolic community. For instance, an apostolic order may live in much smaller groups than we live in. Or they may group around their works, where we would group around the community

We would go to a place to be together, to be a sign of community, and then minister out of whatever gifts were there. An apostolic community may say, "This is a ministry that must be given to these people," and so those people who are capable of giving that ministry would go there. Each of those spiritualities will develop expressions of prayer and community. That's an important distinction to me, in reference to your question.

Your question points to another central question for all of us, which is, does the community exist as a vehicle for my ministry? I would argue that that assumption is false in either a monastic or apostolic community. Even when a common ministry is what draws us into the faith life and community, that does not give me the right to use that group as simply a touchstone for my own work.

The function of community life is for us to be and do together what we cannot possibly do nearly as well alone. Can you pray alone? Yes, you can. Can you pray better in a group that enhances and is a vehicle for your prayer? Yes, you can. Can you work alone? Of course you can. Will you work with more energy and probably more effectiveness if you're working with a group of similarly committed people? Yes, I think you will.

Will you be a sign of Christian presence and sense of community alone? Certainly. Will you be an even stronger, clearer, more capable sign of community if you're being supported by people who think about community the way you do? Yes, you will.

If you find somebody who thinks that the community exists in order to facilitate their own agenda, they haven't formed their communal spirituality. Communities don't exist; they're developed. And community is developed by community members. When I'm not developing community for you, and I'm simply using what you develop for me as a way to go about my interests in life, I'm not living community. I'm allowing you to create it for me; but I'm not living it.

I only live community when I, too, create community. And that means that you can't be the only person in charge of the guests. It can't be just your responsibility. That's when a community will get ineffective and unbalanced—when some of us expect the rest of us to keep it in existence.

That is not to say that everyone does the same things. Everyone doesn't have to be on hospitality, but we must all be hospitable. Everyone doesn't have to perform the same community task, but every one of us has to perform our community task. Everyone does not have to be responsible for the same things in the same ways, but we must all feel a responsibility for this community. No other sign of community will be authentic.

Needful Joy

SOJOURNERS: Your community exudes joy and celebration. How is that related to your prayer life?

CHITTISTER: Let's look at three dimensions of that. A long time ago, the Catholic Church made the distinction between ordinary days and feast days. The church punctuated the calendar year with feasts. The whole notion was to lift moments of time out of the humdrum for special consideration.

Feast days were very important in early Europe, in an agrarian society that worked so hard from dawn to dark. The peasants and the serfs carried the entire economy on their backs. The feast day was one of the ways that the church, like the

Jews in the observance of the Sabbath, brought equality to the society.

It was a long time before the forty-hour [work] week. But the church said this great feast is like a Sunday, and therefore you cannot force these serfs to work. So it was free time. It was the first contribution to the labor movement, the first contribution to equality, and it was a profound theological contribution to the notion of hope. It was a sign that the victory had come for some, that life was a great gift.

Now you take that concept of joy in the Christian tradition and you add it to the concept of redemption and salvation, the Messianic prophecy, and you embody it in your life. You're not talking about cocktail parties, you're not talking about organized laziness, you're not talking about shirking your responsibility, you're not talking about being unreal.

How can Christians celebrate? How can peace people celebrate when you are looking down the barrel of a neutron launcher? How can you women possibly be happy when you live in a church that treats you as if you are less than full human beings? Because the victory has been won. And hope has come. And light has been seen. And some people have shown it.

So it's an absolute theological essential to celebrate. Any religion or any community or any period of history or time that wipes out joy and feast I find very suspect. More neurotic than holy.

Here the church has been faithful as an institution over time. No matter what warped spiritualities might get hold of the people, the church has always been a sign of joy and of celebration.

Now it's an easy move from that consciousness of the face of joy as a theological necessity to joy in prayer. Prayer is not a discipline. Prayer is a dispensation from the humdrum. Prayer is a chance to take a look at other things.

Prayer is a chance to sit down and reflect on something more important than getting out today's mail. The more sincere a Christian you are, the easier it is to fall into that bear trap, and, consequently, to lose a depth of spirituality that's tragic. It's a spirituality that corrupts instead of uplifts.

The function of prayer is to give expression to the signs of joy and hope you see. And it's also the place to count your real joys.

Now if joy is theologically necessary, and if it is provided for in its gentlest form in a regular prayer life, then it is clearly apparent in the life of the community. It has to be. You have a right then. It legitimates happiness!

There used to be this marvelous poster quoting Leon Bloy: "There's no such thing as a sad saint." And I believe Thomas Merton said, "Joy is the infallible sign of the presence of God." The celebrating community, then, is the community that rejoices in its Christianity and in the fact that it is community.

Community comes with a genuine respect and acceptance of one another as people. And you celebrate that. And you make it by celebrating it.

Play exposes us as people. Once you have played with all these people, you just treat them so much more gently in their personal lives, in community meetings, in the discussions of who you are as a group. Joy and celebration enable you to keep humanity in mind.

Joan Chittister, OSB, the author of many articles and books, was prioress of the Mount Saint Benedict priory in Erie, Pennsylvania, president of the Conference of American Benedictine Prioresses, a *Sojourners* contributing editor, and a regular columnist for the *National Catholic Reporter* when this interview appeared. **Joyce Hollyday** was *Sojourners* managing editor when this article appeared in the June 1987 issue.

Is a Contemplative Life Still Possible?

Jonathan Wilson-Hartgrove

Not long ago, a young man stopped me after a sermon and asked a direct question: Is a contemplative life even possible in twenty-first-century America?

He deserved more of an answer than I gave him. His question brought me back to the life and witness of the Trappist monk Thomas Merton, who died forty-nine years ago yesterday. I sadly don't have the young man's address to follow up with him in person, but in memory of Merton, and in gratitude for the challenge, here's my open letter to this young man and his question.

Dear Ben,

I know it has been a while since we met, but I'm writing because I've been seeing your face when I close my eyes. I recall how you stood half-apologetically at the back of a post-sermon greeting line. You lingered until the crowd was gone, asking if I had time. You'd come seeking a word.

The way your face looked at that moment is how it is etched in my memory, your question written in your gaze: *Could a young married man like yourself live a contemplative life in twenty-first-century America?* You wanted to know what it might look like in practice.

I'm sorry that I don't remember what I said. It couldn't have been much—you thanked me and left in time for me to make it to lunch. But now in the quiet of prayer, you are with me.

And this is prayer, I think—paying attention long enough to see what rises to the top. You are here because you are, in some way, a mirror—an image of my own desire that brings me back to prayer, again and again.

The psalms teach, "As the deer longs for living waters, so my soul thirsts for you, O God."

Every hunger and love and longing I've ever felt ultimately points me toward God, my heart's true home. And in a sense, the contemplative life you asked about is as natural as a deer bowing its head to drink from a stream. But you wanted to know whether it is possible for you. Which is to say, you know something about how difficult it is to become yourself in this world.

In the last century—the one in which both you and I were born—the most popular spiritual writer in America was a man named Thomas Merton. Like you, he realized in early adulthood that everything around him was shouting, in no uncertain terms, that he should want the very things that got in the way of what he had begun to sense his heart really wanted. "We live in a society," Merton wrote in *The Seven Storey Mountain*, "whose whole policy is to excite every nerve in the human body and keep it at the highest pitch of artificial tension, to strain every human desire to the limit and to create as many new desires and synthetic passions as possible, in order to cater to them with the products of our factories and printing presses and movie studios and all the rest."

We call this system we have created "advanced capitalism," and we often celebrate its seemingly miraculous capacity for creative destruction and limitless growth. But modernity has its downside, and Merton learned to see it clearly—first from his father, an artist who despised bourgeois values, and later from communists, who emerged from capitalist society's internal contradictions.

Thomas Merton was an intelligent man, who trusted reason as far as it could take him. But his own mind told him that an aesthetic sensibility and a good critique of the status quo was not enough to save the world from the mess we are in. It was, after all, not enough to save him from himself.

This capacity to get beyond our self-deception—to see that the evil of the world is rooted in our own hearts—is the first gift that leads us toward contemplation. I'm not sure any of us can come to this on our own. "We only know sin on the way out," the theologian Karl Barth said.

As we face the twenty-first-century realities of ISIS-backed terrorism and reactionary Christian nationalism, we are grappling with the nature of evil, as Merton and others did in the late 1930s. Given the similarity of our contexts, Merton's insight is prescient. "There was something else in my own mind," Merton wrote in *The Seven Storey Mountain* as he watched World War II coming, "the recognition, 'I myself am responsible for this. My sins have done this. Hitler is not the only one who has started this war: I have my share in it too.'"

If my inner life is as messed up as the obviously broken world around me, your question carries all the more weight: *Is a contemplative life even possible?*

Because Merton had the vocation of both a contemplative and a writer, we have in his writing a record that might serve as a geography of your question. I hesitate to try to sketch some kind of path for you on top of Merton's cartography, which is so intimate, so personal, so inevitably particular. But Merton was always holding his own contemplative journey alongside the written record that preceded him—St. John of the Cross, St. Bernard, *The Cloud of Unknowing*, and the Little Flower. We do not need roadmaps on this journey so much as fellow travelers.

So, a few directions from one who traveled this way before us:

If the source of our problem is at our core, as Merton saw, we need nothing short of an inner apocalypse to open a way toward true contemplation. "Our desire for God must come from God and be guided by his will before it means anything in the supernatural order," he wrote in *The Sign of Jonas*. In essence, we must be born again.

How does this happen? The desire driving your question is itself a sign that God is at work. God grows us up into Christ by forming our hearts in the psalms. Like a fitness enthusiast enjoying a runner's high, Merton delighted in the psalms after his conversion, carrying his breviary everywhere he went and making the world his monastery.

Once he'd settled down into the rhythms of life at Gethsemani, the Divine Office often felt like a burden to him. He so wanted to be alone. Only obedience kept him coming back to sing the psalter seven times a day.

Then, one day some eight years in, a revelation from *The Sign of Jonas*: "This is the secret of the psalms. Our identity is hidden in them. In them we find ourselves, and God. In these fragments he has revealed not only Himself to us but ourselves in Him."

So make time for the psalms, learn to sing them, and keep following their path, even when you no longer want to. Merton's experience echoes millennia of monastic wisdom: God wants to shape our desires as we make the words of the psalms our own.

If we follow this path, where can we expect it to take us? Merton knew that the contemplative life is as concrete and practical as a daily rhythm, as keeping promises to particular people, as the words of psalms passed down to us.

It is simple, as he often wrote, but it is not easy. Some practical formation, like psalms and obedience, is essential. But Merton also knew the temptation to overdetermine our understanding of the path laid out before us. "O Lord, I don't know where I'm going," he famously prayed in "The Merton Prayer." And this is, perhaps, his best summary of what the contemplative life feels like in practice: We must, each of us, give up the false notion that we could be more contemplative if we were somewhere else, if we were surrounded by other people, if we weren't the poor and broken souls that we are.

The contemplative life is fundamentally practical. It must be lived, and with our whole selves. But we do not arrive at contemplation by mastering some technique. We come by way of simplicity.

Merton may have said it most clearly when he wrote in "Day of a Stranger": "What I wear is pants. What I do is live. How I pray is breathe."

Is this even possible? Thank you for asking. Merton lived the question, and my sense is that you and I are called to live it with him. Can we live it in hope that the answer is yes? Not just in general, but for us, here and now?

The words of our Lord are the best answer we have:

"With people this is impossible, but with God all things are possible," (Matthew 19:26).

Trusting with you, Ben,

Jonathan

Jonathan Wilson-Hartgrove, a preacher, author, and community cultivator, was the author most recently of *Strangers At My Door: A True Story of Finding Jesus in Unexpected Guests* (Convergent) when this article appeared on sojo.net on December 11, 2017.

Finding God in the Depths of Silence

Richard Rohr

> Real interior silence, not just the absence of noise, is a foundational spiritual discipline. So why are we so resistant to enter into it?

When I first began to write this article, I thought to myself, "How do you promote something as vaporous as silence? It will be like a poem about air!" But finally I began to trust my limited experience, which is all that any of us have anyway.

I do know that my best writings and teachings have not come from thinking but, as Malcolm Gladwell writes in *Blink*, much more from not thinking. Only then does an idea clarify and deepen for me. Yes, I need to think and study beforehand, and afterward try to formulate my thoughts. But my best teachings by far have come in and through moments of interior silence—and in the "non-thinking" of actively giving a sermon or presentation.

Aldous Huxley described it perfectly for me in a lecture he gave in 1955 titled "Who Are We?" There he said, "I think we have to prepare the mind in one way or another to accept the great uprush or downrush, whichever you like to call it, of the greater non-self." That precise language might be off-putting to some, but it is a quite accurate way to describe the very common experience of inspiration and guidance.

All grace comes precisely from nowhere—from silence and emptiness, if you prefer—which is what makes it grace. It is both not-you and much greater than you at the same time, which is probably why believers chose both inner fountains (John 7:38) and descending doves (Matthew 3:16) as metaphors for this universal and grounding experience of spiritual encounter. Sometimes it is an uprush and sometimes it is a downrush, but it is always from a silence that is larger than you, surrounds you, and finally names the deeper truth of the full moment that is you. I call it contemplation, as did much of the older tradition.

It is always an act of faith to trust silence, because it is the strangest combination of you and not-you of all. It is deep, quiet conviction, which you are not able to prove to anyone else—and you have no need to prove it, because the knowing is so simple and clear. Silence is both humble in itself and humbling to the recipient. Silence is often a momentary revelation of your deepest self, your true self, and yet a self that you do not yet know. Spiritual knowing is from a God beyond you and a God that you do not yet fully know. The question is always the same: "How do you let them both operate as one—and trust them as yourself?" Such brazenness is precisely the meaning of faith, and why faith is still somewhat rare, compared to religion.

And yes, such inner revelations are always beyond words. You try to sputter out something, but it will never be as good as the silence itself is. We just need the words for confirmation to ourselves and communication with others. So God graciously allows us words, and gives us words, but they are almost always a regression from the more spacious and forgiving silence. Words are a much smaller container. They are always an approximation. Surely some approximations are better than others, which is why we all like good novelists, poets, and orators. Yet silence is the only thing deep enough, spacious enough, and wide enough to hold all of the contradictions that words cannot contain or reconcile.

We need to "grab for words," as we say, but invariably they tangle us up in more words to explain, clarify, and justify what we meant by the first words—and to protect us from our opponents. From there we often exacerbate many of our own problems by babbling on even further. In Matthew 6:7, Jesus had a word for heaping up empty phrases: paganism! Only those who love us will stay with us at that point, and often love will also tell us to stop talking—which is precisely why so many saints and mystics said that love precedes and prepares the way for all true knowing. Maybe silence is even another word for love?

Most of the time, "to make a name for ourselves" like the people building the tower of Babel, we multiply words and find ourselves saying more and more about less and less. This is sometimes called gossip, or just chatter. No wonder Yahweh "scattered them," for they were only confusing themselves (Genesis 11:4–8). Really they were already scattered people: scattered inside and out because there was no silence.

We are all forced to overhear cell phone calls in cafés, airports, and other public places today. People now seem to fill up their available time, reacting to their boredom—and their fear of silence—often by talking about nothing, or making nervous attempts at mutual flattery and reassurance. One wonders if the people on the other end of the line really need your too-easy comforts. Maybe they do, and maybe we all have come to expect it. But that is all we can settle for when there is no greater non-self, no gracious silence to hold all of our pain and our self-doubt. Cheap communication is often a substitute for actual communion.

Words are necessarily dualistic. That is their function. They distinguish this from that, and that's good. But silence has the wonderful ability to not need to distinguish this from that! It can hold them together in a quiet, tantric embrace. Silence, especially loving silence, is always non-dual, and that is much of its secret power. It stays with mystery, holds tensions, absorbs contradictions, and smiles at paradoxes—leaving them unresolved, and happily so. Any good poet knows this, as do many masters of musical chords. Politicians, engineers, and most Western clergy have a much harder time.

Silence is what surrounds everything, if you look long enough. It is the space between letters, words, and paragraphs that makes them decipherable and meaningful. When you can train yourself to reverence the silence around things, you first begin to see things in themselves and for themselves. This "divine" silence is before, after, and between all events for those who see respectfully (to re-spect is "to see again").

All creation is *creatio ex nihilo*—from "a trackless waste and an empty void" it all came (Genesis 1:2). But over this darkness God's spirit hovered and "there was light"—and everything else too. So there must be something pregnant, waiting, and wonderful in such voids and darkness. God's ongoing—and maybe only—job description seems to be to "create out of nothing." We call it grace.

God follows this pattern, as do many saints, but most of us don't. We prefer light (read: answers, certitude, moral perfection, and conclusions) but forget that it first came from a formless darkness. This denial of silence and darkness as good teachers emerged ever more strongly after the ironically named "Enlightenment" of the seventeenth and eighteenth centuries. Our new appreciation of a kind of reason was surely good and necessary on many levels, but it also made us impatient and forgetful of the much older tradition of not knowing, unsaying, darkness, and silence. We decided that words alone would give us truth, not realizing that all words are metaphors and approximations. The desert Jesus, Pseudo-Dionysius, *The Cloud of Unknowing*, and John of the Cross have not been "in" for several centuries now, and we are much the worse for it.

The low point has now become religious fundamentalism, which ironically knows so little about the real fundamentals.

We all fell in love with words, even those of us who said we believed that "the Word became flesh." Words offer a certain light, but flesh is much better known in humble silence and waiting.

As a general spiritual rule, you can trust this one: The ego gets what it wants with words. The soul finds what it needs in silence. The ego prefers light—immediate answers, full clarity, absolute certitude, moral perfection, and undeniable conclusion—whereas the soul prefers the subtle world of darkness and light. And by that, of course, I mean a real interior silence, not just the absence of noise.

Robert Sardello, in his magnificent, demanding book *Silence: The Mystery of Wholeness*, writes that "Silence knows how to hide. It gives a little and sees what we do with it." Only then will or can it give more. Rushed, manipulative, or opportunistic people thus find inner silence impossible, even a torture. They never get to the "more." Wise Sardello goes on to say, "But in Silence everything displays its depth, and we find that we are a part of the depth of everything around us." Yes, this is true.

When our interior silence can actually feel and value the silence that surrounds everything else, we have entered the house of wisdom. This is the very heart of prayer. When the two silences connect and bow to one another, we have a third dimension of knowing, which many have called spiritual intelligence or even "the mind of Christ" (1 Corinthians 2:10–16). No wonder that silence is probably the foundational spiritual discipline in all the world's religions at the more mature levels. At the less mature levels, religion is mostly noise, entertainment, and words. Catholics and Orthodox Christians prefer theater and wordy symbols; Protestants prefer music and endless sermons.

Probably more than ever, because of iPads, cell phones, billboards, TVs, and iPods, we are a toxically overstimulated people. Only time will tell the deep effects of this on emotional maturity, relationship, communication, conversation, and religion itself. Silence now seems like a luxury, but it is not so much a luxury as it is a choice and decision at the heart of every spiritual discipline and growth. Without it, most liturgies, Bible studies, devotions, "holy" practices, sermons, and religious conversations might be good and fine, but they will never be truly great or life-changing—for ourselves or for others. They can only represent the surface; God is always found at the depths, even the depths of our sin and brokenness. And in the depths, it is silent.

It comes down to this: God is, and will always be, Mystery. Only a non-arguing presence, only a non-assertive self, can possibly have the humility and honesty to receive such mysterious silence.

When you can remain at peace inside of your own mysterious silence, you are only beginning to receive the immense "Love that moves the sun and the other stars," as Dante so beautifully says in the *Divine Comedy*—along with the immeasurable silent space between those trillions of stars, through which this Mystery is also choosing to communicate. Silence is space, and space beyond time. Those who learn to live there are spacious and timeless people. They make and leave room for all the rest of us.

Richard Rohr, OFM, a Franciscan priest of the New Mexico Province, was founder of the Center for Action and Contemplation in Albuquerque when this article appeared in the March 2013 issue of *Sojourners.*

The Power of Story

Katherine Paterson

> Reading may not change the world—but it changes the reader, and that's a start.

The summer that I was seventeen years old, I, who was born of missionary parents in China, was rooming with a friend whose parents were missionaries in Africa. Although our mothers had been friends long before we were born, Mary and I first met as summer employees at our denomination's conference center when she came back to the United States to go to college. World War II had driven my parents out of China, so I had lived, since the age of eight, in various places in the southern United States.

One night after the day of waitressing was over, Mary began to read aloud to me Alan Paton's novel *Cry, the Beloved Country.* At first it was just the sound of Mary's Africa-haunted voice caressing the beauty of Paton's language that kept me wide awake and enthralled. But gradually, chapter by chapter, that beauty told me of the unspeakable oppression and tragedy that was South Africa's story for too many years. I'm not sure exactly when it happened, but suddenly one night the book came alive for me in a new way. I saw for the first time that the tragedy of South Africa was the tragedy of the American South, where I had been blind to the oppression from which I as a white person had been exempt. I began to cry, sob rather, for my own thoughtless sins and the sins of my people.

I look back on those tears as a turning point in my young life. I did not leave all my sins and fears on that wet pillow—I'm still not free from them—but I know my life began to change that night because of a book.

Caroline Gordon, in her book *How to Read a Novel*, speaks of the reading of a great book as a "conversion experience." You are not the same person when you finish the last page, she says, that you were when you first sat down to read. I believe, from my own experience, that Gordon is right, and that is why I think reading is so important to our growth as wise and compassionate human beings.

To understand and have compassion for others, we must begin by knowing ourselves, and that is the first gift of a great novel. In Eudora Welty's words, a novel "says what people are like. It doesn't . . . know how to describe what they are not like, and it would waste its time if it told us what we ought to be like, since we already know that, don't we? But we may not know nearly so well what we are as when a novel of power reveals this to us. For the first time we may, as we read, see ourselves in our own situation, in some curious way reflected. By whatever way the novelist accomplishes it—there are many ways—truth is borne in on us in all its great weight and angelic lightness, and accepted as home truth."

If we know ourselves and can love and respect ourselves, there is hope that we can reach out from ourselves to love and respect others.

This is a vision that is sadly lacking in our nation these days. We live in a society that seems to delight in division and derision. Each faction seems focused solely on its own agenda, and every faction sneers at those who dare to suggest that problems are complex, that perhaps there is no single solution—that we must listen and learn from each other—that we must consider our neighbor's problem as our own problem. It is a truism that we have become a nation where the first question in the face of any issue is, "What's in it for me?" Few groups, and only the rare individual, seem intent to pursue what might be best for the common good.

I don't think this lack of concern for the whole of society and the fact that many people aren't reading literature these days are coincidental. Of course, we can be deeply affected by music or art. We can be moved to action by photographs and film. The outpouring of money for Haiti came when Americans saw the devastating scenes of the tragedy on television. But what happens to that compassion when the pictures disappear from the screen? The outpouring of money was wonderful and badly needed in those first days after the earthquake, but concern for Haiti is at risk of evaporating now that media attention has gone on to some other story. To truly understand the tragedy of that poorest of countries in our hemisphere, for our initial response to turn into ongoing concern that will make a difference, we need to go deeper. We need to read.

The Sunday after the earthquake, *The New York Times* ran excerpts from books by Haitian writers. I wasn't even aware of these writers before. How can I know the Haitian people except as impoverished victims if I do not read what they say about themselves and their homeland? Justice is not a matter of handouts to those in need; it is a matter of aligning ourselves with those others, learning from them, respecting them, allowing ourselves to be changed, until they are no longer "others," because their welfare and our welfare are one.

Not many of us can or will go to live and work in Haiti, but we can read, and through our reading come to know the Haitian people, learn how we as a nation have contributed to their difficulties, and discover how they might wish us to stand with them in their rebuilding.

I am a writer of fiction, so my bias shows. I love novels because in them you don't only walk in other people's shoes—you eavesdrop on their souls. But great works of nonfiction will also help us to grow as just and compassionate persons. With Haiti so much on my mind, I cannot fail to mention Tracy Kidder's *Mountains Beyond Mountains: The Quest of Dr. Paul Farmer, a Man Who Would Cure the World.* I keep thinking of Farmer's expression, "fighting the long defeat," which is what the attempt to make a difference in Haiti amounts to, and though Farmer says, like any of us in the United States, he would like to be a winner, he has chosen to "make common cause with the loser." "We want to be on the winning team," Farmer tells Kidder, "but at the risk of turning our backs on the losers, no, it's not worth it. So you fight the long defeat."

These words have made me take a deeper look at all the long struggles for justice in the world—William Wilberforce's lifetime fight against the slave trade in England; the long campaign to end slavery in our own country and the many who suffered and died in the civil rights movement, which was the continuation of that long defeat; the struggle for voting rights for women; the ongoing striving for recognition and equal rights by those whose gender orientation is different from those of us in the mainstream. I could go on and on. Throughout human history, in every land, there have been those fighting the long defeat, those who will not turn their backs on the losers.

In many ways, this is the biblical struggle. We have to face it if we read the Bible: God has made "common cause with the losers."

Jesus read the prophets, and they shaped how he grew "in wisdom and stature, and in favor with God and people." After his baptism he took his commission from the book of Isaiah that he was to preach good news to the poor, to release the captive, to set at liberty the oppressed. How did we go from this commission to believing that Jesus' principal desire for his followers was to seek their own salvation from the world he died to save?

It is plain to me that not only the scriptures but many of the books I have read have shaped my own growth. I have to ask myself what this means for me as a writer of novels for the young. I believe strongly that there is a difference between story and sermon. When I am asked what message a book of mine is meant to convey, I answer that as the writer of the book, I know what I learned from writing it, but I don't know what a reader will learn from reading it. I do not have the right, nor do I want the right, to dictate to any reader what he or she will take away from my book.

Barbara Brown Taylor, in speaking of Jesus' narrative style, notes "how courteous it is, how respectful of the listener." Story and image, she goes on to say, "do not come at the ear the same way advice and exhortation do—although they are, I believe, even more persuasive. Perhaps that is because they create a quiet space where one may lay down one's defenses for a while. A story does not ask for decision. Instead, it asks for identification, which is how transformation begins."

But how, in this noisy, plugged-in world, is there hope that a child might read a book that would provide that space—that opportunity for transformation? Recent studies declare that the average eight-to-eighteen-year-old in America spends, each day, seven hours and thirty-eight minutes connected to some electronic device. That does not leave many waking minutes for reading a book that just might transform their lives. So what are we to do? We're not going to turn the clock back to my childhood, when the big threats to good reading were comic books and radio. We're not going to snatch the electronic devices from their ears or their fists.

I don't have the solution, but I do have a few suggestions.

First of all, we can show them that reading matters to us. We can let them see us reading. We can talk about books that we have read and ask them questions about issues that reading a book or an article has raised in our own minds. We can read aloud to and with them. Just the physical presence and the voice of a caring parent lets a child know that his or her parent believes that time spent reading and conversing with the child is more important than anything else on the parent's busy agenda. If we read together and talk about what we read, we create a language and a shared experience that will help us discuss difficult topics in a safe way. It is sad to think that for some children their chief memory of a parent's voice will be that of anger or demands. I am not naive enough to believe that just reading together will save the world, but it just may be a start. Charity, we have long heard, begins at home. And so does justice.

Katherine Paterson is the author of more than thirty books for young readers and a two-time Newbery and National Book Award winner. She was named the National Ambassador for Young People's Literature by the Librarian of Congress and served as an elder in the First Presbyterian Church of Barre, Vermont. This appeared in the May 2010 issue of *Sojourners*.

"Be Still and Know"
An Interview with Thomas Keating

Rose Marie Berger

Father Thomas Keating, OCSO, co-founded the centering prayer movement in the 1970s when he was abbot of a Cistercian monastery, St. Joseph's Abbey, in Spencer, Massachusetts. He and two other Trappist monks, William Meninger and Basil Pennington, began holding retreats to teach this method of prayer, which draws on contemplative church teachings such as those of the Fathers and Mothers of the Desert, John of the Cross, and Teresa of Ávila. Keating co-founded Contemplative Outreach, a worldwide nonprofit organization dedicated to encouraging the practice of centering prayer and Lectio Divina (praying the scriptures). Keating was in his eighties and still teaching and speaking on the riches of contemplation for those seeking a deeper experience of Christian faith when this interview took place. Keating was the author of several books on contemplative spirituality, including Manifesting God *(Lantern Books). He was interviewed at Sojourners by associate editor Rose Marie Berger.—*The Editors

SOJOURNERS: Why is contemplative prayer an essential part of Christian life?

THOMAS KEATING: Contemplative prayer is the movement of becoming acquainted experientially with God, beyond the confines of rational dialogue. It is deeply embedded in the gospel and in the Christian tradition. Jesus' suggestion about how to pray is a formula for contemplative prayer. In Matthew 6:6 he says if you want to pray—if you want to relate more profoundly with God—enter your inner room. Next, close the door, which is an invitation to turn off the internal dialogue. Then he says, "Pray to your Father in secret." That could mean a solitary place, but such were rare in Jesus' time for everybody except the very rich. Nobody else had private rooms; you were lucky to have a roof over your head. It's metaphorical language inviting us to become at ease and present to the divine indwelling, which is the life of the trinity within each of us. The kingdom of God is within you, as well as all around you.

You might define it as the intuitive knowledge in love with God. And so, this formula that Jesus suggests is clearly three steps into ever-deepening levels of interior silence. Then he says, "your heavenly Father will reward you." Actually, that word "reward" isn't very appropriate here. Someone who's praying—in secret, that is, having actually reached a contemplative disposition that's habitual in prayer—is not interested in reward. I discovered in the Aramaic Bible that [the word translated as "reward"] really means "blossom" or "flourish." This suggests that silence is the seedbed in which the Holy Spirit places the mustard seed of divine love. It takes root, and grows, and you blossom.

What is blossoming? The growth of faith, hope, and love—the virtues and especially the fruits of the Spirit listed in the Beatitudes and by Paul in Galatians 5. Contemplative prayer is a process of activating the gifts that we received in baptism.

SOJOURNERS: Do you see the recovery of that type of prayer as particularly essential in the United States?

KEATING: I'm in favor of it in every country, actually. Every culture is deeply distorted by the human condition, and self-interest, and what the Bible calls the "old man," in Paul's words. Which in psychological terms might also be called the false self—which is the only self we know, but it's the self that embodies all of the consequences of the Fall and hence is a program for unhappiness, for human misery.

SOJOURNERS: Many practitioners of contemplative prayer are Catholic. Why has this practice been largely lost in many of the Protestant and evangelical traditions?

KEATING: My observation is that at the time of the Reformation, the contemplative tradition as a practice was at the lowest ebb ever. So the Protestant Reformation unfortunately didn't have a tradition to take with it. So, whatever it has experienced in the way of mysticism has been somewhat limited to certain pockets of renewal.

The list [of contemplative practitioners] is long for Catholics—but it's not nearly long enough. It's barely scratching the surface. The whole thing has fallen out of Christianity. That's why thousands of young people and not-so-young people went to the East in the 1960s and '70s, looking for a spirituality they couldn't find here.

Now the evangelicals are in a special situation: They've had a lot of experience that is very significant, but no roots in the tradition. So they give the impression of having thought that nothing happened in Christianity from the death of the last apostle until they came along. They have a great contribution to make from their renewed perception of certain values in the gospel. But they would be greatly enriched if they became aware of the contemplative dimension, which is a deeper rooting of activity—at least, spiritual activity—in its true source, the experience of God, not just on the level of sense experience, or the devotion that is based on being born again. "Born again" is a wonderful gift, but it's not the end of the journey—it's just the beginning. I think that most serious evangelicals are aware of that. And they're beginning to read about the contemplative tradition.

SOJOURNERS: How do you respond to people who are put off by contemplative prayer because they associate it with New Age spirituality, or with a narcissistic spirituality that is just about a personal relationship with God with no outward focus?

KEATING: Yes, this is a problem. Centering prayer looks a little like navel-gazing. Such criticism has been directed at contemplatives for centuries. What's new is to call it New Age. It's not New Age; it's so Old Age that everything else is post-contemplative prayer. To this we simply say that we don't teach what you think we do. We're convinced that, if you can get an established practice and the mustard seed of divine love is sown in that seed of silence, where there is less resistance than in ordinary, daily levels of consciousness, you'll begin to take part in whatever ministry is appropriate. You cannot sit on divine love. But you can think you've got it, and go out there and then kill yourself with zeal and actually get burned out, if you don't have the inner resources to deal with tragedy, persecution, neglect, failure, and all the other things that accompany the gospel in its preaching as well as in every other human endeavor.

SOJOURNERS: Why is contemplative prayer important for socially and politically active Christians who very much see their ministry as out in the world—serving the poor, serving as peacemakers in situations of conflict, serving in prison?

KEATING: It's important for life. It's important to be whole. It's an essential part of holistic health. Science itself is beginning to recognize that meditation has substantial effects on health. Not just mental health, but physical health, because it reduces tension, high blood pressure, the usual ills that come from stress, or pain that we resist—suffering might be defined as pain that we resist. If we accept it, it's like anything else in life. It comes, and it goes, and it's inevitable, to some degree.

Centering prayer isn't the only way into contemplative prayer. We're putting an ancient prayer practice of the Christian tradition into a contemporary form and language, because people today like how-to methods. But that doesn't mean it's the only way in. The ancient practice of prayerful Bible reading, called Lectio Divina—reading the book we believe to be divine—is still the main focus in monasteries. The evangelical tradition, which is so biblically oriented, is a marvelous base for contemplative prayer. You don't have to do anything except set aside some time after the meeting or before the meeting just to be still. Which is what the psalms recommend: Be still, and you will know that I am God.

All we're asking or suggesting is twenty minutes, twice a day—you'll still have a full day's work. Centering prayer is not in opposition to all the good works of mercy or social action and justice. It will enhance one's capacity to function, especially in difficult ministries, by the activation of the fruits of the spirit.

We're trying to introduce a resource to give strength and perseverance to difficult ministries. We didn't deliberately set out to encourage people to do any specific ministry; we felt that they would find their own. And this is what's happened.

SOJOURNERS: When you speak of "we," are you referring to the Contemplative Outreach work that you're doing?

KEATING: Yes. Contemplative Outreach was founded in 1984 to support those that we had taught to do centering prayer, because it needs an ongoing education and support system.

We've tried to provide monastic means without either calling them monastic or insisting [practitioners] be like people in the monastery. But centering prayer is basically a distillation of monastic spirituality—a dose of solitude and silence, simplicity of lifestyle, and a discipline of prayer. That needs the context of a community. Centering prayer is not just a method of prayer; it's a way of life. It's a countercultural procedure. It doesn't talk loudly, but it challenges the presuppositions at the base of social injustice, at its roots, beginning with one's self. So, if one connects with it, it inevitably leads one to do all one can to end that injustice elsewhere.

We have groups working with the homeless. We have a program to offer retreats for AA groups. We're in at least ninety prisons. Almost any social justice or peace work could benefit from this—centering prayer would simply deepen it by rooting it in the gospel, in a way that's experiential and resourceful.

The heroic exercise of service can also lead to a contemplative state. For some people, nature is a way to God. Or conjugal love. Or art. But centering prayer is available in the literature of the Christian tradition, and people are living it today. So why not consult it? And oddly enough, science has finally started to ask us if contemplative experience is for real. The answer is yes. Judge for yourself.

This appeared in the December 2006 issue of *Sojourners*.

How to Be Alone

Alexander Jusdanis

Long before Karen Fredette became a Fredette, she was Karen Karper: a girl from Kent, Ohio, who everyone thought would become a nun.

The Karpers were devout Catholics. Two of her uncles were priests, and many of her relatives had entered monasteries. But Karen resisted, even if, as she admits now, it was mostly because she didn't want to wear the habit uniform. Then, as a teenager, she had a teacher—"a lovely young nun"—who changed her mind.

"I thought, well, if she can do it, I can do it," she said.

Once out of school, Karen entered a monastery of Poor Clare Nuns in Canton, Ohio.

"My goal was to deepen my prayer life," she said. "And while I could say that glibly when I was seventeen, I really had no idea what I was getting into."

She would stay there for thirty years. At first, she loved the quiet of the monastery, and how the rigid schedule fostered her spiritual development. But she gradually realized that it wasn't enough for her. She was always with her fellow sisters, when they prayed, when they worked, when they ate, and when it was time to relax.

"There's nearly always someone at your elbow," she said.

Late in her time in the monastery, a bad fever left her bedridden and alone. It was then that she got her first taste of true solitude.

"The more I let myself experience it, the more I wanted it," she said. "It's like chocolate candy."

Inspired, Karen decided to leave monastic life. She found a rent-free cabin a few hours away in Colt Run Holler, West Virginia. She moved in with just a hundred dollars and an old Ford Bronco. Alone in the woods, she became a hermit.

Like Karen, none of us had any idea what we were getting into when we paid our last tabs or checked out our last library books and shut our doors many months ago [at the start of the COVID-19 pandemic]. But I had a hunch that hermits like Karen, who have eagerly chosen an isolation more intense than any lockdown, might be able to help us through. Karen has become something of a spokesperson for hermits, coediting a newsletter on hermetic life and writing a number of books on her experiences. I got in touch with her, hoping she might be able to teach us—or rather, those of us with the privilege of staying home—how to be alone.

It is a skill we seem to have left behind. We live at a time when we can talk to just about anyone at any time in any place. And once constant communication becomes a habit, it's almost impossible to stop. Every pause, every moment of downtime, becomes an occasion to check our email.

In this ultra-social world, those who choose to opt out can almost seem like deviants. Consider the stereotypical hermit: a silent, frowning, and possibly bearded man whose misanthropy drove him away from society and forced him to brood his days away in some dark grotto.

But this is not Karen. She didn't choose hermetic life because she hated people. Rather, solitude was a way to free herself from herself.

When she moved into her hermitage, she spent her days walking the wilderness, cutting wood for the fire, writing, and praying. In all she did, she said she tried to open up to "whatever God was saying." Not the "old white man in the sky with a long white beard," she clarified. "The grace-life that is in every green thing, every rock, every tree, every person around us. And we can't see that unless we are less absorbed with what's going on inside us."

It is a foundational—and perhaps paradoxical—truth about the eremitical life: One must be alone to still their ego.

In solitude, self-image fades away, Karen explained.

"Something somehow knocks it up, gives it a 'swift kick in the pants,' like my dad used to say," she said. "You realize, *that's not me, and what I've lost, I don't need.*"

Shortly into our conversation, I felt a sense of calm—not because everything was going to be okay (because it wasn't), and not because I suddenly was okay with a lack of social life (because I wasn't). But through the phone, I felt the peace of the decades she'd spent in stillness and silence. It was a gift she could bestow upon me without losing anything of her own.

When I first emailed her, she responded with delight at the chance to share some of the wisdom that has come from being alone, though she didn't hesitate to dispute my choice of words.

"You know, you use the word 'isolation,' and I'm not happy with that word," she told me. "I like the word solitude better. I think of solitude as a life-giving experience."

I knew what she meant. I was very shy growing up. I was always confused about what people expected of me, and I broke down the minute I felt I'd done something wrong. I often pretended to be sick to avoid going to school and facing the implicit demands of teachers and classmates. As many anxious, unconfident children do, I turned to books to experience the pleasures of social life without the then-overwhelming cost of participation. Solitude was my life-saver.

But I never went full hermit; I never stopped wanting to be with people. Eventually, I forced myself to figure out how to make friends, and now I'm glad to have quite a few good ones. Even though I'm occasionally struck by the desire to leave everything behind and find my own cabin in the woods, I don't believe that I could survive very long without friends and family.

Surprisingly, Karen didn't believe it either, at first. The first few years in the monastery, she said, she stood around waiting for a sign from God that she should go back home to her family. The first Thanksgiving was especially tough. Her relatives always gathered at her family's big house to celebrate.

"I remember standing in the cell, realizing that all my fam is going to be there tomorrow, and I wasn't," she said. "I could hardly bear to visualize that."

She said she felt like throwing open the window and running back home. But she didn't.

"You survive it," she said, referring to the pain of separation. "You become a stronger, better person."

This month, across the country, people have begun to reunite with friends and family—not because it's necessarily safe to do so, but because people are tired of being apart, and because we were never granted the financial means to live otherwise.

Our eagerness to be with one another might explain a big twist in Karen's story.

Four years after she commenced hermetic life, she started working—hermits need money, too—in a parish rectory in a nearby town. Over the next two years, she developed a friendship with the priest, Paul Fredette. One late afternoon, he asked if she wanted to go pray in the chapel.

"I was very glad to do that," she said. She'd always felt a little awkward praying around others. But "sitting next to Paul," she said, "I felt not the least bit self-conscious."

Beside him, she said that she felt the same inner strength and quiet as she did alone. She and Paul got married and decided to leave the parish, "because too many people were going to be horrified."

"You know," she said. "'Look at the father running away with the sister!'"

Karen and Paul Fredette moved to the Smoky Mountains of North Carolina, where they live today.

After decades of self-imposed solitude, she became something of a community organizer for hermits through her and her husband's newsletter, "Raven's Bread." Sent by mail and email, it consists mainly of essays on the hermetic life submitted by some of the 1,160 subscribers, bringing together a dispersed community of people who have otherwise fled community. She's also written several memoirs recounting the lessons of her own journey into solitude.

Karen no longer considers herself a hermit, but she and her husband remain committed to her original hermetic ideals by not seeing friends or going to restaurants or the movies.

"We live a very quiet, hidden life," she said.

Perhaps the desire for others, in one way or another, never fully leaves. Loneliness, says Karen, is simply a fact of life.

"It's just one of those inevitable things that we all have to work our way through. And if you run from it, it's not going to get any better. You just have to sit down and be with it," she said. "You'll discover that there is life within you, and there is life around you, and it is teaching you all sorts of things—if you are listening."

If you're overcome by the pain of loneliness or boredom, she advised, don't just dissociate into a screen. Instead, throw yourself into a coat closet and shut the door. "Just stand there in the dark and the quiet, and let it pour into you for just fifteen minutes," she said.

"You could just come out a different person."

Alexander Jusdanis was a writer with work in *The Outline* and *Dissent* when this article appeared on sojo.net on June 22, 2020.

Why Bother?
An Interview with Kathleen Norris

Julie Polter

Listen in as Kathleen Norris shares how she bears insults and learns humility from the monks.

Writer Kathleen Norris admits that the spiritual concept of acedia is difficult for the modern mind to grasp. "It's sort of untranslatable," she says, with a clutch of English words—including torpor, apathy, indifference, sloth, despair, depression—approximating, but not capturing the fullness of the word as used by early Christian monastics. "Acedia is more than just restlessness, indifference, or despair," Norris explains. "It goes down to the Greek root, absence of care. For me, the essence of it is that inability to care."

In her book Acedia & Me: A Marriage, Monks, and a Writer's Life *(Riverhead Books), Norris explores acedia through monastic literature, contemporary culture, and reflection on her marriage, including the debilitating illness and death of her husband, David Dwyer. As with her previous books* The Cloister Walk, Amazing Grace, *and* Dakota, *Norris' far-ranging intellectual curiosity, gentle humor, and honesty about her own doubts and missteps make it a welcoming read for people of diverse spiritual experience.*

Acedia was, and is, almost a given for those living a monastic life—the commitment to place, work, and daily rhythms of prayer inevitably is dogged by periods of restlessness, malaise, even hopelessness. But Norris believes acedia is utterly relevant for the rest of us too. "Acedia can strike anyone whose work requires self-motivation and solitude," she writes, "anyone who remains married 'for better or worse,' anyone who is determined to stay true to a commitment that is sorely tested in everyday life." And she suspects that the individual experience of acedia is mirrored and multiplied in our cultural and political life. "The more I read about it in monastic literature and medieval theology, the more I realized this isn't just a personal problem, this is a societal problem," says Norris.

Among her primary weapons against acedia, Norris counts self-awareness, prayer, monastic writings, and the psalms. "I can always turn to the psalms and say, 'someone has been here before,'" she says. Hers isn't a precious piety, however; she observes that "the early monks are so great, because if you start thinking too highly of yourself, they really nail you."

Kathleen Norris spoke with Sojourners *associate editor Julie Polter by phone. At home in Hawaii, Norris was preparing to go on a pilgrimage to the Middle East and was looking forward to seeing the Sinai, where some of the desert mothers and fathers once lived.*—The Editors

SOJOURNERS: What impact did writing this book have on your life?

KATHLEEN NORRIS: One very personal thing is that it helped me put a lot of things from my marriage into perspective. I needed to do that, because my husband passed away almost five years ago, and it still feels like yesterday in some ways. This let me put the marriage into perspective and honor it. Another effect is realizing that I'm always going to struggle with acedia—just having written a book doesn't get me off the hook.

SOJOURNERS: What is the definition of acedia?

NORRIS: People would ask what my next book was about. If I said "sloth," they obviously thought it was boring. If I said acedia, unless they were Benedictines and Trappists, they wouldn't know what I was talking about. Acedia is more than restlessness, indifference, or despair. It's that inability to care, inability to even care that you don't care. And that's one of the biggest problems we have in the culture right now—indifference.

SOJOURNERS: Yet you observe that people can keep busy with good, important work and still be in the grip of acedia. So acedia isn't just manifested through inaction?

NORRIS: I'm someone who often runs with all four burners going and can get a lot done in a day. But one of my biggest temptations is to acedia. Keeping busy can foster indifference. You're so busy that you lose the ability to concentrate, to read seriously, because you're so used to skimming—you can't get the big picture. It's almost a form of self-protection. If we're really, really busy and we're running really fast, then nothing bad can happen. We're way too important to die. We're necessary because we're so busy. It's a mindset that many of us get into.

We certainly see compassion fatigue and burnout. People's willingness to use their energy and all their time to do something like work against poverty—there is that turning point where they just get burned out and can't do it anymore and it turns into indifference. Unless you're aware, it is likely to happen. It's the shadow side of caring. You also have to realize that it's okay to be indifferent to some things—you're not going to save the world by acting on every single thing that comes along.

There's a saying from the early monks that says, "A disciple who bears insult is like a tree that is watered every day." That perspective really helps because it makes you realize that whatever someone says to you, it's their burden, not yours. The danger, if you're aware that you're doing good in the world, is that you can start to assume you can do no wrong. If you get too enamored of that image of yourself—as someone who is doing good—you can lose sight of the fact that you're perfectly capable of doing wrong. And sometimes, even the way you're doing good can cause harm.

SOJOURNERS: Do you feel acedia is more of a problem in our current culture?

NORRIS: Yes, I think so. In the process of writing, this became clearer, and I would agree with Bertrand Russell and Thomas Merton—that this "restlessness" really did increase in the twentieth century, and it is more of a societal problem today. Although, it is also just part of human nature to take refuge in indifference, denial, and withdrawal.

Having grown up in the 1960s, with all of the struggles and anti-war movements that went on, I began to look at what happened in Iraq and realized we're holding people without charges in prisons throughout the world and there's no protest movement, really. Some of these revelations, if they'd been made in the '60s, would result in a million people in Washington. Now, there's murmuring, people talking among themselves, but no push. What happened in those forty years? Well, a lot. I wonder how much indifference has really settled in.

I wanted to write about acedia from the personal point of view—how I discovered the word and how it really resonated with me. But one of the breakthroughs in writing the book was when I realized the extent to which the twenty-four-hour news channels fuel our indifference, our inability to really care and act on things. You're inundated. The important news often isn't really reported, because so much that is nonessential is pushed up front and made to sound important.

SOJOURNERS: How is acedia different than depression?

NORRIS: The biggest difference is that clinical depression is an illness that can be treated. Acedia may feel like a kind of a psychological affliction, but it's a temptation. If you're aware of the workings of acedia like the early monks were, you can observe it: It pops up in your mind, you go *ah-ha*, what is it tempting me to do? How is it tempting me to think or feel? So you can analyze in a way that, if you're really suffering from clinical depression, you can't. You need that help from doctors. There is a difference.

SOJOURNERS: How is acedia different from the positive goal of spiritual detachment?

NORRIS: *Apatheia* [spiritual detachment] is detachment from the concerns that keep you unfocused on your spiritual life and distracted from remembering that life has a higher purpose than eating, drinking, and sleeping. It's not callous indifference—*apatheia* only comes *after* you've struggled with callous indifference and acedia. What all religions are looking for is inner peace that translates into living peaceably with other people. You have to seek it over and over again; you may have a really good week and then you get angry and something pulls you back down. It's also peace that's grounded in reality, not illusion. Not just having inner peace while everyone around you is miserable. That's not how it works. It has to translate into other people recognizing that you're a peaceable person.

SOJOURNERS: You talk a great deal about sin and how admitting to sin is a way to freedom. How do you define sin?

NORRIS: My definition of sin, which is more of a medieval definition taken from Gregory the Great and Thomas Aquinas, is to know something is wrong, but to do it anyway. It's a basic definition and so easy to grasp, even a child can. And indifference plays a role in sin—you just don't care what the effect of sin would be until it hits you in the face.

I also talk about how what the church later defined as sin, desert monks termed "bad thought," which to my mind is a much more helpful designation. Thoughts come to everyone—this is a universal thing, because you're human and this is how the mind works. Your job is to figure out which thoughts lead to happiness and real peace with my neighbors and which lead to trouble, both within my own temperament and with my neighbor. It's a whole different thing than looking at acts because it's much more universal. It has nothing to do with religious faith or lack of it—it's simply human psychology.

So, all the baggage, and all the stuff we associate with dos and don'ts, isn't there. Instead, you're simply talking about something that everyone experiences. Everyone experiences the temptation to greed and lust and anger. There's no out. I find it fascinating. You can't claim that lust or gluttony isn't a problem for you, because the thoughts come. And it's our job to figure out how to deal with them when they come.

This appeared in the September/October 2008 issue of *Sojourners*.

My Spiritual Director Told Me I Needed a Silent Retreat

Laurel Mathewson

How the humor and honesty of a sixteenth-century Spanish nun helped me trust God.

The Interior Castle, the best-known text of sixteenth-century Spanish saint Teresa of Ávila, is a tour of the inward ways we relate to God, with varying intensity, awareness, and intimacy. In Spanish, the book is simply *Moradas*, or "Dwellings," a title I find more appealing and helpful than the English title, mostly because "dwellings" sounds approachable, universal, and less precious.

Teresa was a grounded mystic. She is down-to-earth in her prose, her witty and candid teaching, and her lived experience. It could be argued that every "true" mystic or saint is grounded or has some element of both the active and contemplative life. Teresa strikes me as remarkably and robustly balanced, in a way that her basic reputation as a mystic sometimes betrays. She is notably resolute in both her defense of the reality of "supernatural" prayer experiences and her insistence that this loving movement of God to an individual must then extend into the world rather than curve in on itself. What we might call her grounded nature even extended into her prayer dialogues with Jesus: Once, when complaining honestly to Christ about her many struggles, she heard a response to this effect: "Don't be troubled; so do I treat my friends."

Her tart response? "I know, Lord—but that's why you have so few friends!" In many of her waking days, she worried that Christ has so few "good friends," and tried to encourage her contemporaries to become better friends of God. But she is clear-eyed and honest about the things that stand in the way of that friendship, from within and without.

"You Need a Retreat"

From the outside I might not seem like someone who has struggled to have a close relationship with God. I am, in the words of one of my slightly befuddled college friends who asked me to officiate at his wedding, a "real-life religious person." But even as I filled out applications for seminaries and divinity schools, understanding in my mind how the work of ordained ministry aligned with my gifts and values, I wrestled with the vexing question of God's love and personal care for humanity.

I prayed with integrity, trusting that in some mysterious way this was good and right and helpful, even if it was simply a matter of reorientation toward humility and justice. I could talk about following the way of Jesus with integrity—the way of forgiveness, reconciliation, truth telling, humble service, compassion—trusting it as a holy path of justice and healing. It seemed to me a path simple but not easy, full of hope for the world's transformation if we paid heed. But I recognized, even if obscurely, something I felt I could not do with integrity: Proclaim God's love for the world or any particular person.

One afternoon, I admitted this out loud, and received in return a piece of life-changing advice.

"I really think you need a silent retreat," my spiritual director said.

"How long?" I asked.

"Oh," she said plainly, "it takes at least three nights."

The Grace I Sought

And so, ever obedient, I set out for a small Roman Catholic retreat center on the other side of San Diego. When I arrived at the house, I met with the white-haired sister who served as my spiritual director throughout my retreat. I would check in with her once each day; otherwise, my time would be spent in silence and solitude. She provided some basic suggestions for my times of prayer, affirming that "seeking understanding" is my faith, but also noticing that I yearned for something more. "This is what you will be trying to do," she said: "Come to know the heart of God through the word of God. Listen! As you pray these verses, just be noticing, not analyzing." She spoke in direct terms about the kind of prayer that is honest and personal. "What is the grace that you seek?" she asked. "Be very clear about this. What are you looking for? What grace are you asking of God?"

She urged me to pray various scriptures throughout the day, listening, paying attention, and at the end of the day, reflecting on how grace has been given. "In the midst of it all," she said, "trust that God is at work!"

It's like she saw right through my big talk about God. Because she was talking about trust in a personal way, like there might be some point to "paying attention" beyond obedience and discipline—and that's the kind of trust I didn't have. I realized that in my first period of prayer and reflection, right after I met with her, as I considered her question about what I'm looking for. I realized that my honest fear was not that God doesn't exist, but that it is impossible to know God, that God is inaccessible. That God is at work, but not in any way that we can ever know. The grace that I sought was to know that the God of the universe is somehow accessible, that I might somehow hear or know of God's work in my life and the lives of others, even in small part.

The Fourth Dwelling

What happened over the course of the next four days transformed my understanding of God and began a new chapter of faith. Teresa describes the fourth dwelling place as the stage where the natural and supernatural experiences of prayer meet; in symbolic terms, the demanding work of carrying water is interrupted by the feeling of a spring welling up inside. On the second morning of the retreat came a moment where I saw the "messiness" of that fourth dwelling place, where acquisitive seeking and passive receiving comingle.

Around 11:30 in the morning, I sat in my retreat room's recliner to pray, holding a single sheet of paper with Psalm 139 printed on it. I read it all the way through, staying in my head. But I thought back to the instruction to ask for the specific grace I'm seeking, and the invitation to wait, trusting that God would come into the space I managed to clear. I asked for the Spirit to help me pray, too, ever more aware of my need. Then, I started to meditate prayerfully upon these lines: "You have searched me out and known me," repeating them slowly over and over. This repetition soon morphed into the real and deepest question of my heart: Have you searched me? Have you known me?

As I asked, almost accusingly but also very truthfully, with trust that God would answer in some way, my body began to feel warm: My legs were shaking, and a trembling seized me, drawing my attention to warmth and internal movement through my feet. It felt like God was saying, "All the way through the blood in your feet, to the tips of your toes I've known you; every part." I was shocked and moved into a new prayer in response: "You have searched me; you have known me," but even yet this didn't seem right, and I kept trembling when I said "known." I realized through a sense of pressure, correction, that this needed to be in the present tense; it needed to be "know": "You have searched me, and you know me." I kept praying this way, caught up in both fear and awe at what was happening.

I am loathe to describe the specific physical elements of my experience because such descriptions invite skeptical analysis, as they certainly have for Teresa. It is obvious she tries to minimize these aspects, too, though in the end they are present; they are part of her work. And, tellingly, they are the parts of her work that people who have never read her know something about: "Didn't she levitate? Didn't she feel pierced with fiery arrows?" This is the "crazy-mystical" stuff that both attracts and repels attention, in a way that sometimes has little to do with genuine interest in the movement of God. I offer more details for the sake of those who do care.

Presence, Fear, and Awe

What I have written thus far doesn't do justice to the sense of power and otherness that moved my body in fear and trembling. It was frightening in its newness and unexpectedness, the way it ruptured my understanding of how God would or would not be present on this earth in these times, to insignificant individual humans, and more particularly a cold-blooded white girl like me, formed by the staid spiritual expectations of the "frozen chosen." My full journal entry after the fact includes the words fear, scared, frightening, scary, and freaked-out, along with the admittedly "silly" observation that, "I'm not Pentecostal, but this is still happening to me."

This. The overall physical effect might be compared to a mild seizure that just kept shaking me again and again as I prayed, drawing tears, and yet leaving me with full presence of mind, the capacity for observation and bewildered engagement in this foreign conversation, but also the (real and terrifying) awareness of another power affecting my physical being. As I moved further into this prayer of "You know me," eventually the fear and awe overtook me and transformed my words to "Holy God." Later, as the experience intensified, even this gave way to a simpler prayer: "I'm scared."

In my fear I turned to Jesus: the name of Jesus, the idea of Jesus, the Jesus to whom I had never prayed for help more urgently or earnestly. I don't know why I thought Jesus might help me, except that I figured if anyone knows what it's like to be seized by the Spirit of God, it's him. My prayer was like that of Jesus' friends who think they might die in the storm, and so I begged him for relief. Suddenly I grasped—and pinned my hope to—the notion of Jesus as the Christ, the priestly mediator, the one who can stand between small creatures and their Creator, the one who cannot just bridge this cosmic divide but provide a sheltering wing for the frail human psyche.

This thought came later, of course; in the moment I just cried out to Jesus because he was a human and divine figure I trust, despite all my intellectual qualms. There seemed to be no other place to turn when I wanted out of the boat. Slowly, gently, there was relief. Calm settled over my limbs and my heart. I lay there in stillness for a moment, then uttered an exhausted prayer of thanks. Despite the fear, the confusion, I was awake enough to say thank you to God for this gift, this sign that I am known, every particle of me. I opened my eyes and looked across the room at the alarm clock next to the bed; about thirty standard minutes had passed in this time when I felt outside of time.

I stood up, bewildered. As I wandered toward the bathroom, I wondered: Did I just conjure that whole thing? Did I somehow make that happen? I was washing my hands with the light off, and I began to doubt that it was God after all. Suddenly the Spirit seized me again, my knees buckling beneath me. I made my way back to the chair, where I prayed and put my head down in my lap, again asking for Jesus to be with me. I cried, overwhelmed by God's insistence that I not toss this great gift aside. I cried, seeing clearly that I always thought I wanted a mystical experience of God, but I should have been smart enough to fear it a little more. It felt like I had been given the very slap in the face that I had been praying for, and I was embarrassingly surprised.

You dare to ask if I know you? If I have searched you? I am in every part of you! Moving in you even as you don't understand what is happening, knowing your very thoughts before they are on your lips.

I don't know where to go from here, other than to the place that the line from the psalm leads me, where I can rest in wonder, at least for a bit: I am known. It is what I can say with every part of me, even as my mind continues its habits of protest: I am known.

Laurel Mathewson was pastor of St. Luke's Episcopal Church in San Diego when this article appeared in the April 2024 issue of *Sojourners*. This excerpt is adapted from *An Intimate Good: A Skeptical Christian Mystic in Conversation with Teresa of Ávila* (Whitaker House, 2024). Used with permission.

Chapter 2

Lay Me Down

Rest and Sabbath

"Rest is holy," Sandi Villarreal writes, "not a reward for the productive." The U.S. economy is built on an unpaid labor system (slavery) and even today depends on overworking some and under employing others. Rabbis Waskow and Yanklowitz remind us that our ancient stories show that greed and accumulation by the few are not new—but God gives timeless sacred limits to help all live good, balanced, and just lives. "Rest is not disconnected from social wellness and political power," writes Jeania Ree V. Moore, "but vital to it." At Sojourners we ask, who gets to rest when we rest?

We Need Sabbath. In the United States, We Don't Trust Each Other Enough to Take It

Rachel Hope Anderson

In March last year, as I was leaving a medical appointment, a nurse handed me a small, leopard-print cosmetic case with a pink ribbon attached. "A gift from us."

This is not the kind of gift one wants to receive. I had been diagnosed with breast cancer. It was a welcome-and-sympathy gift wrapped up in one. With two young children distance-learning at home, I had considered a wide range of maladies our family might encounter—from "Zoom fatigue" to learning loss to the coronavirus itself. But not cancer.

My unpreparedness for major illness meant that I had no primary care physician, no relationship with any of the major health systems in my area, and no access to paid leave.

All this despite the fact that I was a professional advocate for family leave policies. During the last several years, nearly all my working hours were spent researching, writing about, and promoting more humane work and family policies. I have often made this case to employers and legislators: All workers, at some point in their lives, will experience illness, frailty, or the need to care for someone else. It is wiser to anticipate and honor this aspect of humanity than to ignore it.

Now, the human in question is me.

I had not prepared for an illness requiring rest and extensive treatment. Work—both that for which I earn a living and all that goes into raising children and managing a household—played a defining role in structuring my days. Needing to *not* work was barely imaginable.

Learning about the Sabbath was part of my childhood catechesis in the Lutheran tradition. But the biblical commandment to "remember the Sabbath day by keeping it holy" was presented as a personal exhortation to attend church each Sunday, rather than a practice that might transform the relationship between people and work.

Married to the job?

In the United States, we are a nation accustomed to working "in sickness and in health," more reflective of marriage vows than a labor contract. Americans work more hours, on average, than do workers in most other industrialized nations. There is evidence that today's families devote more time to work than families a generation ago did. Economist Isabel V. Sawhill and researcher Katherine Guyot estimate that average middle-class married parents in the United States now work, collectively, six hundred more hours per year than did a comparable couple in 1975—that's two and a half months more.

Work is not only about volume but also about trade-offs. The dominant role work plays in U.S. culture and life reveals itself not only in the quantity of hours worked but when those hours occur and how those work hours interfere with other aspects of life. At least 20 percent of new mothers—more than seven hundred thousand women each year—return to work just a few weeks after giving birth to a child. Three million Americans work while sick each week. At the precise moment that many Americans would like to be tending a new baby or recovering from a cold, they are working.

During this coronavirus pandemic, the high stakes associated with work became devastatingly clear. Early in the pandemic, there were reports of food processing plants with strict attendance policies where hundreds of workers got sick, and some died. Parents who were fortunate enough to work from home multitasked like never before. Parents and other family caregivers put in a daily average of 6.1 hours of "secondary childcare," engaging in paid work and other tasks while also caring for children. Worry about whether one could take time off to receive and recover from the COVID-19 shot prevented some individuals from securing timely vaccinations.

Problems with a "Meritocracy"

Many in the United States are overworked, but the circumstances that provoke this condition vary. In knowledge-based sectors of the economy, competing for elite educational spots and limited job positions demands large investments of time and focus. Many corporate, financial, and legal firms offer clients round-the-clock service, which requires professionals in those fields to work extensive hours. Meanwhile, those who earn a living by selling must tirelessly jockey for attention, often on increasingly crowded media platforms.

Although it may seem counterintuitive, *overwork* can impact those who are *underemployed*. As of 2016, one in ten Americans, many of whom work in service or hospitality industries, were involuntarily underemployed, receiving fewer work hours than they would like. This workforce faces distinct pressures. Retail workers, for example, are often called to work shifts with little notice, or are asked to arrive early or stay late. Underemployment, combined with job type, can prompt one to accept whatever work hours are offered, no matter the trade-offs.

Research by the Shift Project, a collaboration between Harvard and the University of California San Francisco, illustrates that parents who experience variable scheduling are more likely than others to leave young children alone or with a sibling. Showing up for work despite being unable to secure a safe place for one's children is a kind of overwork. Although there is evidence that a tighter labor market may lead some employers to increase wages, it is not yet clear that those same dynamics will cause employers to change the job structures and workplace norms that lead to overwork.

America's ideology of a meritocracy enables overwork. In the United States, economic security is too often associated with worthiness and worthiness with work. We work to achieve security. We keep working to justify whatever security and success comes our way or to avoid blame if we lack either. A meritocratic ideology suggests that overwork is a natural condition and possibly even a virtuous one, while at the same time rendering invisible those who, because of physical or mental condition, never fit into the meritocratic work structure in the first place.

Finally, of course, there are the paltry sums of paid and protected time off that Americans receive. Most industrialized nations guarantee between five and fifteen days of employer-paid time off for illness followed by a public benefit for longer periods of illness or recovery. The United States lacks such a system for guaranteeing paid sick leave. Likewise, the United States is one of the few nations that fails to guarantee paid leave to new parents. Basic benefits are meted out through the negotiation of employers and employees, a patchwork approach that yields limited benefits and from which one can quickly fall. Those employees who are offered paid sick days through their work secure an average of eight paid days off a year. Fifteen million people in the U.S. workforce do not have an employer at all but rather are contractors, self-employed, or seasonal workers and are rarely entitled to any paid time off.

Our stingy benefits system contributes to overwork in two ways. First, it withholds the material resources required to take necessary breaks from work. For example, of the U.S. parents who had leave available following adopting or giving birth to a new child, slightly more than 50 percent took less time off work than they wanted. The major reason cited for returning to work early was concern over lost wages or salary. Workers without paid sick days are 1.5 times more likely to show up to work when ill and to forgo medical care. Second, our inconsistent system of paid-leave benefits withholds the social signals that enable humans to cease working when needed, to rest. Social signals are direct or indirect communications that provide information through social behavior, emotions, and relationships. American culture is biased toward work, earnings, and production, with less social signaling in support of time spent in cultural, recreational, and relational activities or at rest.

Permission to Rest

When I became sick last winter, I was standing right at the precipice of overwork. Many of the ingredients were present—contingent work without paid time off, family care layered on top of paid work. A lifetime spent on meritocracy's treadmill taught me that whatever supports or benefits I lacked, I did not yet deserve. Even though my Sabbath theology had broadened since I was a child, work's pull had also strengthened. As a parent, Sunday became not only a day of worship but also the temporal staging ground for the week ahead. After church, I would compile a list of meals, parenting responsibilities, and appointments for the next six days.

A cancer diagnosis transformed my fundamental relationship to work. My "job" suddenly became much simpler: to remain alive. I accepted fewer work hours and took time off for treatment. This life-saving shift required, principally, resources.

I rely on a spouse with a steady income. But I also connect the shift to that leopard-print cosmetic case. Stuffed with a pair of pink socks, lip balm, nausea-soothing devices, and other self-care sundries, the gift also carried something invisible yet also essential: permission to rest.

"Time as we now experience it in fact depends heavily on how our culture organizes and uses it," writes Todd D. Rakoff in *A Time for Every Purpose*, a book about the law of time. So much of our time is dominated by work, in part because there are few cultural cues marking out time for rest. Rest is often treated like negative space. It is what's left over when work is done. The pink-ribboned case was a rare cultural cue that sanctioned rest. It signaled my membership in a particular sorority of sufferers—a sorority whose members society agrees to release, at least briefly, from the quest for favor through work.

The biblical tradition is one in which rest has an affirmative and, even, holy purpose. Theologian Walter Brueggemann writes, "The Sabbath sanctifies time through sanctioned forms of rest and in action." God gave the Sabbath to humanity by first modeling and then commanding it (Genesis 2:1–3). Sabbath-keeping mirrors God's decision to rest after six days of creative work. For humans, Sabbath rest is both the fulfillment of the work that precedes it and an expression of worship.

In modern Christianity, Sabbath is often considered a personal practice, but scripture presents it as a social instruction. After God liberated the Hebrew people from oppression in Egypt, God brought them to a daunting wilderness. There, they were offered divine provision in the form of bread appearing outside their tents each morning. Alongside this gift, God issued a time-shaping requirement: On six days the people of God were to gather bread, but on the seventh day they were to rest (Exodus 16:22–26).

The whole community was to desist from gathering bread on the seventh day. God prohibited reward and, indeed, rebuked anyone who sought to secure advantage over their neighbors through an extra day of work. Observing Sabbath both required and engendered communal trust. The Sabbath, suggests Judith Shulevitz in *The Sabbath World*, is a "mutual non-compete clause." Sabbath wisdom teaches that rest and social trust are integrally connected. The human body cannot rest well without trust in the community that surrounds it. It relies on predictability and security.

This connection between rest and trust, and lack thereof, presents itself in the negative in many contemporary workplaces. Research documents a clear association, for example, between variable scheduling and sleep disruption. It is not only that workers who are routinely asked to work late into the night or start before dawn trade sleep for work. Disorders like insomnia also emerge in response to precarious work. It is as if work-on-demand amounts to a perpetual refusal of permission to rest.

The Sabbath I'd practiced before I became sick was a Sabbath in miniature, fixed in time and purpose. To be sure, weekly Sabbath-keeping is a good. As a habitual spiritual discipline, it can become a foundation for a deeper personal and communal trust in God and one another. But in my case, I had instrumentalized the practice, using it to propel me toward the next cycle of work. Despite my post-diagnosis shifts, choosing to rest remains a partial, emergent practice for me. But I have come to experience Sabbath as more capacious and mysterious than I previously had; its gifts—be they prayer or emotional clarity or respite from pain—only revealing themselves once I have stepped into its sphere.

God's Divine Humor

Encountering my permission to rest through a cosmetic case gestures at God's divine humor. But the gift also illustrates a problem with our prevailing culture of time.

Since the late 1980s, breast cancer has been the focus of extensive cause marketing efforts that simultaneously raise awareness and promote commerce. The pink ribbon, popularized by cosmetic maker Estée Lauder, traffics in its association with wellness, tenacity, and womanhood. The pink ribbon's ubiquity helped me claim time for rest. But what about illnesses that are not poised to move an audience or suited to product sales? What about the diseases that lurk less visibly in sufferers' lives? A community that approves rest only for those maladies that acquire cultural cachet and commercial power cannot be a just or a trustworthy one.

The last widespread social sanction for rest occurred eight decades ago. The five-day work week and, its companion, the weekend, reformed the industrial era's excessive work patterns. Contemporary movements for paid family and medical leave, fair scheduling practices, or a guaranteed month of paid time off per worker per year all build on the legacy of affirming time for work and for rest.

Just as the material resources required for rest depend on chance—the nature of one's job or one's familial safety net—so does the social permission to rest. But it does not need to be this way. Wisdom-rooted traditions, rather than marketing campaigns, should shape our time. Time for rest should be predictable, trustworthy, and universal. Everyone, at some point in our lives, will experience sickness, frailty, or the need to care for someone else.

Rachel Hope Anderson was a resident fellow at the Center for Public Justice and director of Families Valued when this appeared in the January 2022 issue of *Sojourners*.

The Sabbath
An Ancient Vehicle for Social Progress

Shmuly Yanklowitz

We live in an oppressive age where there are few potential breaks from the enormous demands of surviving in our rapid-paced global economy. As the demand for more products delivered at a quicker, more insatiable pace becomes normalized, workers are more susceptible to oppression, animals are more easily abused, the land is mistreated, and leisure time rarely goes towards self-nourishment or reflection. All these factors lend themselves to an unhealthy workforce and, looking more broadly, a sick society. This is where the Sabbath comes in. The Sabbath acts as the great adjuster of temporal and intangible time.

In this way, the Sabbath is about labor law: One may not work one's worker one day a week.

The Sabbath is about animal welfare: One may not work their animal one day a week.

The Sabbath is about environmental justice: One may not work the land one day a week.

The Sabbath is about taking care of one's inner being: One must refrain from working themselves one day a week to recharge for the next six.

Today, lamentably, many progressives do not think to turn toward this biblical prescription in their efforts to advance society. Maybe due to a lack of interest in aspects of religion in society, progressives often overlook the benefits derived from the Sabbath.

For those who feel the Sabbath is solely a religious imperative, I would caution against such a sentiment. One doesn't have to be religious to embrace the principles that the Sabbath offers. Taking a day to shut off digital and worldly distractions is a gift. It is an ethical enterprise, one that is sorely needed in our time. Political thinker Michael Walzer, a professor emeritus at the Institute of Advanced Study at Princeton, wrote in his book, *Spheres of Justice: A Defense of Pluralism and Equality*, about the vitality of a day set aside for rest and growth: "Sabbath rest is more egalitarian than [a] vacation because it can't be purchased: it is the one thing that money can't buy. It is enjoined for everyone, enjoyed by everyone."

Furthermore, consider the wisdom of Rabbi Abraham Joshua Heschel on this topic. In his book *The Sabbath*, written more than sixty-five years ago, he wrote:

> To set apart one day a week for freedom, a day on which we would not use the instruments which have been so easily turned into weapons of destruction, a day for being with ourselves, a day of detachment from the vulgar, of independence of external obligations, a day on which we stop worshipping the idols of technical civilization, a day on which we use no money. . . is there any institution that holds out a greater hope for man's progress than the Sabbath?

So then, what are the benefits of observing a sabbath in a mostly secular society? At its core, the Sabbath is about protecting the rights of workers. Employers may not mandate work seven days a week; logically, one day must be free of work. Laws banning work—and related activities—on the Sabbath are nearly as old as the English colonies in America. Puritan settlers in the Massachusetts and the Virginia colonies passed laws as early as the 1620s outlawing commercial activities on the

Sabbath, followed by other colonies as they joined the nascent American territory. Though these statutes grew steadily less prevalent and less enforced after the American Revolution, some persisted. In the early nineteenth century, Calvinist New Yorkers literally put chains across their streets to prevent business and travel on the Sabbath.

In the twentieth century, after years of hard-fought struggle, the Fair Labor Standards Act of 1938 established a minimum wage, overtime pay, and maximum hours for most full-time workers, although it did not specifically ban work on the Sabbath. Some states, such as New York, state that employers must give their employees "twenty-four consecutive hours of rest in any calendar week," while elsewhere it is made clear that such protection is only offered to full-time workers. In California an exception is made if a job would usually require working more than six days in a row, as long as time off reached an equivalent of one day in seven. Laws banning work on the Sabbath, called "blue laws" (first used in 1762), became popular again by the 1960s, when thirty-four states had blue laws; today, only Bergen County, N.J., keeps a blue law on the books.

This is all pretty recent and still evolving. Yet, thousands of years ago, the Bible already came and taught that we may not work our worker, our animal, our land, or even ourselves for one day a week.

In our modern lives, each of us should feel challenged to embrace a sabbath where we do not work, where we do not employ others, and where we refrain from the pressures of consumer capitalism. I am, of course, not suggesting that everyone follow the strictures that I do as an Orthodox rabbi. From Friday night until the following Saturday evening, I cease all use of cars, phone, or any electricity at all; my work life immediately ceases. I understand that completely turning off all electronic usage would be difficult cessation for many people without preparation. What I am proposing, instead, is that we can turn off all of our technology and use that time to talk with family and friends, to read and learn, to pray and meditate. We can build commitment to one another and reflect upon our lives. We can become more intellectually and spiritually creative. We could focus on cultivating positivity and shutting out toxicity. Those of us who observe the Sabbath religiously could learn a lot from new ways that some might come to observe it more secularly.

Dedicating one day a week to refrain from activity will not solve all the problems found in society, but it may give everyone a deserved respite from the incessant stresses of the world. Including a regular day of pause and reflection, perhaps, will have an effect on our outlook during the other six days of our busy, productive weeks.

Rabbi Dr. Shmuly Yanklowitz was the president and dean of the Valley Beit Midrash, the founder and president of Uri L'Tzedek, the founder and CEO of The Shamayim V'Aretz Institute, and the author of fourteen books on Jewish ethics when this appeared on sojo.net on January 3, 2017.

"All Is Calm"
Scripture's Radical Call to Rest During Advent

Julian Davis Reid

Five suggestions for stillness despite the busyness of the season.

The fervor at church during the Advent season is a remarkable sight. Both clergy and laity work like the shepherds, tending to their flocks late into the night. And many move like the wise men, traveling to foreign places and spending extensive resources to celebrate Christ's arrival with family.

This time of heightened activity makes sense given the story of scripture and the story of our current world. The shepherds could not help but tell others once they learned of the Savior's birth. And as we now await his return, we *should* work hard to share the riches of the nativity with a world that is a little more open to matters of faith at this time of year.

But if increased activity is the only melody we pick up from the nativity story told in Matthew and Luke, we neglect a needful counterpoint: the importance of rest. The nativity story is replete with theological, familial, and political lessons about rest that quietly proclaim God's goodness to this weary world. With exhaustion rampant in the church—perhaps especially so at Christmastime—we would do well to hear notes of rest sounding from the manger.

1. Listen to Your Sleep

God uses sleep as a vehicle for saving Joseph's family (Matthew 1:18–25). God instructs Joseph to honor his marriage to Mary because her pregnancy was not a sign of infidelity. To the contrary, it was a sign of immense devotion to God. Furthermore, this miracle child would save all his people, including his parents, from their actual sins, as opposed to their alleged ones. In obedience, Joseph listened to the message heard in his sleep and thus participated in God's saving of his family.

Through this dream, God helped Joseph navigate the tension between commitment to religious expectation and commitment to family—a tension prominent in the life of church leaders during busy times of the year such as Advent. Can you be faithful to your public ministry life and to your family equally, or does one have to give way to the other? I am thankful to be the son of a pastor who intentionally maintained her family life alongside her ministry life (Rev. Adonna Davis Reid pastors First United Methodist Church of Oak Park in Chicagoland). But I know that for many families, the demands of ministry can lead to distance between spouses as well as distance between parents and children, sometimes causing enduring harm.

If you ever face this tension over priorities, try looking to Joseph's example for guidance. Joseph reminds us that God is ultimately in control and that we have a role in the story because God chooses to involve us. God told Joseph that his seed was not needed but that he was still part of God's salvific plan. Joseph could have ignored this dream and divorced Mary anyway, but he instead listened to the instruction heard during sleep. As earthly father to the child of the Holy Spirit and Mary, he would always remember that ministry is not ultimately by or about him.

So it is with us: The God who protects us when we are drooling on our pillow is the same God who freely chooses to use us.

These lessons from Joseph's sleep can keep needless weight off our shoulders during Advent and Christmas—which, funnily enough, might help us sleep better at night.

As you sleep, if you are one who remembers your dreams, can you gain insights from them about your family? Another angle is to think about your last thought before you nod off or your first thought in the morning. (The psalms routinely talk about how our nighttime self-monologue is a good place to hear instruction from God.) You might find God helping you hold together your commitment to your public ministry and to your family the way God did for Joseph.

I pray that your family ties are stronger this Advent because of how you listen to God through sleep. And as those ties are strengthened, may fruit come that blesses the world. Because Joseph listened to God through his sleep, he was able to participate in God's deepest vision of rest: the saving of creation from the restlessness wrought by sin.

2. Pause to Tend Sacred Memory

Luke's gospel depicts Jesus' tumultuous delivery, with Mary giving birth in an animal stable (2:1–7). It is hard enough to deliver a child in normal circumstances, but to do so in a stable would have been all the more disorienting. And on top of that, shortly after Jesus is born, the Holy Spirit sends unfamiliar shepherds to the new parents to pay homage to the new king (verses 8–20). Since the Spirit had to give them specific instructions on locating and identifying the child ("you will find a child wrapped in bands of cloth"), these shepherds most likely did not know Mary and Joseph beforehand, which would have added to the strangeness of the event.

But after the shepherds moved with haste to the stable and described their conversation with the angels, Mary "treasured" and "pondered" their report in her heart (verse 19). These two verbs may appear to describe benign contemplation, but their use elsewhere in Luke and the other gospels suggests they are about protecting something valuable from danger. In Mary's case, that might mean protecting these memories of Jesus' divine glory as the angels detailed it. Perhaps she would return to these pondered memories when Jesus was crucified, which is predicted just a few verses after the shepherd's report when Mary talks with Simeon in the temple square (verses 25–35).

The stakes and vicissitudes of Advent can make it hard to keep our attention still enough to remember anything in front of us. There are so many concerts to attend, ugly sweaters to sport, and gifts to wrap that we can get to December 26 with nothing stored up or treasured. But when we rest our attention on special times of God's gracious presence in our lives during this season, we can store up memories for facing future travails. In this way, Christmas can be seen as a harvest of what my mom would call "God sightings" that can nurture our faith as we move into the New Year. Lest we forget, an African American spiritual reminds us: "There's a storm out on the ocean / and it's moving this'a way / If your soul's not anchored in Jesus / you will surely drift away."

My wife and I moved from New England to Atlanta for graduate school at Emory from 2016 to 2020. This was our first time living in the Southeast, and so it was quite the experience being there amid the uptick in public racialized terror: A white gunman had massacred the Emanuel Nine a year prior, Black churches were being burned, COVID-19 hit, and then George Floyd was murdered. And on top of these national spectacular headlines was our work in settings marked by quotidian anti-Black violence: health care disparities at Grady Memorial Hospital, where my wife worked as a medical student, and an almost all-Black population at Metro Regional Youth Detention Center, where I served as a prison chaplain while in seminary.

Through it all, the Black elders at the churches we attended modeled how to be like Mary as they treasured in their hearts the joy of being in God's presence on Sunday morning with fellow saints. We all knew that there was always a possibility that an acolyte of the Charleston shooter might come into our church and open fire, and so despite that and because of that, we protected the shepherds' testimonies in our midst. We instead chose to still our souls such that we could draw on those memories of glad tidings of great joy when the next headline hit. Our faith was not, and is not, contingent on the predictability of safety but on God's grace.

How can you still your attention this Advent season and treasure the presence of God in your midst as Mary did in her pondering?

3. Find Sanctuary from Violence

In the book *Rest Is Resistance*, the "Nap Bishop" Tricia Hersey argues that claiming our rest resists the violence wrought by capitalism and white supremacy. She encourages these politics of refusal by creating art installation projects that are sleep sanctuaries where people can nap together. When we rest, we can dream of other worlds that are not violated by the death we experience in our waking hours. This dreaming can help us act in our present to move our current world toward others yet to be.

Hersey's vision helps us understand the political implications of rest in the nativity story. After Jesus is born, God visits Joseph in another dream, this time to instruct him to take his family to Egypt to avoid King Herod's infanticide (Matthew 2). By sending the Holy Family into political sanctuary, God sidesteps Herod's lust for political power. In so doing, God uses sleep to help God's children resist the violence of the age.

Because Advent brings Christmas and the changing of seasons from fall to winter in the northern regions, it is traditionally a time where much of society can sleep a little longer (for church folk, that rest may start on December 26). How can this season of longer sleep help you see the violence of our age better? Maybe your sleep habits give you perspective on others' lust for power. For instance, by choosing healthy rhythms of sleep whenever I can, I see better how greed keeps others from doing so. Or maybe God is telling you that the violent systems that keep people from sleeping regularly need to be avoided if not altogether dismantled.

For many years God has spoken to me through dreams about violence in our society. I often dream at night about being physically hurt by fellow Black men—a dream I am not proud to confess. The frequency of this dream indicates the violence that my people are encouraged to commit against each other and against ourselves. I pray that my ministry can always address these violent realities, and that I can lessen the fear of my own people that whiteness has ingrained.

4. Rest May Not Lead to Comfort

Joseph's obedience to what is revealed in his second dream would lead his family into a place of discomfort. To flee King Herod, they had to become vulnerable immigrants in a new land. While I do not believe God opposes all comfort and leisure, I do know that being well rested in our society might lead to unexpected risk. This can contradict greater society's overtures toward rest, which capitalism has domesticated. The health and wellness industry often sells us rest for the sake of increasing our creaturely comforts, but that is not always what God has in mind for us. One day we will rest in paradise with God, away from all evil, but today is not that day. In this life, our rest helps us avoid violence and move into discomfort for the sake of caring for others. But rest assured: The Holy Spirit goes with us.

5. Rest Begets More Rest

The four kinds of rest in the nativity story feed each other. God's plan for salvation leads to the message in sleep to Joseph about ushering Jesus into the world. Because Jesus comes into the world, Mary stills her attention to treasure that memory. Because Joseph and the wise men listen to God through their dreams, Jesus escapes to political sanctuary in Egypt.

I hear these four kinds of rest as a metaphorical music chord, with salvation being the bass note and sleep, stillness, and sanctuary sitting on top. In music, the bass note defines the chord, meaning the other notes derive their identity from their relationship to it. Joseph's sleep, Mary's inner stillness, and the family's political sanctuary all are defined in terms of God's plan to save humanity, through Jesus, from the restlessness of their sins.

These notes in the nativity story ring together for the sake of God's glory and our rest in God, offering a reflection on how we can sing the melody of rest found throughout the Bible. This Advent, we can let the good news of salvation lead us to listen to God through our sleep, to protect our inner stillness no matter the external circumstances, and to find sanctuary for ourselves and others from the worldly economic and political systems that seek our death. As we celebrate Jesus this Advent, may the body of Christ listen for the notes of rest from the One who has come to give us rest eternal.

Julian Davis Reid, a Chicago-based artist-theologian, was the founder of Notes of Rest, a spiritual formation ministry grounded in scripture and Black music that invites the body of Christ to receive God's gift of rest, when this appeared in the December 2023 issue of *Sojourners*.

Rest Is Holy, Not a Reward for the Productive

Sandi Villarreal

Pope Francis, in his first public appearance after returning to the Vatican following an eleven-day hospital stay for a scheduled surgery, told those gathered in St. Peter's Square to "learn to take a break" and truly rest. "Let us beware, brothers and sisters, of efficiency," Francis said, "let us put a halt to the frantic running around dictated by our agendas." He was reflecting on Mark 6:30–34, in which Jesus instructs the disciples to "come away to a deserted place all by yourselves and rest a while," after they told him all the preaching and teaching they had been doing.

"Rest a while," he told them. Holy, ever-elusive rest—it's a simple command but, in my experience, a complicated practice.

The COVID-19 pandemic has forced workers and corporations to engage in conversations around overwork, death-by-a-thousand-efficiencies, and the trauma that burnout unearths, but we still lack the vocabulary to really talk about rest.

When I was recovering from my own surgery and accompanying hospital stay in late January, my body forced bed rest. I had planned for a couple of days off of work, but it stretched into more than a week; the severity of what had just happened caught me off guard. And I was restless. I wanted a lesson; this all had to mean something. So I took doses of books like medicine; I thought I could force a healthy mind and spirit with the wisdom of others, giving purpose to my newly foregrounded mortality. Friends sent me reading lists; my husband teased me about my emotional support pile.

I meditated alongside the poetry of Rupi Kaur and Mary Oliver; I was undone by Kate Bowler and recovered with Samantha Irby and Jenny Lawson. I finally read Joan Didion's *The Year of Magical Thinking*, and was reminded in this long year of mourning that "we also mourn, for better or worse, ourselves. As we were. As we are no longer. As we will one day not be at all." Dust to dust, but human in between.

In *Wintering: The Power of Rest and Retreat in Difficult Times*, writer Katherine May points to the seasonality of rest—that as human beings, we'll invariably encounter seasons throughout life that require intentional escape. "[Wintering] is a time for reflection and recuperation, for slow replenishment, for putting your house in order," she writes. "Doing those deeply unfashionable things—slowing down, letting your spare time expand, getting enough sleep, resting—is a radical act now, but it is essential."

But the reality is that I wasn't wintering. My brief attempt at recuperation from major surgery was not *rest*. Capitalism has taught us that rest is a cyclical but most importantly *temporary* state and that by optimizing our habits and schedules and bodies, we can actually require less of it. Abysmal leave policies in the United States have ingrained in us a quick-fix approach to medical crises, leaving those with chronic conditions and those who care for them behind.

As I considered my needs, Audre Lorde's journal writing from the mid-1980s, after breast cancer metastasized to her liver, felt like a more honest approach: "As a living creature I am part of two kinds of forces—growth and decay, sprouting and withering, living and dying—and at any given moment of our lives, each one of us is actively located somewhere along a continuum between these two forces." Decay happens over time; so does growth.

Another way we often think of rest is as fuel for ongoing work. This is common in justice movements, recognizing that the journey is long and resistance requires recovery. But the concept has more recently been adopted in corporate culture. Studies show that taking breaks from work increases capacity for creative thinking, and daydreaming engages different parts of our brain that enables us to solve problems. Business leaders have taken these lessons to incorporate various methods of employee "free" time, whether by installing foosball tables in common areas or by giving unlimited personal time (while doing little to lessen unrealistic workloads). Even conversations around the benefits of a four-day work week tout sustained or increased productivity as a result. This line of thinking isn't bad: More breaks and less scheduled work tend to result in higher happiness levels, work-life balance, and overall job satisfaction.

What it presupposes, however, is a definition of rest that still relies on a person's utility to give them value—that a break is earned through enough output and, upon return, will launch a person into an even higher level of productivity. This is why we can take all of our vacation days (if we're lucky enough to have them) and still be filled with anxiety the days before we return. Sunday scaries on steroids.

By instead recognizing a person's inherent value, rest is no longer a reward for the productive but an essential part of the human experience. Rest can be part of a regular rhythm, built into the week as a practice, as sabbath. It can also be a season, a recognition that some things take time to repair and require boundaries and self-compassion.

Rest finds home throughout scripture, whether through exhortations to "Be still, and know that I am God!" (Psalm 46:10) or in concrete examples of Jesus stealing away to pray in silence (Mark 1:35). In Matthew 11:28–30, it's an invitation: "Come to me, all you that are weary and are carrying heavy burdens, and I will give you rest," Jesus says. "Take my yoke upon you, and learn from me; for I am gentle and humble in heart, and you will find rest for your souls. For my yoke is easy, and my burden is light."

Rest is found if we accept the invitation, unburden ourselves, and learn the way of gentleness and humility. But so often we put off rest because we are convinced that our work—our jobs, our families, or even our service for others—requires our constant attention. Rest necessitates a change of pace and a laying down of self-importance.

"If we learn to truly rest, we become capable of true compassion," Pope Francis said in his July 18, 2021, address. "If we cultivate a contemplative outlook, we will carry out our activities without that rapacious attitude of those who want to possess and consume everything; if we stay in touch with the Lord and do not anesthetize the deepest part of ourselves, the things to do will not have the power to cause us to get winded or devour us."

A few months after my surgery, as I struggled (I still struggle) with the realities of a crisis-turned-chronic condition, I did take a longer break. While not a full season of wintering, those few weeks enabled me to spend time in reflection and true rest even as I navigated the daunting health care system and adapted to a new normal. I sat on a rocky beach and let my noisy mind fade into the sound of the waves. I spent mornings hiking, giving thanks for the reminder that despite its limitations, my body is still good. I went on near-daily trips to a new bookstore, a never-ending project to add to my emotional support pile. My husband and I caught small glimpses of the people our three young children are becoming as we spent time in long conversation instead of quickly ushering them through the usual evening routine. I took hundreds of photos, each one a small prayer that we would all remember this. Very importantly, I deleted my email app.

I think back on this time fondly, somehow erasing the pain and fear from my memory. It's a strange feeling to look back on the most harrowing time of your life with a melancholic longing. I was learning and becoming and realizing that while I'm here, I'll never stop learning and becoming. I'll never stop needing rest.

Sandi Villarreal was editor-in-chief of *Sojourners* when this appeared on sojo.net on July 29, 2021.

Jesus' New Economy of Grace

Ched Myers

A biblical vision of Sabbath economics.

The Hebrew Bible's vision of Sabbath economics contends that a theology of abundant grace and a communal ethic of redistribution is the only way out of our slavery to the debt system, with its theology of meritocracy and private ethic of wealth concentration. The contemporary church, however, has difficulty hearing this as good news since our theological imaginations have long been captive to the market-driven orthodoxies of modern capitalism.

Our fears have persuaded us that the biblical Jubilee is at best utopian and at worst communistic. Yet we find it awkward simply to dismiss the biblical witness, so an alternative objection inevitably arises, as if on cue: "Israel never really practiced the Jubilee!" If genuine, and not simply a strategy of avoidance, this challenge is best addressed by considering both the "negative" and "positive" evidence.

By "negative" evidence I mean the fact that Israel's prophets repeatedly and relentlessly criticized the nation's leadership for betraying the poor and vulnerable members of the community. This strongly suggests that the Sabbath vision of social and economic justice remained a measuring stick to which they could publicly appeal.

There can be no question that the Sabbath disciplines of seventh-year debt release and Jubilee restructuring were regularly abandoned by those Israelites who wished to consolidate social advantages they had gained. The historical narratives in the Hebrew Bible indicate that as the tribal confederacy was eclipsed by centralized political power under the Davidic dynasty, economic stratification followed inexorably. Indeed, the prophet Samuel warned that a monarchy would be linked intrinsically to an economy geared to the elite through ruthless policies of surplus-extraction and militarism (1 Samuel 8:11–18).

Prophets and Jubilee

Israel's betrayal of its Sabbath vocation became a central complaint of the prophets. When Isaiah charged the nation's leadership with robbery (Isaiah 3:14–15), he was echoing the manna tradition's censure of stored wealth in the face of community need (see also Isaiah 5:7–8; Malachi 3:5–12). Amos accused the commercial classes of regarding Shabbat as an obstacle to market profiteering, and of treating the poor as an exploitable class rather than guaranteeing their gleaning rights (Amos 8:5–6; see Exodus 23:10–11; Leviticus 19:9–10; Micah 7:1).

Hosea laments that fidelity to international markets had replaced Israel's allegiance to God's economy of grace (Hosea 2:5). Most telling of all, however, is the tradition that attributed the downfall of Jerusalem to the people's failure to keep Sabbath: "God took into exile in Babylon those who had escaped the sword . . . to fulfill the word of the Lord by the mouth of Jeremiah, until the land *had made up for its Sabbaths.* All the days that it lay desolate it kept Sabbath, to fulfill seventy years" (2 Chronicles 36:20–21; see Leviticus 26:34–35).

But there is also positive evidence that the Sabbath vision was practiced. Jeremiah blasts King Zedekiah when he reneges on his declaration of Jubilee manumission (Jeremiah 34:13–16). Naboth resists King Ahab's attempt to assert eminent domain by invoking his traditional "ancestral rights" to the land (1 Kings 21). And the reformer Nehemiah resurrects the Levitical prohibition of interest (Nehemiah 5:6–13) as well as the Sabbath strictures on commercial production, transaction, and finance (10:31).

There are also eschatological visions of Jubilee. Sabbath redistribution is remembered by Ezekiel (Ezekiel 45:8; 46:17–18; 47:13–23), and the most well-known appropriation of the Jubilee vision is found in Isaiah 61:1–2: the prophetic commission that begins with a call to "bring good news to the oppressed poor" and ends with a proclamation of "the year of the Lord's favor." Of all the possibilities in his scriptures, it is this text that Jesus of Nazareth chose to define and inaugurate his mission, according to Luke's gospel (Luke 4:18–19). And it is in this latter-day Hebrew prophet that the vision of Sabbath economics is wholly rehabilitated.

Jesus and Jubilee

It was late Mennonite theologian John Howard Yoder, in his now classic work *The Politics of Jesus*, who popularized for my generation the notion of Jesus as a Jubilee practitioner. Yoder rightly pointed out that Luke's gospel is organized around Isaiah's proclamation of "good news *for the poor*" (Luke 7:22; see 14:13, 21). Only real debt-cancellation and land-restoration could represent good news to real poor people—unless we would spiritualize the entire tradition (against the specific advice of James 2:15–17). Similarly, a Jubilee gospel is usually unwelcome news to the wealthy (as in the Magnificat's annunciation that God "has filled the hungry with good things, and sent the rich away empty," [Luke 1:53; see Mark 10:22]). But the evidence goes far beyond a few widely acknowledged texts. In fact, a revisioning of Sabbath economics defined Jesus' call to discipleship, lay at the heart of his teaching—and stood at the center of his conflict with the Judean public order.

The gospels agree that Jesus' first substantive clash with the authorities arose as a result of his practice of "unlicensed" forgiving of sins, which has clear Jubilee overtones (Mark 2:1–12; John 5:9–17). Although the words "sin" (*hamartia*) and "debt" (*opheileema*) are different in Greek, there are many indications of their semantic and social equivalence in the gospels. Most of us have noted it, for example, in the Lord's Prayer according to Luke: "Forgive us our *sins*, for we ourselves forgive everyone *indebted* to us" (Luke 11:4). Their correlation is further suggested by the fact that here and throughout the New Testament the same verb (*aphiemi*) is used to "forgive" sin and "release" from debt. Unlike our society, which refuses to see the economic dimensions of moral and criminal dysfunction, the gospels do not spiritualize "sin" and ignore the realities of "debt," but rather see the two as fundamentally interrelated.

We see this correlation in Luke's version of the story of the woman who washes Jesus' feet with her hair (Luke 7:36–50). Jesus prefaces his "absolution" of the woman's sins (verses 39, 48–50) with an object lesson describing how a creditor forgave debt (verses 41–43). Matthew does the same in his instructions on reconciliation within the community of faith: The exhortation to forgive sins "seventy times seven" (perhaps an allusion to the jubilary "seven times seven" of Leviticus 25:8; but also to Genesis 4:24) is illumined by a thoroughly political-economic tale about the settling of accounts in the debt system (Matthew 18:15–35).

In Mark's gospel Jesus identifies himself as the "Human One" who has the authority to forgive sins (debts) (Mark 2:10). Shortly thereafter Jesus instructs his disciples to help themselves to field produce, justifying it on the basis of a story about the right of hungry Israelites to food regardless of social convention (Mark 2:23–26). Then comes his punchline: "The Sabbath was created for humanity" (2:27). This is neither a proprietary statement nor a Messianic abrogation of the Sabbath discipline! Quite the contrary: It reiterates the Sabbath as part of the order of God's good creation (Genesis 2:2-3) and confirms that its purpose is to humanize us in a world where so much of our socioeconomic reasoning and practice is dehumanizing. Jesus then asserts his authority to interpret true Sabbath practice (Mark 2:28). In fact, Jesus' central struggle with the political leadership was not over theology, but over the meaning of Sabbath (Mark 3:1–6; Luke 13:10–17; John 7:22–24, 9:14–16). This "Human One," claiming the authority to cancel debts and restore the Sabbath, is a Jubilee figure indeed!

Jesus' Jubilee orientation is also seen in his efforts to rebuild community between socioeconomically alienated groups. His "outreach" to tax collectors, who made their living exploiting debtors, is a case in point. Luke begins and ends his narrative of Jesus' ministry with such stories. Following Jesus' call to discipleship, Levi renounces his tax-collecting work and throws a banquet for Jesus and his clientele of "sinners" (5:27–32). Why does this provoke strenuous protests from the authorities? The answer is made explicit in the story of Zacchaeus (Luke 19:1–10). This wealthy creditor is also invited to host Jesus—but he (rightly) understands this to mean he must first practice substantial economic reparation. It is to this program of socioeconomic "leveling" that the official adjudicators of debt object—in Jesus' day and our own.

Leave and Follow

But while Levi and Zacchaeus embrace Jubilee liberation through redistribution, another man with "much property" rejects it (Mark 10:21–23). Jesus expects his followers to enter into the new economy of grace. Interestingly, the formulaic discipleship phrase "they *left* and followed" (Mark 1:18–20; Luke 5:28) uses the verb *aphiemi*, which we have seen also means to forgive sin/cancel debt. Jesus promises that whoever *leaves* "house or family or fields" (the symbols of the basic agrarian economy: site of consumption, labor force, site of production) will receive the same back "hundredfold" (Mark 10:29–30).

Discipleship thus means forsaking the seductions and false securities of the debt system for a recommunitized economy of enough for everyone. In such an economy, which Jesus calls the "kingdom," there are no longer any rich and poor—by definition, therefore, the rich "cannot enter" it (Mark 10:23–25). So contrary is this vision to our accepted horizons of possibility, however, that disciples ancient and modern have difficulty truly believing (10:26).

Jesus' call for radical social restructuring at all levels, from the household (Mark 3:31–35) to the body politic (Mark 10:35–45), is summarized by the Jubilee ultimatum: "Many who are first will be last, and the last first" (Mark 10:31). He typically chooses the venue of table fellowship in order to both show and tell object lessons that illustrate this. Meals lay at the heart of ancient society: Where, what, and with whom you ate defined your social identity and status. Thus the table was a "mirror" of society, with its economic classes and political divisions.

In the extended banquet story in Luke 14, Jesus systematically undermines prevailing conventions and proprieties, while advocating a new "table" of compassion and equality. The opening episode deals (not surprisingly) with a dispute over the Sabbath practice (Luke 14:1–6). Next comes Jesus' attack on the dominant system of meritocracy, with its hierarchies, prestige posturing, and ladder-climbing, and his invitation to "downward mobility" (verses 7–11). He then offends his host by criticizing his guest list, rejecting the reciprocal patronage system of the elite, and calling instead for a focus upon "those who cannot repay" (verses 12–14). The series concludes with Jesus' pointed little fable about an exemplary host who finally understands the bankruptcy of meritocracy and decides instead to build a Jubilee community with the poor and outcast (verses 15–24).

Grace vs. Mammon

There is no theme more common to Jesus' storytelling than Sabbath economics. He promises poor sharecroppers abundance (Mark 4:3–8, 26–32), but threatens absentee landowners (Mark 12:1–12) and rich householders (Luke 16:19–31) with judgment. In order to teach the incompatibility of the economy of grace with the dictates of "Mammon," Jesus spins a parable that portrays a hapless middleman caught in the brutal logic of the debt system who decides to "trade" instead in Jubilee-style debt release (Luke 16:1–13). When faced with a dispute over inheritance rights, Jesus counters with a parable about the folly of storing up wealth (remember the manna!), and then exhorts us to learn the lessons of grace and subsistence from the "great economy" of nature (Luke 12:13–34; see James 5:1–6).

The notorious parable of the talents (pounds) shows how Sabbath perspective as an interpretive key can rescue us from a long tradition of both bad theology and bad economics (Matthew 25:14–30; Luke 19:11–28). This story has, in capitalist religion, been interpreted allegorically from the perspective of the cruel master (= God!), requiring spiritualizing gymnastics to rescue the story from its own depressing conclusion that haves will always triumph over the have-nots (Matthew 25:29). But it reads much more coherently when turned on its head and read as a cautionary tale of realism about the mercenary selfishness of the debt system. This reading understands the servant who refused to play the greedy master's money-market games as the hero who pays a high price for speaking truth to power (Matthew 25:24–30)—just as Jesus himself did.

In light of this evidence, it should come as no surprise that the archetypal manna story, which as we saw in part one represents the foundation for Sabbath economics, should have a central place in Jesus' consciousness. At the outset of his ministry, Jesus must face again the wilderness temptation concerning bread and sustenance (Matthew 4:1–4 = Deuteronomy 8:2–3 = Exodus 16). At key junctures he re-enacts that wilderness feeding—and all who participate "have enough" (Mark 6:42; 8:8). And at the heart of the prayer he teaches his disciples is the double petition: "Give us enough bread for today, and forgive us our debts as we forgive others" (Matthew 6:11–12).

These are some of the "Jubilee footprints" in the Jesus story. It is important to note that the early church that produced these gospels also *practiced* Sabbath economics. The most obvious example—similarly maligned or ignored by modern exegetes—is the Acts account of the coming of the Spirit at Pentecost—the Jubilee-tinged celebration of Shavuot (Acts 2). This occasions a portrait of the church's first experiment in wealth redistribution, echoing the manna story with the report that "assets were distributed to any as had need" (Acts 2:45, 4:35). Similarly, central to the itinerant ministry of the apostle Paul was his invitation to the new Gentile churches to learn Sabbath economics by practicing interchurch mutual aid. Significantly, in his most elaborate articulation of this commitment (2 Corinthians 8–9), the one scriptural justification Paul employs is a citation of the manna story: "As it is written, 'Those who had much did not have too much; and those who had little did not have too little,'" (2 Corinthians 8:14–15)!

Biblical interpreters skeptical of the Jubilee tradition have not found evidence for its practice because they have not been looking for it. But once we restore Sabbath economics to its central place in the Torah, we hear its echoes *everywhere* in the rest of scripture. The standard of economic justice is woven into the warp and weft of the Bible; pull this strand, and the whole fabric unravels.

If we are going to dismiss the Jubilee because Israel practiced it only inconsistently, we should also ignore the Sermon on the Mount because Christians have rarely embodied Jesus' instruction to love our enemies. But it is time to move beyond such rationalizing theology in our churches. We must rediscover the gospel as good news for the poor, and the economic disciplines of *Shabbat* as the path of humanization.

Fortunately, the "subversive memory" of Jubilee has kept erupting throughout church history, among early monks, medieval communitarians, and radical reformers. Even with the ascendancy of modern capitalism—with its fierce antipathy toward Sabbath economics—this vision has not been extinguished. We see it in tracts by the eighteenth-century "leveler" Thomas Spence in his struggle against the move to enclose (i.e., privatize) the Commons in early industrial England: "Since then this Jubilee/Sets all at Liberty/Let us be glad/Behold each man return to his possession." And we hear it in the nineteenth-century spirituals of African slaves sung in American fields: "Don't you hear the gospel trumpet sound Jubilee?"

Those of us who would insist that the Bible's ancient socioeconomic and spiritual disciplines remain relevant today have hard work to do. We must diligently and creatively explore what contemporary, concrete analogies might be to Jubilee practices of old. The task is as imperative as it is daunting; the alternative is the "capital-olatry" of the runaway global economy. In all of this, the church can help nurture commitment and creativity by promoting "Sabbath literacy," a spirituality of forgiveness and reparation, and practical economic disciplines for individuals, households, and congregations.

"Who, then, can be saved?" (Mark 10:26). Mark's epilogue to the call of the rich man (Mark 10:17–25) anticipates our incredulity: Does Jesus *really* expect the "haves" (that is, us) to participate in Sabbath wealth redistribution as a condition for discipleship? Can we imagine a world in which there are no rich and poor? To the disciples' skepticism, and to ours, Jesus replies simply: "I know it seems impossible to you, but for God all things are possible" (10:27). In other words, economics is ultimately a theological issue. And this is why our churches must talk about it, and talk about it in light of our unique tradition of Sabbath economics.

Ched Myers, an activist theologian, had worked in social change movements for more than twenty years when this appeared in the July-August 1998 issue of *Sojourners.* Myers, author of *Healing Affluenza and Resisting Plutocracy: Luke's Jesus and Sabbath Economics* (Fortress), co-directs Bartimaeus Cooperative Ministries (www.bcm-net.org) with his partner Elaine Enns in the Ventura River watershed of southern California.

Rest Is Resistance, Too

Jeania Ree V. Moore

> Sleep deprivation is a racial and social justice issue of white supremacy and capitalism.

What is rest and what does rest look like during a time of pandemic?

Over recent years, the multiple pandemics we have faced have upended many things, not least of which has been our language. "Essential" has been revealed to be simply another word for "disposable," with "essential frontline workers" being those whose lives society deems expendable, not irreplaceable. "Safe" has been shown to be so shoddy, subjective, and circumscribed a reality in this country that protesting for Black lives in a pandemic is indeed safer than failing to protest at all. And "rest"—what *is* rest?

Many of us were struggling with healthy notions and practices of rest prior to COVID-19. Now? "Rest" seems both undefined and unattainable. Biblical images of rest have often been interpreted to emphasize separation, distance, and juxtaposition. For example, Jesus withdrawing from the crowds is often read as modeling rest distinct from the activity, the hubbub, the movement, the people. There is value in this reading of rest, particularly in how it spatially mediates self-care (thus, "retreats"). The thing about pandemics, however, lies in the *pan-* prefix denoting "all" or "every." As safer-at-home policies and seemingly limitless racial violence make clear, whether facing COVID or white supremacy, withdrawal to elsewhere is not an option. So, what does rest mean when one cannot "retreat," spatially or politically or otherwise?

After wrestling with what rest is and looks like for me over the past several months, I only have initial thoughts. Rather than understanding and practicing "rest" as something that takes me "away," I am moving toward rest as a crucial form of relationship to the world, to others, and to myself.

As "no justice, no peace" conveys, true rest—peace—is not found in flight from social ills. There is a deeper integrity, one that not only links rest and activity but also frames rest itself as active. St. Augustine reflects on this integrity at the close of the *Confessions* in contemplating divine apatheia as the coherence of God's rest and work in the Sabbath. Tricia Hersey, founder of the Nap Ministry, frames this integrity within contemporary, liberation theological terms. Identifying sleep deprivation as a "racial and social justice issue" of white supremacy and capitalism, she affirms rest as a "form of resistance" and helps people resist through immersive workshops and installations.

The site of rest, the source of peace, and the offering of justice are one and the same. This identity, reflected in Jesus, tells us something about how we can and should live in this moment. If our struggles preclude or exclude rest—if they are cultivating fear, anxiety, and a dwindling sense of hope—then we need to find a different way. This does not mean rest is easy; on the contrary, like justice, it may be hard-won.

Rather than displacing the possibility of rest, the multiple pandemics underscore its centrality. Rest is not disconnected from social wellness and political power but vital to it. Rest is liberative—rest *is* resistance.

Jeania Ree V. Moore, a writer and United Methodist deacon, was a doctoral student in religious studies and African American studies at Yale University when this appeared in the January 2021 issue of *Sojourners.*

Sabbath as Resistance

J. Dana Trent

Practicing Sabbath can create space to engage in the "holy work of mending the world."

"America first" is not a new mantra. While Donald Trump used the phrase during his campaign and in his inaugural address, some of its most telling roots are in the America First Committee of the 1940s, which advocated staunch isolationism (and less explicitly, antisemitism) and sought to prevent the United States from entering the Second World War.

For Trump, the phrase is connected to economic wealth. "I'm 'America First,'" Trump told *The New York Times* in a pre-election interview. "But you can't make America great again unless you make it rich again."

When Trump declares he will make "America" first and rich, he's clearly not referring to everyone in the United States. "America first" is a battle cry for the privileged, those who already reap tremendous benefits off the backs of the marginalized. When Trump wants America to be first by being rich, he means white Americans at the helm of corporations and lobbies, whose success comes at the expense of others.

"Prosperity Breeds Amnesia"

Christianity is rooted in a gospel narrative that urges its adherents to strip ourselves of attachment to worldly treasure and the egoism of being first (see Matthew 20:16). Despite that,

Trump's most supportive base is among white evangelicals. As Frederick Douglass put it, "Between the Christianity of this land, and the Christianity of Christ, I recognize the widest possible difference."

Why has so much of modern (white) U.S. Christianity—with its scriptures of the "first shall be last" and in light of hard-earned historical lessons of slavery, the Civil War, and the civil rights movement—aligned itself with values so antithetical to Jesus' message? Perhaps some of the answer can be found in an insight from Walter Brueggemann's *Sabbath as Resistance*: "Prosperity breeds amnesia."

Have we forgotten the story of Exodus? Norman Wirzba of Duke Divinity School described Pharaoh's frenetic "Egypt first" policy of brick-building—the original pyramid scheme—as "the wealth of the few . . . secured at the expense of the many." Scripture is clear, Wirzba says: We simply must do better than this.

Like Pharaoh, Trump wants his "mammon" (Hebrew for money, wealth, or riches) to grow. But Brueggemann warns that mammon comes at the cost of "endless desire, endless productivity, and endless restlessness." Restlessness is a trait we've become accustomed to under Trump. It arrives in the form of angry tweets, ill-informed executive orders, and wall-building rhetoric that condones and perpetuates white supremacy.

How did God's people resist under Pharaoh to become free? They fled to the desert, under Moses' leadership, where they had nothing, but built community shaped by cooperation and love. God then gave them commandments of rituals and ethics—including the obligation to rest—a mitzvah completely antithetical to Pharaoh's (and Trump's) dictatorial agitation.

Have the sons and daughters of Abraham—and the people of the New Covenant in Christ—forgotten tyranny as we've enjoyed American prosperity? Have we stripped the gospels and the story of Exodus so sharply from our canon that we've proof-texted our way into forgetting Pharaoh's tyranny or Jesus' commandments?

Negative and Positive Duties

How will the people of God break free from the modern Pharaoh's enticing chains of first and rich? By acknowledging that we actually serve a God who is neither obsessed nor preoccupied with being first or rich. Rather, this is God who incarnates as a servant, who commands *shabbat* and love for neighbor.

Bowing down to the God of love, and not to Pharaoh, means that we utilize the fourth commandment ("Remember the Sabbath day, and keep it holy") as both a negative and positive duty. First, we must embrace a negative duty to cease from conscious or unconscious participation in this system of violence and oppression accentuated, perpetuated, and maintained by Pharaoh.

An institutional approach to human rights, according to Yale's Thomas Pogge, emphasizes that citizens have a moral duty to refrain from participating in oppressive institutions. And the economic institutions that surround us, as Wirzba describes, are built on oppression. "Whether we care to admit it or not," Wirzba writes, "the church bears a great responsibility for the fact that we are abettors and willing participants in one of the most rapacious, violent, and destructive economies the world has ever known, an economy in which natural habitats, families and local communities, and moral principles are regularly sacrificed for the sake of financial gain."

The problem with worshipping at the altar of mammon—often a cloak for systemic racism—is that it's the altar of Pharaoh, not Jesus. The white American dream so many evangelicals voted for stands in sharp contrast to the gospel—a challenging narrative of inclusion where love, not bricks, is the commodity, freely shared and given to all. But love—cooperation—is the enemy of capitalism, because it fosters community and collaboration, not competition, among peoples.

Second, in Pogge's view, Christians have a positive duty to create systems of care to protect and empower the oppressed from coercive institutions. These systems of care fulfill the greatest commandment: loving God and loving our neighbor. By opting out of Trump's mammon empire, we can opt in to rightly centered systems. From the Israelites to Gandhi's obstructive and constructive programs of resistance, the idea of negative and positive duties has for centuries led to societal change. Using this lens for the fourth commandment of ritual rest from our labor, we opt out of tyranny and opt into care for one another.

Opting Out

Sabbath—the longest of the ten commandments—is both the tie back to Egypt and the fulcrum to the future. Remembering the Sabbath to *lekadsho* ("sanctify it") becomes the bridge from our ritual way of life with God to our ethics toward family and neighbors. But Sabbath is not only for individuals and Israelite families; God says it must be extended to servants, animals, and strangers. Everyone—not just those in Trump's America First—gets a day off.

"Sabbath-keeping is a way of making a statement of peculiar identity amid a larger public identity, of maintaining and enacting a counter-identity," Brueggemann explains. It is a "bodily act of *testimony* to alternative and *resistance* to pervading values and the assumptions behind those values."

As much as our privilege allows, we can use Sabbath to opt out of the mammon machine one day per week. If all U.S. Christians did this, we'd harness and mimic the enormous economic power of the most successful boycotts. But nothing will change if we remain in our silos, allowing the allure of prosperity and the power of empire to obstruct the true meaning of the gospel.

And Sabbath is practiced in community: "God did not give this commandment to a person but to a people, knowing that only those who rested together would be equipped to resist together," Barbara Brown Taylor writes in *The Christian Century*. Keeping Sabbath not only prevents our own exhaustion but also defends against the exploitation of others.

Opting In

Real Sabbath, Brown Taylor insists, is done in community each week and every seven years, Leviticus 25–style. Everyone and everything are affected: Land and animals are given rest; debts are forgiven; those who work in bondage (literally or metaphorically) are freed. It's the kind of wild community cooperation we've come to expect from a triune God. Traditional order is turned upside down; the rules of the game are changed; new systems are created.

But such a radical interweaving of community dependence will not arrive in a white American Christianity that has too much invested in benefiting from Trump's ethos of "America first and rich." Resistance as a community, Brown Taylor insists, comes from those who remove themselves from the merry-go-round to join God in *tikkun olam*, the "holy work of mending the world."

Sabbath as resistance is nearly impossible to practice in isolation. We must opt out of mammon to create new systems of care for the marginalized in our communities. Like Mohandas Gandhi's *satyagraha* ("truth force") movement, our positive duty is to create spaces that foster truth, love, nonviolence, fearlessness, tolerance, and the dissolution of the U.S. "caste" system.

May we, like the Israelites, turn to God each week, to remember and keep holy the fulcrum commandment that connects us to the divine and to one other. May we be reminded that systems of oppression and coercion can only be perpetuated by our participation. If we, as Christians, use Sabbath as a tool of resistance—both in a negative and positive duty—we free ourselves and others from the bigotry of America first and rich.

J. Dana Trent was a graduate of Duke Divinity School, professor of World Religions, and author of *Dessert First: Preparing for Death While Savoring Life* when this appeared in the June 2018 issue of *Sojourners*.

Chapter 3

When Enough Is Enough

Simplified Life

When culture links a person's value to the amount they can consume, writes Faith-Marie Zamblé, "the desire to take one's fiscal habits seriously is radical." Capitalism invented consumerism to preserve its own momentum, addicting ordinary people to stuff. Our addiction is strangling us and our planet. Céire Kealty's examination of the fast fashion industry paints a stark picture. The interview with Christopher Carter on Black veganism examines cultural foodways and eating mindfully. These "simple living" counter-movements have deep religious roots, including in Christianity. Jesus said, "Do not be anxious about your life, what you shall eat, nor about your body, what you shall put on. For life is more than food, and the body more than clothing" (Luke 12:22–23). At Sojourners, we remember that our "extra" belongs to the one who has less; joy is found in life, not stuff.

The Demon, the Desert, and the Wardrobe

Céire Kealty

> Monstrous mountains of our own making are growing in number in the driest non-polar desert on Earth.

In the Christian tradition, the desert serves as the rugged backdrop against which biblical figures and mystical successors encounter God and the ungodly. The desert is a place to grapple with fear, temptation, and self-understanding. From the patriarchs to the Desert Mothers to Christ, the desert is a place of great consequence.

Moses' numinous encounter with the burning bush in the desert directs him from bewilderment toward understanding his mission for God's chosen people. David's time in the desert, spurred by the threats of Saul, inspires him to write poetry and prose to articulate his deep desire for God. Jesus, too, journeyed into the desert in preparation for his public ministry. For forty days, he fasted and endured temptation from the devil—equipping himself well for the trials he would later face.

The Christian tradition continues to uphold the desert as a place of encounter and renewal. For example, the Eastern Orthodox tradition reveres the spiritual endurance of St. Anthony who battled demons in the desert for decades, scorning intimidation while asserting his devotion to Christ. His trials and time in the desert granted him *apatheia*, a Greek word that loosely translates to "emotional equilibrium." For many believers today, these stories provide inspiration in navigating one's own deserts, whether literal or metaphorical.

I find the desert portrait useful when confronting the disturbing forces that persist throughout the world. Though they may not resemble the spirits tormenting Christ and the church's saintly successors, we might be so bold as to call them demons. The demon that has caught my eye in recent months lingers near; it nestles carefully against our skin. We think that the clothes we wear are ours to don, wash, and discard—that they take a tidy journey from drawer to donation bin. In reality, they often land in piles of clothing castoffs in the Atacama Desert in South America. Thousands of miles away, these monstrous mountains of our own making are growing in number in the driest non-polar desert on Earth.

Dumped in the Desert

In November 2021, *Al Jazeera* published an article exposing an environmental problem plaguing Chile: excess clothing waste. The country receives a whopping fifty-nine thousand tons of clothing from Europe, Asia, and the United States every year.

The garments begin their journey through Latin America at the Port of Iquique, which sits in a free trade zone of northern Chile. From here, they can take three paths: Some clothes may be bought by merchants from Santiago, the country's capital. Others will likely be intercepted by smugglers who will distribute the clothes to other countries in Latin America. The third path is bleak: Garments that cannot be sold, whether due to prior wear or damage sustained before or during transport, are dumped in the Atacama Desert.

To make sense of Chile's clothing dumping problem, I contacted Beatriz O'Brien, a Chilean sociologist based in Santiago. When I first spoke with O'Brien about Atacama, she sighed deeply. What we in North America were just now seeing, she had witnessed in-person five to six years earlier. Even then, she said, the waste was staggering. "You feel anguish," she said. "How did this [clothing] get here?"

I share her sorrow. For the last eight years, I have studied the humanitarian and environmental impacts of the global garment industry. I've combed through reports, testimonies, and photos documenting the tangible harms done by industry excesses. While reading reports on Atacama, I struggled to reconcile the images of discarded garments occupying space meant for the desert flora and fauna and, as Christian history notes, spiritual inspiration.

Juxtaposed against the arid backdrop of Chile's largest desert, the mounds are intrudingly garish, scattered like confetti—a rainbow panoply of environmental ruin growing by thirty-nine thousand tons each year, according to *Al Jazeera*. And no one is coming to clean them up.

Because the clothes reside in a free trade zone, a designated area where foreign goods can be moved without paying taxes and duties, there's little incentive for local government to resolve the waste accumulation or pay out of pocket for tariffs to clear the existing waste. So, there the clothes sit. Economically disenfranchised residents of North Chile and neighboring countries travel to the dumps to find garments suitable for their families to wear or for resale in their communities, risking exposure to toxins and pollution caused by the piles. Items that are not retrieved remain splayed across the desert floor, left to rot.

Many of the clothes were treated with chemicals at the time of production or are synthetic, made of polyester and other plastic fabrics. As they degrade, toxins seep into the ground, contaminating soil and injuring surrounding animal and plant life. The process is agonizingly slow, O'Brien reminds me, as many of these garments will take hundreds of years to break down, and there is limited data on the long-term environmental impacts to the region. And, as O'Brien notes, those who have tried to take samples have faced intimidation by smugglers.

Though our discussion was rich with systemic analysis, O'Brien doesn't shy away from sharing the sensorial gravity of her encounter with Atacama. In surveying the desert and its fabric fragments, she sensed an energy that was, in her words, "not good." Perhaps this sensation, this energy, was simply a manifestation of the vices wrought on the desert ground, from environmental abuse to smuggling to illegal activities. Perhaps the sheer gravity of the waste before her—and now, before us—was overwhelming in itself. But what forces are embedded in the rotten, burnt, ruined castoffs of our closets?

More than Meets the Eye

In 2019, the Vatican's Synod on the Amazon urged believers to understand "acts and habits of pollution and destruction of environmental harmony" as "ecological sin." We would be right to interpret the waste that accumulates in Atacama as sin. Yet there is still more than meets the eye. When I indulge in shopping excursions and purchase clothes that I don't need (but certainly *want*), I sense something more behind that want—something persistent, pushing me toward unbridled accumulation, fueling and endorsing my temptation to buy with abandon.

It is here that I find helpful the image of the demonic. At first blush, it might seem inappropriate to frame clothing waste—something so banal, so ubiquitous to many North American households—as demonic. Yet how could we not regard such widespread waste, which denigrates the handiwork of oft-underpaid garment workers, degrades the natural environment, wreaks ecological harm on vulnerable ecosystems and vulnerable people, and hides the hyper-consumptive vices of the materialistic West from view, as ungodly?

The demon of clothing waste materializes most shockingly in the clothing mounds of Atacama. It is embedded deep in the soil. Yet this demon also lurks in every overstuffed closet. It lingers in the filled-to-the-brim donation bags of well-meaning believers who march their excesses to the nearest Goodwill drop-off site, whispering assurances that "a poor child somewhere will wear the stained T-shirt, too-big or too-small pants, and battered sneakers." But these assurances are lies, manufactured by corporations, endorsed by churches, and reinforced by colonialist attachments to white-savior narratives and impersonal acts of charity. And the rotten fruits of these lies are hellish for the world's most vulnerable.

When we face the demon of clothing waste, we face a great shame personally and systemically. The demon of clothing waste forces us to confront the vicious afterlife of our sartorial castoffs. In doing so, the demon exposes the rot underlying our systems of consumption *and* production. Vox reports that the global garment industry produces between 80 billion and 150 billion garments a year; nearly three-fifths of these garments are incinerated or discarded in landfills within a few years of being made. Despite this baffling waste, clothing corporations continue to impose massive production quotas, forcing burdened workers to churn out stock that ultimately goes to waste.

Facing the Demon

We may be tempted to despair after considering the expansive waste in the Atacama and in other areas of the world that haven't caught the radar of mainstream media. It appears that our deserts—literal and spiritual—burst at the seams with vice and strife. Yet we must remember that these deserts house more than devastation. O'Brien spoke affectionately of the flora and fauna indigenous to the Atacama. Though it's one of the driest deserts in the world, and the driest in Latin America, the desert supports numerous creatures, from ferns to Andean condors. These critters bespeak creative joy, reminding us of how the desert is a holy space of generative encounter.

The heralded figures of Christianity remind us of this truth. It is in the desert that God spoke to Abraham, urged Moses to guide the Israelites out of slavery which birthed the revelations of Mount Sinai, rejuvenated Elijah at the point of death, and sustained John the Baptist during his ascetic residence in the wilderness. We ought to consider the steadfast words of John the Baptist who, when asked who he was, turned to the words of the prophet Isaiah, saying, "I am the voice of one crying out in the wilderness, 'Make straight the way of the Lord'" (John 1:23). I envision God's call reverberating through the waste-laden Atacama Desert. This call decries the results of our collective and corporate greed. But it also urges the hearer toward the promise of salvation, posing the challenge to "make straight the way of the Lord." In the face of thousands of tons of rotting garments, how can we even begin to prepare this way, to atone, and to make things right and just?

We might start by approaching Atacama as a spiritual crossroads. Shall we be tempted once more by the demon of conspicuous consumption, of fast fashion, of disregard for laborers' handiwork? Shall we choose the path of indulgence and detached disposal, while disregarding the harm inflicted on God's green Earth? Or shall we heed the desert cry, scorn the demon of clothing waste, and turn toward more just ends?

Latin American innovators have already heeded this cry. Ecocitex converts textile waste into upcycled products. EcoFibra Chile transforms textile waste into insulation panels. Both companies are addressing clothing waste through creative action. We can be inspired by their work to be more innovative with our excesses and take seriously the call to reduce, reuse, and repair our wardrobe.

Interpreting Atacama as a tangible, spiritual desert, plagued by the demon of clothing waste, proves generative for believers. Atacama exposes the spiritual relevance of clothing waste, laying bare our disordered desire, haywire appetites, and our multitude of sins—environmental, interpersonal, and transnational. The problem of clothing waste, highlighted by Atacama, exists not only as a concern for ethicists, environmentalists, and sociologists, but also for theologians. Here, the desert and demon awaken us to the spiritual rot made manifest in clothing castoffs, bursting wardrobes, crowded garment factories, and choked Earth. From here, we can see how clothes—and how we purchase, care for, and discard them—deserve theological attention.

The portrait of the demon and the desert hastens our response to God's call, guiding us toward renewed action. Repenting from the systems in which we are ensnared, and regarding them as they are—demonic and in disrepair—frees us to live differently, to pursue accountability in personal endeavors and structural participation. Facing the demon compels us to consider the resonant call of God weaving through the deserts of our lives.

The creatures persisting throughout Atacama despite the demon of clothing waste make manifest the enduring joy of created life and encourage us to live, act, and even consume anew, for the sake of these lives—and for our own. My hope is you can be moved by Atacama to act in ways that eschew the temptations of conspicuous consumption, secure justice for the communities burdened by our clothing waste, and replenish the Earth with rich soil devoid of discarded dresses.

Céire Kealty holds a doctorate in theology from Villanova University, where she studied fashion theory, spirituality, and ethics. This appeared in the August 2022 issue of *Sojourners*.

You Can't (Fully) Blame Your Distraction on Your Phone

Rose Marie Berger

> An unsettled, restless, disquiet mind is as old as humanity—and makes it hard to meet God.

Have you ever had one of those perfect moments?

My wife and I sat on a bench at the farmers market with a plate of steaming hot tamales before us and a bag of crisp fennel bulbs, Pink Lady apples, and fresh spinach at our feet. The air smelled of salt and cooking oil. A deep yellow and iridescent gold light wrapped around us. Every noise fell away in a holy hush. We met, however fleeting, the "still point of the turning world" described by poet T.S. Eliot. Held and beheld.

To be honest, I usually miss these moments. Though I try (religiously) to keep custody of my mind and attention, the world we live in now beeps, dings, buzzes, and updates 24-7. It's hard for God to break in. Perhaps this description of digital architecture's pointed intrusions into our one beautiful life is too minimalist. Most days, I'm holding my breath against the crushing dynamics of digital onrush and knowledge outflow. I miss the still points between the crest and lip of that wave.

But I won't blame my "monkey mind" wholly on instant communication. An unsettled, restless, disquieted mind is as old as humanity (and perhaps distinct to us). My guess is that we've been prone to distraction since we first glimpsed that shiny, delicious apple, just exceeding our grasp. Nearly every religious tradition teaches techniques for training attention and concentration—not to detach or parade a black belt in "mindfulness," but because the taproot of anxious toil consists of pride, ego, and fear, each of which separates us from God. Pride because whole universes of social need appear to have me at their center. Ego because the ease with which digital messages puncture my private life makes me feel that no place is safe, no time can't be breached, and that I must react or risk, as a result, a plummet in self-value. Fear from my brain's ancient amygdala that if I don't react (with nearly involuntary muscle response), I might die, might be cut from the herd.

More than two millennia ago, the Jewish sage Ben Sira of Jerusalem offered a precise diagnosis: "The beginning of pride is stubbornness in withdrawing the heart from one's Maker" (Sirach 10:12). Prayer and contemplative practices, service that centers community rather than self, and sabbath disciplines that reattach one's heart to that of our Maker: All teach us to attend to the "still points."

Ben Sira warns not to interfere in other people's business (11:9). Seriously? What would happen to social media? And not to undertake too many activities because, as theologian and mystic Howard Thurman writes in *Meditations of the Heart*, "There is some strange magic in activity." Chasing after activity leads to failure, and one will never be free, no matter our escape plans. Ben Sira points to my present condition: "There are those who exhaust themselves, tire themselves out and become anxious, yet in the end they are only the poorer" (11:11).

In *The Spirit of Life*, theologian Jürgen Moltmann reflects on those moments when our souls rest in God. "If we become one with ourselves, the Shekinah [presence, of God] comes to rest." But the encounter with God's Shekinah is one born of suffering with the world, not escaping from it or its pain. When we meet those still points, then activity can transform into action with holy purpose. When our life force drives toward God alone, then we are linked with our Maker in "indescribable joy."

Ulrich Duchrow, an economist and theologian, once told me, "In Germany, we have a movement with a slogan that says, 'If you live differently, you live better.' If you go to a local farmers market where the vegetables are still wet with the water of the morning, it's just a joy to get your vegetables." Maybe that explains our "perfect moment."

Rose Marie Berger, author of *Who Killed Donté Manning?* and *Bending the Arch: Poems*, was senior editor of *Sojourners* magazine when this appeared in the February/March 2023 issue.

Lives of Compassion and Meaning

Ann B. McClenahan

The great irony about today's "simple living" trend is that it really isn't simple, or about simple things, at all. Two volumes—*Simpler Living, Compassionate Life: A Christian Perspective*, edited and compiled by Michael Schut, and *Graceful Simplicity: Toward a Philosophy and Politics of Simple Living* by Jerome M. Segal—nicely illustrate this observation.

In Schut's collection of twenty-nine articles and two brief stories, "simple living" serves as the umbrella under which are grouped themes ranging from the value of contemplative prayer, leisure time, and daily attentiveness to the need for profound economic and ecological change. From a somewhat different perspective, Segal defines "simple living" as graceful living, a way of life in which the aesthetic dimension and the role of service are central. "Simple living" thus begins to emerge as a catch phrase for a number of personal, social, environmental, economic, and political initiatives that have both micro and macro implications.

Focusing on the latter, Harvard University's Timothy C. Weiskel offers in the Schut volume one of the most powerful and provocative presentations, where he describes the increasingly catastrophic impact of growth and consumerism on the global ecology. Referencing scientific indicators that suggest we have entered a global "extinction event" affecting numerous species, Weiskel calls for a theological revolution to unseat our dual Western commitments to human dominion over nature and to unlimited growth and consumption. He calls upon theologians—and readers—to take on the very un-simple task of articulating and acting upon a theology that locates the human species within, not above, a larger whole and that stands as a challenge to contemporary conditions of global human and ecological suffering.

Weiskel reminds us that while theology—literally talk about God or, more broadly, reflections on God, the world, and ourselves—does not determine evolutionary processes, it can "determine the character of our engagement with natural processes and thus conditions the outcome." The reader is left to reflect on the important relationship between theological thought and subsequent acts—and the potential consequences if this is ignored.

From a more micro perspective, the Schut volume includes James T. Mulligan's essay, "The Great Hunter-Gatherer Continuum." Mulligan, executive director of Earth Ministry, leads the reader through the pros and cons of patronizing various food outlets. The cultural norm, the supermarket, is contrasted with six other less convenient but more "earth friendly" options. Mulligan asks us to consider the community-supported agriculture farm, for example, where subscribers receive a portion of the weekly harvest throughout the year. What is traded for convenience and availability (tomatoes in December would be out for most of us) is made up through "keeping one more farm and one more farmer an active part of the local food economy."

Other essays compiled by Schut address issues of time, money, material consumption, and community-building advocated by nineteen contributors, including Frederick Buechner, Juliet Schor, Wendell Berry, and Henri Nouwen. A useful feature of this collection is the fifty-five-page study guide at the end, designed to facilitate small group discussions. For each of ten sessions, Schut has included discussion topics, meditations and prayers, and suggested action steps.

Jerome Segal, a political activist and former staff member of the House Budget Committee, sketches his vision of what American middle-class "simple living" might look like and how it could be accomplished. Drawing on Aristotle and various utopian and anti-consumptionist strands in American thought, Segal argues that the purpose of an economy is to "liberate us from the economic—to provide a material platform from which we may go forth to build the good life."

Segal has written an easy-to-read, wide-ranging, and impassioned manifesto for social and economic policy change, but readers may stumble—or derail entirely—as a result of some of his assumptions and recommendations. I cannot speak as an African American or member of the urban poor; but as a woman who spent twenty years in American business and the past three in the academy, I do not share Segal's perspective that our society is "substantially along the way to overcoming historic legacies of slavery, mass poverty, and the subjugation of women." Nor do I share his backward-yearning observation that the "world we have lost was in many ways more interesting, more diverse, and often more beautiful than the world we have created."

After spending several weeks reflecting on "simple living," I find myself left with two lingering questions. First, which segments of society are driving this movement and which are not? I can't help wondering about the voices that are largely missing from these two volumes—the voices of people of color, of people without multiple college degrees, of people just starting to climb the economic ladder, and, yes, even of people in the business community. Is "simple living" a social, economic, and political way of life that really embraces all? I would like to hear more.

Secondly, I wonder why ideas such as these are presented under the rubric of "simple living." Is it "simple living" to initiate and effect the many social and economic changes advocated?

Does the concept of simplicity serve us well in addressing enormously complex issues of hunger, homelessness, and human and ecological violence in our society? These books wrestle with how we can make time and create commitment to lives and communities of compassion, justice, respect, dignity, and meaning. But these are not simple goals, and it is hard to imagine that they will be achieved by a curiously nostalgic call to a "simple life." As a former marketing executive, I wonder if there are marketing fingerprints on that moniker.

Ann B. McClenahan spent twenty years as an advertising and marketing professional before entering Harvard Divinity School, where she completed the Master of Divinity program in June 1999. This appeared in the July-August 2000 issue of *Sojourners*.

Ten Ways to Live "Almost Amish"

Nancy Sleeth

"What are you, Amish or something?" a large man with a booming voice asked from the back of the room. I was not surprised by the question, but the tone rattled me a bit.

Open your eyes! I wanted to reply. *Am I wearing a bonnet? We arrived in a Prius, not on a pony.*

The question came at the close of a long day, at the end of a long speaking tour. I was tired, but that's no excuse for my less-than-gracious thoughts. It was not the first time my family had been compared to the Amish, nor would it be the last. So why did this question stay with me, long after the workshop ended?

Over the previous few years my husband, Matthew, and I had gone around the country giving nearly a thousand talks, sermons, seminars, and retreats about the scriptural call to care for God's creation. We wrote books on the subject. We made films. From Washington State to Washington, D.C., we had fielded questions on everything from light bulbs to the light of Jesus, from water bottles to living waters, from soil erosion to the four kinds of soils. The Q&A session was usually our favorite part of the seminar.

As a teacher, I often say that there are no bad questions. This one, as it turns out, was especially good because it forced me to examine my life in new ways. Now, a few years later, I feel nothing but gratitude for this man's question, for it started me on my *Almost* Amish journey.

Principles to Live By

The Amish are by no means a perfect people, and there are dark sides to their history. Their example, however, does have much to teach us. How can we incorporate the best of Amish principles into our modern lives? To answer this, I did some reading. And some visiting. And some listening. I in no way pretend to be an expert on the Amish, but the more I read and visited and listened, the more I found to admire. The Amish are islands of sanity in a whirlpool of change.

Along the way, I discovered some Amish principles that we can all try to emulate. These principles (similar to the list that Wendell Berry laid out more than two decades ago in *Home Economics*) provide guidelines for a simpler, slower, more sustainable life. They offer me hope.

1. Homes are simple, uncluttered, and clean; the outside reflects the inside.

Most modern American homes are burdened by the accumulation of mass-produced junk, bought on impulse, and paid for with credit, which either falls apart or no one uses. Cluttered homes lead to cluttered lives, and cluttered lives can harm families.

Our homes reflect our values. They reflect who we are inside and what we hold most precious. If our houses are cluttered, our hearts are too. Possessions should work for us; we should not work for them. Too easily, our homes and the stuff that fills them can become false idols, tempting us to break the first of the Ten Commandments. The Amish offer a less cluttered, more sustainable alternative.

2. Technology serves as a tool and does not rule as a master.

Recently, I sat down and made a list of the things I love about our twenty-first-century technology:

- I can work anytime, anywhere.
- I can check email anytime.
- People get back to me immediately.
- I can access entertainment anytime.
- I can stay informed all the time.
- I can get in touch with almost anyone, anytime.
- I can buy almost anything, anytime.
- I can multitask.
- There's always something to do.
- I never feel alone.

And then I made a list of what I *hate* about modern technology:

- I can work anytime, anywhere.
- I can check email anytime.
- People get back to me immediately.
- I can access entertainment anytime.
- I can stay informed all the time.
- I can get in touch with almost anyone, anytime.
- I can buy almost anything, anytime.
- I can multitask.
- There's always something to do.
- I never feel alone.

I know I'm not the only one feeling this love-hate relationship with technology: We love the convenience technology affords. We hate how technology is taking over our lives.

The Amish are different—famously so. They understand that technology is neither fully good nor fully bad, but a tool to be used; we should not become either slaves or gluttons on account of it. In the upside-down world of Christ, setting boundaries with technology can be one of the most liberating things we can do.

3. Saving more and spending less brings financial peace.

Amish attitudes toward money are based on biblical principles. Saving is encouraged; frivolous spending and coveting are not. The Amish stay out of debt, give generously, and make investments in keeping with their values. Amish businesses thrive when others fail because the goal is to make a living, not make a killing.

Think about where the U.S. economy would be today if we applied Almost Amish principles to personal, corporate, and governmental finances. We would not spend money we did not have. We would restrain our tendencies toward greed. We would plan for the future, sacrificing immediate gratification for the long-term good. We might not have the mercurial highs, but we also would avoid the devastating crashes that have left so many homeless and hopeless in recent years. We would take care of the poor among us. Those with more would help those with less.

4. Time spent in God's creation reveals the face of God.

One of the most frequent *places* where God speaks to us is in nature.

I like to call these "Romans 1:20 moments." In this verse Paul says, essentially, that we can get to know God by simply taking a stroll in our backyard. Once again, we can take a cue here from the Amish, who make the outdoors a central focus of life. The more time they spend in God's creation, the more they come to know the Creator. But the opposite is also true. The less time we spend outdoors, the more alienated from God we can become.

Scripture tells us to live in the world, not of the world. The Almost Amish extension might be to live less in the manmade world and more in the God-made world. Adjusting the ratio can be the difference between a paradise imperiled and paradise restored—an abandoned lot or a community garden.

5. *Small and local leads to saner lives.*

If the Amish made bumper stickers for their buggies, the best-seller might read, "Be not conformed to this world" (Romans 12:2). The world believes bigger is better, yet recent history has revealed the high cost of our mega-sized world. Now we are slowly relearning what the Amish have always known: infinite growth is not only impossible but in many instances undesirable. Focusing on an infinite God, not infinite growth, frees us from so much striving and allows us to lead simpler, less burdened lives.

6. *Service to others reduces loneliness and isolation.*

The Amish understand that the key to a joyful life is simple: serve God and serve your neighbor. Interdependence can be more holy than independence. But how does that play out?

The Amish serve their children by doing the hard work of parenting, teaching them the skills and habits that will make them healthy spouses, colleagues, and neighbors. Instead of short-term distraction or coddling, they aim for long-term character and strength.

In acting kind, we become kind. In serving others, we are served. Blessed are the merciful and the pure of heart. As the physical arms of God Almighty, we comfort those who mourn. In doing so, we serve him gladly, all the days of our lives.

7. *The only true security comes from God.*

Half a century ago, Martin Luther King Jr. gave a sermon entitled "Paul's Letter to American Christians." In it, King warns that moral advances are not keeping abreast with our technological advances: "Through your scientific genius you have made of the world a neighborhood, but through your moral and spiritual genius you have failed to make of it a brotherhood."

We are all brothers and sisters in Christ. As the family of God, we must reach out to protect and care for others, even when it is inconvenient or costly.

The Amish build stability, routine, and tradition into their lives, all centered on God. We, too, can build a firm foundation based on an all-powerful, all-knowing, and all-loving God. Family and friends, acting as the hands and feet of God, can provide comfort along the way. Yet it is God—first, last, and always—who is the Truth, the Light, and the Way.

8. Knowing neighbors and supporting local businesses build community.

The Amish have avoided many of our social ills because they build community into their lives. People know and care about one another. They support one another's businesses, worship together, take an active role in their children's education, welcome neighbors into their homes, and engage in group activities to break up the routine of work. Because of this emphasis on community, virtually no members are homeless, unemployed, or living on government subsidies. Almost no Amish people are incarcerated, and rarely do Amish couples divorce.

Here's the good news: the power of community is not limited to those born Amish. It can start with you, in your neighborhood, beginning today.

9. Family ties are lifelong; they change but never cease.

Broken families have become the norm in modern society, but they are an anomaly in Amish communities. The main reason families do not break up is because their first allegiance is to God, not self. Children are not idols to be worshiped. Husbands and wives are not disposable. The (top) Ten Commandments are not optional. Harmony takes precedence over self-interest.

The Amish have a saying: "A happy marriage is a long conversation that always seems too short." And, of course, happy marriages tend to make for happy families. Do everything in your power to make gatherings with family part of a long conversation, full of joy, harmony, and faith in an all-powerful Father who loves every one of his children. Keeping your family on track might be the most important job you ever have.

10. Faith life and way of life are inseparable.

We are God's children not just on Sundays, but every day of the week. Whether we are at work, at home, in the car, or on the soccer field, we are to act with compassion and love. What we do and say does matter, not only to our friends and family, but to our Father.

Where we seek spiritual guidance also matters. The Bible warns of a time when people "will follow their own desires and will look for teachers who will tell them whatever their itching ears want to hear" (2 Timothy 4:3). The Amish example helps us counter such impulses, reminding us time and again, as C. S. Lewis advises in *Mere Christianity*, that "Going back can sometimes be the quickest way forward."

The Almost Amish life is a conscious life. Though the choices we make may vary, it is a journey that we can take together—and above all, with God.

At one time or another, many of us have been amazed when God puts *exactly* the right Scripture before us, at precisely the moment we need it. In my regular Bible reading, I have been studying the teachings of Jeremiah.

> *This is what the Lord says:*
> *"Stop at the crossroads and look around.*
> *Ask for the old, godly way, and walk in it.*
> *Travel its path, and you will find rest for your souls."*
> (Jeremiah 6:16)

This wisdom bears repeating: *Stop at the crossroads. Ask for the old, godly way. Travel its path, and you will find rest for your souls.*

Thanks to that man in the back of the room with the booming voice, I now have an answer to his question, "What are you, Amish or something?"

"Not Amish—*Almost* Amish!"

My prayer is that wherever you are along the Almost Amish path, you have the will, passion, and energy to make one change—however small—this very day. My prayer is that you gain joy in drawing closer to God and lean on him for the strength needed to carry through. My prayer is that you find the peace that surpasses all understanding as you continue along the Almost Amish journey. May God bless you with his love and protection every step of the way!

Nancy Sleeth was co-founder of the faith-based environmental non-profit Blessed Earth when this appeared on sojo.net on August 2, 2012. This article includes adaptations from her book, *Almost Amish: One Woman's Quest for a Slower, Simpler, More Sustainable Life.*

When Enough Is Enough

William T. Cavanaugh

The contrast between consumerism and simple living at first glance seems fairly straightforward: Consumerism is about having more stuff, simple living is about having less stuff. Consumerism seems to be a permutation of the age-old vice of avarice, whose "special malice," says the *Catholic Encyclopedia*, "lies in that it makes the getting and keeping of money, possessions, and the like a purpose in itself to live for." As the old vitamin commercial from the '80s so bluntly put it, "I want MORE for ME."

Avarice, however, does not really exhaust the phenomenon of consumerism. Consumerism is not so much about having *more* as it is about having *something else.* It is not buying but shopping that captures the spirit of consumerism. Buying is certainly an important part of consumerism, but buying brings a temporary halt to the restlessness that typifies it. It is this restlessness—the moving on to shopping for something else no matter what one has just purchased—that sets the spiritual tone for consumerism.

In the Christian tradition we are accustomed to thinking that the greatest temptation associated with material things is an inordinate attachment to them. Since biblical times and before, some people have accumulated great stores of wealth, and the Bible is often quite severe in its judgment of them. When we hear that the "love of money is a root of all kinds of evil" (1 Timothy 6:10), and that the "poor in spirit" are blessed

(Matthew 5:3), we resolve to cultivate an attitude of detachment from the material things we have. The problem is that consumerism is already a spiritual discipline of detachment, though one with a very different way of operating than classical Christian asceticism.

What marks consumerism as something new is its tendency to reduce everything, both the material and the spiritual, to a commodity able to be exchanged. Things that no other culture ever thought could be bought and sold—water, genetic codes, names (Tostitos Fiesta Bowl), human blood, the rights to emit pollutants into the air—are now routinely offered on the market. The recent story of the Nebraska man who auctioned off advertising space on his forehead is only the latest example of the commodification of everything. This story is not so much a lesson about greed—his forehead was apparently not big enough to garner bids for more than a few hundred dollars—as a statement about the extent to which we are able to become detached from even those things, like our foreheads, to which we are most obviously attached. We stand back from our bodies, faiths, vocations. Our very identity is something to be tried on, chosen, bought, sold, and discarded at will.

The Satisfying Nature of Dissatisfaction

Consumerism is a spiritual attitude that is deeply entangled with changes since the Industrial Revolution in the way goods are produced. In pre-industrial society, the home was a place not merely of consumption but of production. Most people lived on farms and made the majority of the goods that they needed. Starting with the enclosure of common lands in England and elsewhere in Europe, the bulk of the population was moved away from subsistence farming and into factory labor. Cottage industries were wiped away by the production of cheap goods from mechanized factories, compelling people to enter the market as wage laborers.

With the relentless pressures on the family farm that continue today, the home as a site of significant production has all but disappeared. We make almost nothing of what we consume. The process of globalization has accelerated this detachment from production. Fewer and fewer of us have any idea what factory work is like, since manufacturing jobs are more and more being transferred overseas. Nor do we have much more than a vague idea of the wages or working conditions of the workers who make what we buy.

There are two significant results to these historical shifts. First, many people have become detached from their labor, seeing work not as a creative vocation but as a commodity to be sold in exchange for wages. Part of our very selves and the impress we make on the world is commodified. Second, our connection to things has become very tenuous. We know almost nothing about how products are made and how they end up in our shopping cart. The bananas we meet in the grocery story refuse to tell us how they ended up in Minnesota in the dead of winter. We eat cows without ever having been near more than a few pounds of beef flesh at any one time. We simply pull products off the shelves, dump them in our carts, and keep shopping.

Detached from their origins in human work and the networks of human community, commodities take on a life of their own. In the moment of encounter between product and consumer, the connection to other people and places falls away. The consumer has little or no connection to the producer, and more than likely has little connection to the seller either, since most local stores have been replaced by giant, impersonal chain stores. The relationship of consumption has been reduced to the bare encounter of consumer and thing, with nothing to connect the two except the utility of the product to the consumer.

The story does not end with the detachment of consumers from production and from things, however, for alienation and detachment do not explain the appeal of consumerism. If the consumer and the inert thing were left staring at each other across the store aisle, consumption would not keep pace with production. The product must be made to sing and dance and create a new kind of relationship between itself and the consumer.

Histories of marketing commonly trace the rise of mass advertising to the need to create mass consumption in the wake of industrialization. Factories were capable of producing goods at a heretofore unimaginable rate. The value of manufactured goods increased more than sixfold during the last four decades of the nineteenth century. Markets had to be created for all those products. People had to be trained to act as consumers, to be attracted to items to which they had no natural connection. Marketers began talking about "building relationships" between consumers and products. The catch is that these relationships could not be too durable or, once again, the pace of consumption would not keep up with the pace of production. People could not become too content or attached to products; desire had to be kept on the move. So began what the marketing department of General Motors—in a reference to changing car models every year—once called "the organized creation of dissatisfaction."

What has happened in consumer society is that dissatisfaction and satisfaction have ceased to be opposites. Pleasure resides not in having but in wanting. Insofar as an item obtained brings a temporary halt to desire, it becomes undesirable. This is why shopping, not buying, captures the spirit of consumerism, and why shopaholism is being treated as an addiction. Consumerism is a restless spirit, constantly in search of something new. Consumerism is typified by detachment, not attachment, for desire must be kept on the move. Consumerism is also typified by scarcity, not abundance, for as long as desire is endless, there will never be enough stuff to go around.

Being Consumed

If detachment is the problem, should the Christian respond with greater attachment to material things? Not exactly. St. Augustine famously prayed to God "our heart is restless until it rests in you." Augustine knew that mere created things fall far short of the glory of God, such that ultimate satisfaction can never be found in created things on their own. Nevertheless, created things are good because they participate in the goodness of their creator. They contain vestiges of the Creator in them, vestiges that ought to lead us beyond the things themselves to the source of their being.

In this spiritual universe there is no such thing as an isolated commodity confronting an isolated individual. All created things sing and dance and shout of the glory of God. People and things are united in one great web of being, flowing from and returning to their Creator. Our dissatisfaction with things does not lead us endlessly on to the next thing but to our true end in God. The Christian view elevates the dignity of things by seeing them as participating in the being of God, but simultaneously causes us to look through and beyond things to their Creator.

Participation in this great web of created being informs the way that Christians view production. Work is not simply a means to gaining money so that we may consume. Work establishes an intimacy with God's creation, so that we become, as Pope John Paul II reminds us, "co-creators" with God in our work. Participation in God also informs how we view one another. Human persons are not only connected to things but to other persons. We are all made in the image of God, and all made to participate in the body of Christ. Such is our close connection that we share the same sufferings and the same joys (1 Corinthians 12:26). It is as impossible to ignore sweatshop labor as it is to ignore pain in our own bodies.

In the Christian view, we do not stand apart from the rest of creation as individuals, appropriating, consuming, and discarding. We are rather consumed, as it were, by something larger than us. When we consume the body of Christ at the Lord's table, we are in fact consumed by the larger body, the church. In his *Confessions*, Augustine hears Christ's voice say, "Grow and you will feed on me. And you will not change me into you like the food your flesh eats, but you will be changed into me." At the communion table, the act of consumption is turned inside out, such that in eating we become food for others. True consumption, in the Christian understanding, is thus a kind of self-emptying, a decentering of the self into a larger web of participation. Thus Jesus connects the "abundant life" in John 10:10 to laying down one's life in 10:11. True abundance is never realized by the competition of insatiable desires for scarce goods. It is realized by emptying the small self into the larger reality of God's superabundant life.

The Christian task in a consumer society, then, is to create economic spaces that underscore our spiritual and physical connection to creation and to each other. We must strive to demystify commodities by being informed about where they come from, who makes them, and under what conditions. We should support products, such as fair-trade coffee, that pull back the veil from the production process and offer a sustainable life to their producers. We should attempt to create local, face-to-face economies, where consumers and producers know each other well enough that their interests tend to merge. My parish's connection to a local cooperative of family farms is a hopeful example.

Finally, we should attempt to close the gap between work and consumption by supporting worker ownership of the means of production. The first step toward doing so is turning our homes back into sites of production. To bake bread, to make our own entertainment, and do so in community with others: These are small but important steps in turning from consumers to celebrants of God's abundant life.

William T. Cavanaugh was associate professor of theology at the University of St. Thomas in St. Paul, Minnesota, and author of *Theopolitical Imagination* (T&T Clark) when this article appeared in the May 2005 issue of *Sojourners.*

What Minimalism Lacks

Faith-Marie Zamblé

> The trendy aesthetic often means giving up everything . . . except privilege.

Certain strains of consumerism are easy to spot. Think Beverly Hills and walls stacked with brightly colored shoes and purses, like heaps of fresh produce. Closer to home, perhaps, is the caricature of suburban consumption—gas-guzzling SUVs, expensive outerwear.

And then there's minimalism, an ideology defined by its emphasis on intentional efforts to spend less. At its best, minimalism provides a healthy alternative for people of faith seeking simplicity and thoughtful economic practices. At its worst, the minimalist aesthetic looks an awful lot like the system it was designed to critique—oblivious, privileged, and disconnected from reality.

"You need less stuff than you think!" minimalists cry, their authentic Peruvian bracelets clinking together in agreement. From a theological perspective, the minimalists are right. From a social perspective, they're missing a critical caveat: A person can make do with less *if* they have more. Would the person whose closet consists of three shirts out of necessity be considered a minimalist? Probably not, because minimalism is marketed to and for the wealthy. Somehow, the exhortation to "buy less" has morphed into "buy less, but buy expensively—I mean, ethically!"

With corporations vying for both our wallets and our hearts, where and how a person spends her money matters. The choice to invest in an item, and its maker, rather than enter the breakneck cycle of throwaway consumerism, is shot through with good intent. It is also a choice threaded with privilege.

In a world that often links a person's value to the amount she can consume, the desire to take one's fiscal habits seriously is radical—and for people of faith, essential. But after we look at our daily practices, we need to ask why we have so many resources while others have so few. We need to look compassionately at broken systems that make poorer folks feel that their worth is directly proportional to the things they own. We must confront toxic materialism even within ourselves.

Buying handmade items, decluttering our lives, or shifting the palette of our wardrobes to grayscale are value-neutral choices that only accrue ethical value when other areas of our lives also shift. If our hearts do not grow larger in proportion to the spaces we clear in our homes, if we do not discipline our unruly consumerist impulses, minimalism is nothing more than a class signifier disguised as social consciousness.

Privilege shouldn't pressure us into guilt-stricken immobility. After all, Christians are called to examine privilege when we have it and use it for the common good. Fortunately, in true biblical fashion, there are conditions for this. When Jesus told the rich young ruler to sell all he had, the next step wasn't for him to turn around and buy fewer (but more elegant) items from Anthropologie. The next step was to give the money to the poor. Are we willing to give up what insulates us from our neighbors' suffering because we trust that God will provide, because our resources are better spent in the service of others?

Though the quest for less stuff is a noble one, without self-awareness minimalism can quickly become a shallow fix for the more complicated work of economic justice and spiritual depth.

Faith-Marie Zamblé, an artist and writer, was a MFA candidate in dramaturgy and dramatic criticism at the Yale School of Drama when this appeared in the July 2018 issue of *Sojourners*.

Simple Living Becomes Sexy

Valerie Weaver-Zercher

Christians concerned about poverty and the environment aren't used to sitting at the popular table in the cultural cafeteria. So, when Cindy Crawford waxes poetic about her "eco-awakening" in *Vanity Fair* and a Proctor & Gamble advertising circular shows a smiling woman icing a cake beside the words "Do more with less"—well, we can be forgiven for not knowing whether to applaud or grimace. Beg your pardon if we ask questions about the monetizing of our values, or if we doubt that Zac Efron's use of an "eco-limo" has anything to do with what we've been talking about all these years.

By now, many Christians are accustomed to being branded "green" because they freeze corn or bike to work. The corporate hijacking of the environmental movement is old news, writes Lauren Weber, author of *In Cheap We Trust: The Story of a Misunderstood American Virtue*. What is new, Weber claims, is the extent to which "cheap is the new green." Stories about the new frugality have hit most major news outlets, and what Weber calls the "eco-cheap" economy—the world of secondhand commerce, bartering, and freeganism—is drumming up increasing attention.

So when simple living becomes sexy, what's a Christian to do? It seems a little priggish to insist on drawing distinctions between the pop culture iteration of living more with less and "our" version. Besides, many different environmentalisms and movements toward thrift are afoot today, and Christians are often at the forefront of both, making the comparison between Christian "more-with-less-ness" and popular movements a little muddy. And despite the *More-with-Less Cookbook* by Doris Janzen Longacre and its companion volume, *Living More with Less*, Mennonites (and other Christians) don't own the phrase any more than Proctor & Gamble does.

Plus, isn't this exactly what we've been hoping for—more people detoxing from their consumptive and earth-destroying addictions? Who cares whether people are motivated by authentic concern for the poor and the planet—or by how gorgeous Cameron Diaz looks in a YouTube video about the environmental crisis when she tilts her head and asks earnestly, "How do you get people to care?"

On the other hand, an uncritical embrace of all things touted as thrifty and green could weaken the kind of rigorous approach that more-with-less living can entail. Is it really possible for Hollywood to contribute to the cause without cheapening it?

At the risk of sounding pedantic, I offer three things that the fashionably green and cheap movements might learn from Longacre and the contributors to her more-with-less books, most of whom were living eco-frugal existences long before Cameron Diaz hit the big screen.

Styles pass; standards have staying power. Doris Janzen Longacre couldn't have seen it coming. Longacre, who died in 1979, knew her cookbook about eating responsibly in light of global hunger was selling wildly (200,000 copies within the first two years), and she wrote *Living More with Less* in part because the oil crisis and stagflation had readers scrounging around for practical tips on how to live with less in all areas of life, not just cooking. Longacre knew the planet was being stressed by human habits of extraction, consumption, and fuel burning, and a few other folks did too, but their concerns remained marginal to the still-ballooning American dream.

Eco-couture items such as $350 sweaters of cashmere and spun milk protein and 400-thread-count bamboo sheets—part of what Jeff Yeager, author of *The Cheapskate Next Door*, calls a "cause de stuff"—were still decades off.

Still, Longacre had a hunch that her ideas might someday become chic. She avoided the word "lifestyle" because it "bears the stamp of the new, the distinctive, the fun," choosing instead the term "life standards" to describe a "way of life governed by more than fleeting taste." It's as if she foresaw—and rued—the day that Matt Petersen, president and CEO of Global Green USA, would gush, as he did at a celebrity-studded Oscar week fundraiser: "The solutions [to global warming] are . . . fashionable. They can be fun! They can be sexy!"

The language of Longacre's five life standards—do justice, learn from the world community, nurture people, cherish the natural order, and nonconform freely—may sound frumpy to contemporary ears accustomed to a vernacular of fashionable, fun, and sexy. But they interlock to create what theologian Malinda Berry, in the thirtieth-anniversary edition of *Living More with Less*, calls "a more-with-less theology." And while theologies and standards aren't as appealing as styles, they also don't topple over when the winds of public opinion change direction.

Because here's the thing: As author Lauren Weber reminds us, Americans' commitment to frugality waxes and wanes. "History shows us that in hard times, we hunker down and make do with less," Weber writes. "It also shows that as soon as the danger passes, we cheerfully reset our appetites a notch or two higher than before." Only when (or if) the economy rebounds will we know whether the new frugality is a durable virtue or passing fancy.

Changing habits may require—are you serious?—hard work. Despite chirpy checklists of five simple ways to save the planet, it's not always easy being green. Hanging up laundry takes more work than tossing it in the dryer. Biking takes longer than driving. Making food from scratch, repairing broken items, and taking care of your neighbors might mean sacrificing recreational or even vocational pursuits.

Of course, there are payoffs in contentment and spiritual health—those constitute the "more" in "more with less." But frugality for the sake of the environment and the poor isn't some accessory value that you can splice onto a maxed-out, harried lifestyle. It's a set of practices that displaces some priorities and disrupts others. It's not always convenient, and it's not always easy. Expecting it to be either means that, when the going gets tough, you'll be more likely to throw in the organic cotton towel.

Living more with less is about more than personal—and even planetary—health. When it is not moored in concern for those with less, commitment to sustainability and simplicity can fold in on itself. Local living can contract its way toward narcissism, or at least provinciality. Being cheap saves *me* money. Eating organic lettuce helps *me* be healthy. Growing a garden feeds *my* family.

Even though such actions are inarguably good for the planet and often for the poor as well, self-interest can sneakily supplant concern for the poor or for the earth's crisis that is endangering the most vulnerable first. Books such as *Living More with Less*, rooted in the Mennonite Central Committee's relationships with the global poor, can remind a movement in danger of navel-gazing that sustainability has at least as much to do with the climate refugees crowding into the slums of Dhaka because their coastal villages are being flooded as with the fact that asparagus and morel quiche tastes lovely in the spring.

So, if cheap is "the next cool," as Jeff Yeager of the Cheapskate books predicts, so be it. The fact that U.S. and Canadian citizens are wasting less, borrowing less, building smaller homes, and staying around home more, as Yeager claims, is undeniably a good thing. Perhaps the role of more-with-less Christians is to gently support adherents to the new frugality if or when thrift once again moves from chic to passé. Perhaps then we can remind them that, when the planet and the poor are concerned, responsible living never goes out of style.

Valerie Weaver-Zercher was a contributing editor to *Sojourners* and editor of the thirtieth-anniversary edition of *Living More with Less* (Herald Press, 2010) when this appeared in the December 2010 issue of *Sojourners*.

A Black Christian Approach to Veganism
An Interview with Christopher Carter

Mitchell Atencio

My first introduction to animal rights activism was not one I welcomed. My favorite football player had participated in something horrendous—dogfighting—but all my preteen self could focus on was the punitive and vengeful way some animal rights activists treated Atlanta Falcons quarterback Michael Vick.

"[Vick] should be given a brain scan that will show if he's capable of remorse," said Ingrid Newkirk, the president of People for the Ethical Treatment of Animals. "Have your Vick spayed or neutered," read one protest sign. Conservative political pundit Tucker Carlson said Vick should have been executed for his crimes. Even the more benign protesters explicitly argued that Vick didn't deserve a second chance, something that never sat right with my Christian upbringing.

Worse than mocking signs and inflammatory statements, animal rights groups successfully fought to increase Vick's jail sentence. Prosecutors recommended twelve to eighteen months, which was already more than the usual recommendation for first-time offenders. The judge sentenced him to twenty-three months; animal rights groups had lobbied for more than double that amount.

So, despite my beliefs that something is seriously wrong with the way American society treats animals, particularly in factory farming, I have had my trepidations about engaging in animal rights work. Even as I've largely stopped eating beef and attempted to integrate more vegan/vegetarian meals into my diet, I've been mostly doing this because of my concern for the environmental impact of meat.

Rev. Christopher Carter is a virtue ethicist, commissioned elder in the United Methodist Church, and professor of theology. He has spent much of his professional and personal life learning to better the treatment of animals as part of an integrated approach to justice for all. Carter, the author of The Spirit of Soul Food: Race, Faith, and Food Justice, *defines his work as a practice of "Black veganism," which "forces us to examine how the language of animality and 'animal characteristics' has been a tool used to justify the oppression of any being who deviates, by species, race, or behavior, from Western Christian anthropological norms."*

In our conversation, we discussed food security and factory farming, developing better cooking habits, and how animal rights affect all species.—Mitchell Atencio

SOJOURNERS: What's the right term for this type of work? Is it animal rights? Animal liberation?

CHRISTOPHER CARTER: It depends on what we're discussing, right? I am a virtue ethicist. So, while I think a lot about how ideology and cultural norms shape behavior, and how we can see that there are limitations to a "rights" approach or just a rules approach, it's not to say that rights aren't important. They are.

Rules are deeply important. Rules give us boundaries and frameworks for having conversations and discussions about what is morally right and what is morally wrong. But rules also are limited because of human sin. And to be clear, I describe sin as a failure to love, or a "failure to bother to love," to borrow a phrase from Jim Keenan.

What we're invited to in Christianity is much more of a "both/and," a "transcend and include." The "rights" language is important and useful, but we need to recognize that it has limitations.

This, [coming from] a Black person, ain't surprising, right? We technically got all kinds of "rights" that we don't actually have access to. The intersectional approach or analytical lens that I bring to [animal rights] is unique because I'm gonna be thinking about rights in a fundamentally different way than a white person. By nature of the racial hierarchy and caste system in America, even though I technically have the same rights on paper that you have, in practical reality, I do not.

SOJOURNERS: So then, how did you get involved in working on animal rights and animal liberation?

CARTER: It was a little bit of happenstance, a little bit of suffering, and luck. I'm the first person in my family to even have an undergraduate degree. My grandpa was a migrant picker. My mom worked at a factory. My dad's a janitor. I didn't go to college until I was twenty-two. I had a good job, bought a house, and in my family, that was considered very well-off. My wife—she's brilliant, she's a veterinary oncologist—she essentially forced me to go to school. It was there that, not only I accepted my call to ministry, but I began to be interested in oppression and oppressive systems, particularly racial oppression because I grew up in a poor neighborhood that was multiracial.

When I finished my master of divinity and decided to do a doctorate, I happened to be driving between Los Angeles and San Francisco for the American Academy of Religion conference. And what I saw [farmworkers] looked so much like slave camps. It looked like what my grandpa—born in 1938 Mississippi, in the deep Delta—would tell of stories about how he was treated by white people, the work he did in the field, and the racism he endured. And he would always end those stories by saying "Oh, it could have been worse." And when I was driving to San Francisco, I saw the same things happening to other brown people. And it clicked with me in a way that I hadn't really ever noticed before.

The dehumanization of industrial agriculture; the ways people of color, particularly Black and Indigenous people, are "animalized"; how the language of the "animal" is really the linchpin of race. It all just rushed to me. I knew, in my soul, that I had changed. I had a conversion experience, quite honestly.

At that point, I became a vegetarian. And I didn't become vegan because I knew I needed to continue to find ways to eat that were in alignment with my identity. I wasn't going to rush into it. I was one of the handful of Black people at my school and I felt very culturally isolated. To leave my cuisine behind—which was one of the ways I felt connected to my community—just seemed like a terrible idea. So, I had to figure out how to cook and eat in ways that allowed my moral values to align with my cultural identity. And then, in addition, figure out a way to explain this theologically, ethically, and morally.

I love animals. But I don't do my work for the animals. It's really for people. I'm vegan for my people. Because this industry disproportionately harms people of color. We get a [disproportionate amount of harm] based on the ways animal agriculture and industrial farming impact Black and brown communities.

SOJOURNERS: What would look different if we had a better approach and dismantled the systemic oppressions of food production, particularly around meat?

CARTER: Now, I am going to give you an answer that other vegans are probably going to disagree with—I'm just going to lay that out there. I come, not only from a family of rural folk, but family who hunt. Even though we Black. We didn't have school on the first day of the second week in November—that was the first day of bowhunting season.

[That said], individually, we need to take seriously the reality of the structural racism embedded in our food system. That means considering where we purchase our food and taking seriously the reality of the ecological oppression that comes along with that. That typically means buying from a farmer's market.

You have to do some research to figure out where is best to buy food. Thinking about where we purchase our food is probably going to be the most important way to begin to make a change.

The other thing we can do is advocate for structural changes within the organizations that we are tied to. My son's school has a great food lunch program in [the Los Angeles Unified School District]. So much of [the program's food] comes direct from farmers . . . a lot [of them are also] people of color.

I would argue that unless you are buying [meat] directly from the place where it was grown, raised, and slaughtered, you are essentially complicit in systems that do harm to people of color and the planet. Also, we fundamentally eat way more meat than we actually need to. We should practice "soulful eating," which includes a kind of veganism. While recognizing that not everybody can do that.

I talk in [*Soul Food*] about how to practically do that. I grew up on food stamps, we couldn't have [eaten] purely vegan. But we could have practiced "Black veganism" as I define it.

SOJOURNERS: What about organizations like churches?

CARTER: Churches can work together to establish and create food sovereign communities. A great example of what this looks like in practical terms is the Black Church Food Security Network. They're doing amazing work. Rev. Heber Brown III is a good friend of mine. Soul Fire Farm too—they're not religious [but] they are in alignment with the values of the radical prophetic tradition.

Churches can be food hubs. We could be working together to connect with local farmers so that we can buy food at a price that's fair to the farmer and allows [churches] to cover overhead, but doesn't have to "make money," because that's not the goal; the goal is to feed people.

Theologically, churches should probably be vegetarian. It's hard to make the argument for eating meat, given how difficult it would be to procure it in a way that's sustainable. We have to take life seriously and [the fact] that life has sacred meaning and value. [At minimum] they should opt out of factory-farm meat.

SOJOURNERS: Growing up in the American church, I had this idea that all of creation was "good," but humans were "very good." Or that humans are made in the image of God, but animals are not. And that we're supposed to "steward" the earth, which in most people's minds could include raising and eating meat. When you say churches should be vegetarian, what's the theology behind that?

CARTER: How things would be different if the Bible started with Genesis 2 versus Genesis 1, right? The second [creation] narrative is written by farmers, [and it] fundamentally talks about the interconnectedness that we have with all life. It talks about stewardship and responsibilities that we have and that we're supposed to exercise . . . It's about appropriate relationships.

We have to take seriously the reality of human sin, fundamentally. To make the argument that "it's okay as long as we're doing it right"—we have yet to do it right.

I really focus on the second [Genesis] narrative. Not to dismiss the first narrative, because it's important [and] there's something to be said about being created in the image of God and that order structure, but if I am going to talk about the first creation narrative, I'm definitely going to emphasize the fact that the seventh day is the only day that is blessed. And the seventh day is holy.

[That should cause us to ask]: What does it mean to not extrapolate and externalize our resources such that the planet is blessed and livestock and everything can actually rest?

SOJOURNERS: How long have you been vegan?

CARTER: Since 2018. But I don't really know because I went through this whole complex around purity culture. I was a vegetarian, and I was slowly becoming a vegan, figuring out how to do it. I called myself a "dirty vegan" for years. [I would be vegan except when I traveled because it made it harder to be strict.]

The notion of purity is so embedded in Christianity. Honestly, [rejecting that] shaped my approach to thinking about the beginnings of Black veganism.

SOJOURNERS: I think a number of people feel like a fully vegan diet would be impossible, and so they don't take any steps to change their food sources. Do you think those small changes are worth it?

CARTER: As a virtue ethicist, I'm all about the cultivation of habits. We have to cultivate habits that help us embody practices that move us toward—as we Methodists would say—perfection [or] sanctification.

I want to apply this to food, but I want to also emphasize that I apply this to my spirituality: You should be growing toward God every day. That's just how I fundamentally live my life.

It's a matter of making progress. There is no way of being perfect, but it's about improving every day and taking improvement seriously. Unfortunately, a lot of Christians practice that kind of Christianity that demands very little of them on a day-to-day basis.

SOJOURNERS: If I were to try and get more hands on with this—let's say you're somebody who eats an average American diet, what would be a helpful first step toward less oppressive food habits? What does it look like to find new recipes? What does it look like to create those new habits?

CARTER: When I became a vegetarian, it required me to do a couple of things. We have to reclaim the kitchen as a sacred space. It's hard. We don't live in a culture that values cooking. This is an American thing; capitalism requires us to place little value on the kitchen as a sacred space or a place of community.

So, some of this is changing our relationship to cooking. Some of this is finding recipes or veganizing and vegetarianizing recipes that you already have.

I live in Southern California. I like to eat a lot of tacos. I like to eat a lot of pizza. I like to eat a lot of soul food. I just got on Amazon and bought cookbooks, looked up recipes, and just tried them out. The hardest part was the investment in time and seasoning. But, what I found is that I grew to love it so much that there's recipes in my book [*The Spirit of Soul Food*].

SOJOURNERS: What would it look like if the kitchen were a sacred space?

CARTER: We need to take more time because cooking does take time. We also need to remember that we are a people who love stories and narratives. My son, who's little, helps me cook. I have pictures of him helping me cook since he was two. And that's the only way he's ever going to get a chance to know his great-grandmother because she died really young. I talk about the stuff I learned [to make] from her. I talk about my grandpa. I talk about my mom. And I talk about [my son's] day.

I can't [cook with him] every day, but I do it once a week and it's important. I want my son to know the story of the liberation and growth of his family, but also to see himself as a part of the story.

That's how the kitchen becomes sacred. Yes, we need to take more time. That's fundamentally important, but we need to talk to each other.

SOJOURNERS: What do you think about the ethics of lab-grown meats or Beyond Meat and products like that?

CARTER: I am impressed by the work that they've done. To an extent, it does solve a lot of problems ecologically. But it also can create other environmental problems. You have to also consider who's working in those factories and the wages they're getting paid.

There is no silver bullet. We have to actually think about food, not only through a local process and a local lens but also a systems lens. We need to talk much more about access and public transportation; all of these things are interconnected. You can have lab-grown meat, but if people can't afford to get to the store or afford to buy it, then what good is that going to do?

SOJOURNERS: If you could change one law around animal protection, what would it be?

CARTER: We need to get rid of ag-gag laws. We don't have any space to hold these organizations accountable. These mega-industrial agricultural organizations have created a system such that if you try to record anything or "spy" on them, it's called domestic terrorism. That's evil.

We've created a system that's so bent on capitalism and exploitation that we don't actually want to hold people accountable. If we hold these places accountable, if people see what's happening in them, you could have a lot of grassroots activism. People want to believe that animals are being treated better than they actually are.

Mitchell Atencio was senior associate news editor of sojo.net when this appeared on sojo.net on April 2, 2024.

Five Simple Living Tips for Millennial Christians

Timothy McMahan King

Jesus was clear.

You cannot serve both God and money.

Throughout my twenties, this was not a problem I thought I struggled with.

First of all, I didn't perceive myself as having all that much money. So, how could I be serving it? (I deal with the inaccuracy of how I perceive of my own wealth here.)

Second, money was never a part of my thought process when choosing my career. If money wasn't the motivator for choosing my job, how could I be in danger of "serving two masters?"

It's been said that one of the greatest tricks devil ever played was convincing most of the world he doesn't exist. His greatest encore might be wrapping up vice in the midst of a big ball of virtue and letting the whole thing rot from the inside out.

I might not struggle with being a slave to money in the sense that I obsess about how much I make. But, in looking back over the past ten years of my life, I've found myself serving the master of mammon precisely in the ways that I DIDN'T think about money.

The accumulation of things that aren't necessary is warned against (see the lilies of the field in Matthew 6), but the wise stewardship of resources also allows us to invest in other values (see Joanna and Suzanna in Luke 8).

I've prided myself that "I don't think that much about money." But it is exactly because I haven't been thinking about financial decisions that I have not been able to be as generous, hospitable, or responsible as I could have been.

The money that we DON'T spend on things we DON'T need can be money that we DO give for things others DO need.

I don't write this from a perspective of having mastered a "Christian approach to finances" or being a sterling success story of generosity, but rather from one of having just finished my third decade of life, which was full of the most significant financial decisions of my life to date.

There are a lot more things to be said about the way we should spend the money we do have. But here are a few lessons I've been learning about how to save money so I can be more responsible, generous, and hospitable.

1. Live with People

Never pay all that you can afford to pay in rent. You might be coming off years of sharing a room during college and are thrilled to get your own apartment. But just because you can afford to live alone doesn't mean you have to. Rent (or mortgage) is likely going to be your single largest monthly expense for years to come. Saving even just $200 to $300 dollars a month over the course of your twenties can mean $24,000 to $36,000. And it is a lot harder to get a nice place early and then have to downgrade later than going as cheap as you can at first and then spending more as your needs change.

2. Be Creative About Community

When I first graduated college, one of my priorities was investing in friends and building community. What that often meant was that every time a friend invited me out for dinner or a drink, I would say yes. This got pricey. But I didn't want to skip out on building relationships with people I cared about. Things got a lot cheaper (and the quality time together improved) when I started being more proactive about how I spent time with my friends. Hosting them (at my group house) or offering to bring a bottle of wine to their place was a lot less money than splitting the check at a restaurant.

3. Make Your Coffee. Make Your Lunch. Seriously

I get it. Everyone forgets lunch sometimes. I do too. There might be times when it's a choice between a trip to the coffee shop or falling asleep in a meeting. But there is a BIG financial difference between making that the exception or a habit. Scenario A: $3 a day on coffee at Starbucks and $10 a day on lunch at a sandwich shop. Scenario B: $0.33 a day on coffee and $3 on leftovers from dinner or a homemade sandwich. Five days a week, fifty weeks a year for ten years, and Scenario A is going to run you $32,500 over your twenties. Scenario B is going to run you $8,325. That's a $24,175 savings your first decade in the work force.

4. Watch Your Monthly Expenses

To date, there are no known fatalities as a result of not having a cable subscription. Netflix might be a nice cheap alternative, but do you also need Hulu Plus? Do you need a car? The most expensive cell phone plan? I'm highly in favor of supporting high quality journalism and writing through having magazine and newspaper subscriptions but . . . If you aren't sure, try this test: Take a look at your weekly, monthly, or annual cost for something. Project your total cost over the next ten years and then ask, "Will I look back and still be glad I spent $XX on Y?"

5. Redefine Entertainment and Relaxation

Enjoying music, theater, and film isn't a bad thing. Neither is being proactive about having a healthy mind, body, and spirit. But achieving your personal goals doesn't have to be expensive. Just as you can cultivate a taste for the "finer things in life," you can develop a taste for the simpler. Hosting a local amateur musician at your house for a concert can be far more fulfilling (and go further to build community) than purchasing tickets to the concert of a well-known artist. A walk through a public park, a short hiking trip, or a nice cup of homemade tea can all ultimately do more to restore your spirit than the costly "relaxation" options marketed to us every day.

These lessons aren't comprehensive and are written by an unmarried guy who just hit thirty—and are limited as such.

Timothy McMahan King was chief strategy officer for Sojourners when this appeared on sojo.net on November 18, 2014.

What Would Jesus Buy?
On Rev. Billy's Church of Stop Shopping

Walter Brueggemann

Before there was Reverend Billy, there was Bill Talen, born and raised in Minnesota, in the midst of conservative Dutch Calvinism, a faith he rejected as a teenager. He became a playwright, performer, and producer, working for years in San Francisco before he moved to New York City in the mid-1990s. "Rev. Billy," Talen's alter ego, was created in 1997, when Talen/Billy began street-corner preaching near the new Disney Store in Times Square, using the cadences and mannerisms of a TV evangelist to decry the chain-store commercial excesses of gentrification.

Rev. Billy began to take his preaching into the Disney Store, and later into Starbucks, often joined by supporters who would help him stage "shopping interventions," during which he might, for example, perform an "exorcism" of the cash register. In the process, the Church of Stop Shopping was born, a performance activism nonprofit staffed almost entirely by volunteers, including many professional musicians, singers, and actors who turn up as they're able at actions and rallies promoting free speech, local communities, and anti-consumerism; tour with Rev. Billy as the Stop Shopping Choir; and help lead periodic "revival" productions.

Talen uses elements of parody in Rev. Billy. But the persona reflects much more than over-the-top mannerisms and rapid-fire wordplay. Rev. Billy seems to have grown out of Talen's genuine soul-searching and his delving into the writings and work of activists, theologians, and radical performers. This preacher and his church that is not a church has a distinct philosophical—some might even say theological—basis. Talen, it should be clear, professes not to be a Christian and distances himself from all organized religion. But much of the political and spiritual truth in Billy's "sermons" will seem familiar to followers of Jesus with ears to hear, and believers of other traditions as well. And as he struggles, sometimes awkwardly, to express something both incarnate and transcendent without using any known religion's terms, one can see the fire of a devotion that mere political rhetoric could not contain. Agree with him or not, Rev. Billy's call to seek "the god that is not a product" seems to be a mission statement, not a joke.

Given that there is a long tradition of prophetic theater and theatrical prophets, we asked eminent biblical scholar Walter Brueggemann to examine whether and how Rev. Billy might relate to the prophets of the Bible.—The Editors

That day Starbucks was busy but quiet. People were relaxed and talking, sipping six-dollar venti lattes. Then there was a phone conversation, readily heard by the sippers, about being in the wrong Starbucks and missing each other. There was another cell phone call, this one raising the question of buying all the "extras" sold by Starbucks. Soon two more calls occurred over the same issue—then a dozen calls, enough to disrupt the entitled relaxation. Finally there was a disturbing hubbub and the phone-callers shrieked with joy and celebratively removed themselves from the shop, to the great relief of management.

It was a prophetic disruption by the Church of Stop Shopping, a fairly typical enactment of "guerrilla theater" by the folks around Rev. Billy, a dramatic performer of prophetic faith.

Reverend Billy, also known as Bill Talen, has gotten the strange idea that the Big Corporations, notably Disney, Starbucks, Nike, and Wal-Mart—and their shameless commitment to profit at the expense of human infrastructure—constitute a destructive force in our society. He has, moreover, reached the critical judgment that such a negative ideological force in our society must be resisted, and can best be resisted from a self-aware theological perspective that operates with parody and irony. The purpose of such parody and irony is to expose what seems like an economic operation as an ideological force of totalizing scope in our society. This force seeks to situate U.S. consumers in an uncritical way in the "life world" of consumer capitalism.

The specific discipline that is expected and required by this corporate "life world" is endless shopping without reflecting on the needs of or obligations to the community that might curb patronage at such shops. That is, Rev. Billy takes these organizations (and many others like them) as agents of consumerism that has become a "consuming" ideology in our society. In the end that consuming ideology distorts not only social resources but eventually neighborhoods, practices of neighborliness, and social vision as well.

Thus the Church of Stop Shopping, Rev. Billy's congregation, dispatches its members in protest against the Church of Shopping and engages in deliberate, sustained resistance to shopping as a way of participating in an alternative covenantal life.

After hearing his disc of preaching and music and reading his two books—*What Should I Do If Rev. Billy Is in My Store*? and *What Would Jesus Buy? Fabulous Prayers in the Face of the Shopocalypse*—I have no doubt that Rev. Billy is a faithful prophetic figure who stands in direct continuity with ancient prophets in Israel and in continuity with the great prophetic figures of U.S. history who have incessantly called our society back to its core human passions of justice and compassion.

In thinking about Rev. Billy, I have had recourse to an old article by my friend and Hebrew Testament scholar Sibley Towner, "On Calling People 'Prophets' in 1970." I take from Towner four marks of a prophet that are easily identified in the talk and walk of Rev. Billy.

First, prophetic practice has a *style* that gives dramatic form to what is said and done. That is, prophets are "performers." That style, characteristically, is one of enormous, passionate conviction. One would not situate one's self in a risky challenge to such great corporations, as Rev. Billy does, were there not deep conviction that is grounded in thoughtful social theory that, as in the ancient prophets, is kept mostly hidden in more-popular modes of discourse. That social theory in ancient Israel focused on the concentration of wealth among the urban elites in Jerusalem that would bring destruction because the poor were not honored or taken seriously. Rev. Billy's conviction concerns the super-corporations (and their uncriticized ideology) that serve the insatiable monopoly of the urban-suburban elites. That style of the prophetic, moreover, consists in parody that teases and makes fun of both corporate seductions and the long list of consumers who sign on for lattes and much else.

It is the power of parody to call attention to the unstated but powerful intentions that are mostly kept hidden in advertising and public presentation. The parody of the prophetic regularly slides over into irony, in which things are renamed and re-identified so that their truth cannot go unnoticed.

Second, prophetic practice has a *rhetoric*. While Bill Talen in fact is not a "reverend," he is closely enough allied with the church that he can easily and readily appropriate church lingo and terminology. His "sermons" reflect all of the passion and rhetorical force of an evangelistic preacher accompanied by devoted listeners who respond with engaging verbal support, affirming what he says and urging him on.

The rhetoric of this preacher is saturated with religious terminology that talks about "change" (repentance), "real love," and "freedom." In an important riff, Billy says he must be "surreal" if he is to talk about reality; he is in need of being "exorcised" if he is to escape the demonic power of consumer ideology; and he must be "impossible" if he is to be understood.

That triad of "surreal, exorcised, and impossible" shows the prophet seeking a mode of discourse that is not contained in and domesticated by market ideology. That is, the consumer ideology is so totalizing that anything outside of it must, perforce, sound outrageous. We are able to see ancient prophets practicing daring, scandalous rhetoric (and conduct) in an attempt to make sense outside the dominant ideology of their time. Billy is an echo of their work.

Third, prophetic practice is *located institutionally* in society and appeals to a particular *constituency*. In ancient Israel the prophets were variously situated amid the temple and the central institution of monarchy (thus Isaiah could speak of a "messianic king"), or among the peasants who regularly faced economic emergency brought on by the exploitation of the urban elites. Their work is always context-specific. Billy is, for sure, a voice "crying in the wilderness," located in a risky environment outside the ordered domain of Pharaoh but well short of any new place of prosperous well-being. Billy is indeed swimming "upstream" against enormous odds.

But he is not alone. In his practice, he is the voice of a "church"—albeit a curious church—but one rooted in the visible historic church. His practice would not be possible without "church" in that he has disciples, a choir, and a congregation that responds to his preaching. This institutional form, partly serious and partly parody, lends a certain kind of authority and gravitas that provide standing ground for his testimony.

Beyond that, it is clear that Rev. Billy is identified with and has wide support among the company of believers (religious and secular) who know that our current market ideology is a path to death. As always with prophets, Billy's vocation is to be a presence visibly at work in concrete acts of protest, resistance, and alternative possibility. Thus the talk he offers is rhetorical insistence of a most concrete kind that has a chance to impinge upon settled authority and unquestioned social assumptions.

Fourth, what counts in prophetic practice is *the message* of a truth rooted in God and enacted in concrete society. Billy quite explicitly situates himself in the tradition of Mohandas Gandhi, César Chávez, and Rosa Parks, three he names. Without being reductionist, it is fair to say that prophetic utterance characteristically concerns divine judgment and divine hope.

The divine judgment Rev. Billy pronounces concerns a condemnation of religion that has been "hijacked" by the right wing, the resignation that we have "nothing to love but fear itself," and the self-deceptive illusion that commodities can make us safe and happy. The shopping he assaults is seen to be an ideological practice whereby we keep "the demons in the zoo." All of that will come to a sorry end for which he uses the term "shopocalypse," a play on "apocalypse," that imagined end of the world in a divine judgment as a great conflagration. Like every good poet, Billy has no interest in when or how that may happen, but only a conviction that this ideology that drives our society can only end in failure and raw disappointment.

But prophetic practice is not finally about judgment. It is about hope. Hope for Rev. Billy is the deep conviction that there is a viable, choosable alternative to shopping that will make possible a human community of neighborliness, peace, and justice. At one point he even uses the phrase "eternal life," but he would not want that phrase misconstrued, as if it referred to enduring life as "pie in the sky." I understand his usage to mean a possible human neighborhood. And as with every prophet, that hope requires committed embrace. Billy urges his congregation to "use your bodies for your freedom"—that is, to vote against the slippery consumer ideology with your feet, even to use your bodies in the practice of corporate "interruptions" as a way of testimony to an alternative. He also urges active remembering that is an act of radical neighborliness, a difficult act of specificity against great corporations that want to encourage timeless amnesia.

The discipline of Stop Shopping by itself is only a negation. But Billy intends for that discipline to help us redeploy our energy and attention toward the neighbor. Like all prophetic figures, Billy's aim is not to entertain but to recruit. It is now clear, given the current betrayal of our constitutional rights, the erosion of an independent judiciary, and the stifling of an independent media, that the human crisis in our society is deep. Billy's stratagem is a way to think and to act appropriately.

Amos Wilder, the wise New Testament scholar of the last generation, observed that the parables of Jesus are a form of "guerilla theater," action against settled conviction and an invitation to listeners to come "on stage" into the action. Before Jesus, this same guerilla theater was the enterprise of the ancient prophets. That theater continues with Rev. Billy. We are surely apt candidates for the Church of Stop Shopping. With enough new recruits for the action, perhaps we need not be subjected to the Shopocalypse.

Walter Brueggemann was professor emeritus at Columbia Theological Seminary in Decatur, Georgia, when this appeared in the November 2007 issue of *Sojourners*.

Chapter 4

"Strange Mutations"

Spiritual Thriving and Paradox

Spiritual thriving is not the same as "happiness," but joy is one of its fruits. Kentucky writer and farmer Wendell Berry recalls how cultivating human art—playing an instrument, singing together, painting, and so on—are essential for feeding our spirits. Humanizing work, mutual aid, lifting one another's burdens, and sharing meals are all integral to life's soulful invitation. Such thriving should never be a luxury for the privileged—it must be feral and free like jazz. When God's profligate grace does not provide good news for those "with their backs against the wall," as Howard Thurman wrote, then Christianity has become a "strange mutation" of the teachings of Jesus. At Sojourners, we remember that spiritual thriving is magnified in community with all beings.

Heaven in Henry County
An Interview with Wendell Berry

Rose Marie Berger

Kentucky farmer and essayist Wendell Berry talks about what makes people happy.

Sojourners *associate editor Rose Marie Berger and photographer Ryan Beiler spent a February Sunday afternoon with novelist, essayist, philosopher, and poet Wendell Berry at his farm in Henry County, Kentucky. Berry is the author of more than forty books of fiction, poetry, and essays including* The Unsettling of America, What Are People For?, Life is a Miracle, Citizenship Papers, *and* The Art of the Commonplace. *He has farmed in a traditional manner for nearly forty years.*—The Editors

SOJOURNERS: How does your identity as a writer connect to this region and land?

WENDELL BERRY: I was born here in Henry County. I grew up in these little towns, and in the countryside, on the farms. All my early memories are here. All the voices that surrounded me from the time I became able to hear were from here. This place where we're sitting today is the old property known as Lane's Landing. Twelve acres, more or less, the deed says. My wife, Tanya, and I came back here in 1964 and have lived here for thirty-nine years, raised our children here. How could you draw a line separating this place and my identity? If you've known these places from your early youth, that means that you have a chance to know them in a way that other people never will.

We're on the west side of the Kentucky River, in the Kentucky River Valley. Some people call this the Outer Bluegrass. An old ocean laid down these layers of limestone in the soil. There are lots of trees here. There are white, chinquapin, red, black, and shumard oaks. Those are the principal ones.

SOJOURNERS: What are the models used here in Kentucky to resist the economic pressure from the larger market?

BERRY: Community-supported agriculture, farmers markets, direct marketing of meat—that sort of thing. There's an effort under way to develop a retail market for local produce. But this is hard to bring about.

The local landscape used to contribute food to Louisville, Kentucky. There was a significant amount of truck farming in those days. That's gone. The stockyard's gone, the packinghouses are gone. Louisville became economically and culturally isolated from its rich agricultural landscape. Now we are trying to build commercial linkages between the city and its local countryside. You've got the prospect, to begin with, of better, fresher food. You've got the possibility that consumers could influence production.

You have the possibility that urban consumers, by fulfilling their responsibility to local producers, can make secure their local food supply in the face of various threats. The paramount one, now on everybody's mind, is terrorism, but there are also the threats of epidemic and disease. In other words, the influence of local consumers could work not only to maintain farming in the local landscape, but also to diversify it. And American agriculture is badly in need of diversity.

SOJOURNERS: Genetically modified organisms are being promoted by agribusiness as "a way to feed the poor people of the world." What ethical values should we bring to bear on genetic engineering?

BERRY: The first ethical requirement is a decent suspicion of the claims of people who have something to sell. I'm not reading anything that suggests that genetic engineering is increasing production. Some recent things I've read suggest that productivity of Roundup Ready soybeans is less than that of other varieties.

I think that the real reason for genetic engineering is to put absolute control of the food system into corporate hands. They don't want anybody—farmer or urban consumer or anybody else—to have anything whatsoever that they don't buy from a corporation at the corporation's price. In other words, economic totalitarianism is the goal. I don't think the difference between political totalitarianism and economic totalitarianism is worth lingering over. If you're not economically free, if you don't have economic choices, you're not free. You can remove choice by making it impossible for small economic enterprises to survive.

SOJOURNERS: Some people defend their locale by becoming "lifestyle activists." Your friends Harlan and Anna Hubbard are early examples of people who experimented with nomadism and rootedness, while maintaining fidelity to a place.

BERRY: Harlan and Anna Hubbard were a married couple who began their life together by building a shanty boat and making a sort of epic drift down the rivers from Brent, Kentucky, above Cincinnati, Ohio, to New Orleans, Louisiana and then on out into the bayous. In the early '50s, that journey having completed itself, they returned to Kentucky and bought a remote property, known as Payne Hollow, on the Ohio River in Trimble County. They built a house there and remained there, living mostly from their land and the river until they died.

A friend and I met them by accident while on a canoe trip. We stopped there to see if we could get some drinkable water. We had replenished our water supply with the city water of Madison, Indiana, and we were finding it hard to swallow.

They were musicians; they played duets every day of their life together. They played Mozart, Brahms, and Bach. Harlan made prints, drawings, oils, and watercolors. And he was a writer. He published in his lifetime two wonderful books, *Shantyboat: A River Way of Life* and *Payne Hollow*. Their life was exemplary. They did little harm. They lived abundantly, by their own efforts, and with a very small expenditure of money. In their frugal life they experienced much joy and made much beauty. They were teachers to a lot of people, and I'm one of them.

SOJOURNERS: What was your relationship with Thomas Merton, the Trappist monk and writer who lived in Kentucky?

BERRY: Merton was a man who understood how to be a companion. He had a lot of humor, and I think he knew something about how to be happy or how to enjoy happiness when he had it. He had a very lively countenance; a very bright, curious, amused eye.

When we went down to the Abbey of Gethsemani the first time, he just dropped it out casually, and I think with great secret amusement, that he was thinking about joining an Indian tribe. Merton was a profound Christian. Some people seem to think that when he went East he was abandoning his faith or his vocation. I don't think he was at all. His talks to religious groups in Alaska on his last trip before he died were wonderful.

SOJOURNERS: Merton was skeptical of the post-Enlightenment era that shapes modern Christianity. He called into question the myth of progress. You take on these same issues in *Life is a Miracle: An Essay Against Modern Superstition.*

BERRY: The myth of progress substitutes this infinite advance toward better and better life in the material sense for the old pilgrimage, which you make by effort and grace, to become a better person. That's the reason you need to subvert it if you can. It takes people's minds off the important things. It becomes a kind of determinism: All we have to do is just passively go along and things will get better and better, and we'll be happier and happier. That's why we need honest accounting.

What is the measure of progress? It is possible to measure the progress of the last two hundred or three hundred years in soil erosion. We can measure it in the rate of species extinction. We can measure it in pollution, in the toxicity of the world. Those things, like power and speed, are perfectly measurable.

But we need also to raise the questions that are not quantitative. How happy are people? What do we make of all this complaining? How healthy are people? How are love and beauty faring? What do we make of all this doctoring and medication that's going on all the time at such a great expense? That's not to deny that this so-called progress has given us things that are worth having. A hot bath every night is a good thing. I affirm that it is good, and wish to record my gratitude. There are other good things, but real harms also have been done.

SOJOURNERS: The epigraph to *Citizenship Papers* is 2 Peter 2:3, "And through covetousness shall they with feigned words make merchandise of you." In the current economic and political context this verse becomes revolutionary.

BERRY: Yes. The gospels, and sometimes the epistles, are pretty revolutionary. They propose a revolution of about 180 degrees.

Christ was quite explicit, for instance, about his pacifism. You can't be more explicit than "Love your enemies." He did run those people out of the temple, but he didn't kill them.

People are always talking about the first church. The real first church was that gaggle of people who followed Jesus around. We don't know anything about them. But he apparently didn't ask them what creed they subscribed to, or what their sexual preference was, or any of that. He fed them. He healed them. He forgave them. He is clear about sin, but he was also for forgiveness.

Any religion has to have a practice. When you let it go so far from practice that it just becomes a matter of talk, something bad happens. If you don't have an economic practice, you don't have a practice. Christians conventionally think they've done enough when they've gone to the store and shopped. But that isn't an economic life. If you take seriously those passages in the scripture that say that we live by God's spirit and breath, that we live, move, and have our being in God, the implications for the present economy are just devastating. Those passages call for an entirely generous and careful economic life.

SOJOURNERS: In the movement to develop local, sustainable economies, is there a danger of balkanism—of establishing enemy tensions and prejudice between different locales?

BERRY: We're a pretty bad species in a lot of ways and in other ways a pretty good one. We can become a warrior civilization and live by piracy; on the other hand, we're capable of lovingkindness, of genuine affection, of generosity, of friendship, of peaceability, of forgiveness and gratitude. It's a question of where you want to put your influence, how you want to apply the little means that you have. It's too easy to say that country people are provincial and prejudiced, as if the worst things that humans are capable of hadn't also risen up in cosmopolitan, highly sophisticated, urban civilizations. That's just a passing of blame. If you can blame it all on people out in the provinces then you don't have to worry about what's going on in your urban neighborhood or in your urban soul.

One of the oldest human artifacts is the trade route. People were trading in obsidian and other rare things long before [recorded] history. So, we know there's going to be trade, we know that you can't isolate a culture and keep it going without cultural interchange.

The serious question is whether you're going to become a warrior community and live by piracy, by taking what you need from other people. I think the only antidote to that is imagination. You have to develop your imagination to the point that permits sympathy to happen. You have to be able to imagine lives that are not yours or the lives of your loved ones or the lives of your neighbors. You have to have at least enough imagination to understand that if you want the benefits of compassion, you must be compassionate. If you want forgiveness you must be forgiving. It's a difficult business, being human.

This appeared in the July 2004 issue of *Sojourners*.

Why We Must Honor the Worker, Not Just the Work

Julie Polter

My grandfather died late in the afternoon on an October day. My dad was called with the news in the middle of the second shift at the candy factory. They let him leave early. He stopped at home, changed into his daytime work clothes—jeans, white T-shirt, work boots, quilted nylon jacket—then headed to my grandfather's farm, a mile away, to take the cornpicker back to the field. It was harvest season. There was work to be done.

I can't separate questions of work and faith from a host of other things in my mind: Class and privilege. The labor movement and downsizing. The drive to create, the hunger to possess, the call to serve. Efficiency and monotony. Material needs and spiritual wants. Loving my neighbor and expressing myself. Economics, power, justice, prayer. The difference between savings and being saved. Everyday idols and everyday worship. Social status and unconditional love. Bread and roses.

"The basis for determining the value of human work is not primarily the kind of work being done, but the fact that the one who is doing it is a person," Pope John Paul II writes in the encyclical *Laborem Exercens* (On Human Work). Much work that isn't interesting or fun is vital to human life and community, and the ones who perform it—good people, bad people, just plain people—serve as the hands of God's providence. Work is good because the worker is made in God's image.

Beyond that, individuals may bring spiritual value to their work through their prayer and the way faith leads them to live in right relationship with coworkers and the job they are doing. Likewise, a person may produce a good product or perform a valuable service for intrinsically sinful motives (greed, status, domination). So, we can't judge the religious value of work solely on its glamour or pleasantness or intricacy, or on the state of the soul of the worker.

While there are varieties of gifts and varieties of service, and sometimes the same Spirit, human sin also distorts work and creates working conditions that are simply awful. Every day people do work that is underpaid, dangerous, exploitative, or ultimately serving nothing other than someone's profit or another one's destruction. In a sinful world, sometimes not even the innate, God-given dignity of the person doing a job can redeem the work itself. The distortion is too deep.

A woman locked in a sweatshop, a prostitute, an international arms dealer, a cigarette-industry marketing executive—each is a person, reflecting the image of God. But work that is a trap, work that demeans, work that slaughters, work that destroys souls or the world—this isn't divinely ordained, nor divinely blessed.

Can any work take place in a total vacuum, with no effect on anyone, for good or ill? Almost any employment sits in an intricate web of relationships. A family is affected by the employment (or lack thereof) of its members. The workplace is a social location as well as an economic one, where for many people the majority of their interactions with others occur. A company or other employer—the structure that employs a group of people—has some sort of corporate relationship to those who work there as well as to other companies and other people who contribute to or handle its product or service. A person's work, whether it is service, art, or a product, is somehow received by others.

We can assert the dignity of all work, the sacramental potential in even humble tasks. But if we then turn away from those who work in conditions that are demeaning or dangerous, it is little better than saying, "Go in peace, be warmed and filled," to our brother or sister lacking clothes or food (James 2:15–16).

Follow the can of tomatoes on your shelf or the parts in your television back through stores and warehouses, trucks and trains; tumble with them back through machines and hands. Follow them back to the vine in the field, the never-pausing assembly line—and then look into the eyes of the one who is stooped over the vine, the one doing the same task thirty times a minute. She is God's sacred creation—not the TV part or even, perhaps, the tomato (modern hybrids being what they are). How much in wages does she need to feed her children? Is she getting it? Are the chemicals put on the fields poison? Is his workplace safe? If someone sexually harasses her or mocks her with a racial epithet, can she seek redress without losing her job?

These questions aren't rooted in privileged guilt, but rather in the responsibilities of relationship. Support unions and boycotts; train to be a better manager of people, not profits or status; speak up in support of the colleague in the next cubicle, workstation, or church; hold yourself and others accountable to doing work well and to being fully human in interactions with others. Even if you don't know their names, even if you are safe and secure in your own employment, even if you sometimes feel helpless in the face of global economics and office politics, even if: Honor the worker, not just the work.

Talking to my dad, years after he's retired from both the factory and the farm, I ask, "What do you do when you're a candy sucker cook?"

"The ingredients for a batch fed continuously into one of the kettles. We added the flavor and food coloring by hand after the kettle dumped it on the slab."

"Any flavor you wanted?" I ask.

"Naw, in order. You'd run through the flavors in order, then it would go out to the right wrapper machine." Cherry, grape, lime, pineapple, orange, lemon, strawberry, peach. . . .

"The mixer would work it. You would too, reach in from both sides and pick up the candy and rotate it forty-five degrees and drop it back in the middle between strokes by the mixer.

"Then you hauled the batch over to the batch roller. Sometimes it got stuck going into the machine and you'd help the girl get it into the machine. After the suckers were molded, they were carried by belt to the wrappers in the next room."

"How often did you do a batch?"

"Oh, every three minutes."

In his book on the theology of vocation, *The Fabric of This World*, philosopher Lee Hardy describes how the Christian church—and the Western culture it so profoundly shaped—has swung back and forth between an understanding of work as self-fulfillment and work as self-denial, work as blessing or curse.

"The contemplation of divine truth . . . is the goal of the whole of human life," wrote Thomas Aquinas in *Summa Theologica*. At that time, in the Middle Ages, the only truly holy vocation was that of withdrawal to a monastery to pray and add to the indulgences bank. (This was in marked contrast to the first monastics, who did not withdraw from labor, but did what they could to become self-sufficient in order not to participate in the wider economy, which was based on slavery.)

Then Renaissance philosophers rejected the emphasis on contemplation. As Hardy writes, God was "no longer the passive and distant pure mind," but "a cosmic craftsman." The way to draw close to and emulate God was through productive activity and domination of the earth.

Sixteenth-century reformer Martin Luther (driven in large part by a polemic against monastic orders) rejected withdrawal from the world as a path to holiness. God calls people where they are, he insisted—butcher, baker, candlestick maker; child, mother, husband. A true vocation was to love our neighbor through faithful performance of the duties that come with our "stations" in life.

Each of these approaches holds truth, and each has been subject to great distortion: For a time, corruption made monastic holiness a commodity; an emphasis on unfettered human capacity and skill collapses under the weight of pride and a scarred creation; some have insisted that life stations are divinely ordained to stifle uprisings and betterment by those lower on the ladder. The "Protestant work ethic" that began with Luther and was refined by John Calvin and other Reformed theologians had God's glory as its goal, but it has constantly been subsumed by industry and ideology to divert peoples' labor to political and economic glory.

Search for "meaning" or for an integration of spiritual longing and gifts with a paid vocation is not an esoteric, trivial, or foolish luxury. Striving for basic justice and dignity for workers who lack safety, a living wage, or job security is not an unspiritual pursuit. The call of the heart and the call of justice are both in the Bible. The prophets combined them. One or the other—or neither—may be the main focus of a person's work life. But an awareness of both is vital to a balanced and full faith life.

I strain to lift a box of something at my father's house. "When I was your age, I could carry a hundred-pound sack of seed on my shoulders while walking across plowed ground," he snorts.

It is left unsaid by both of us that I neither need nor want to carry a hundred-pound sack across my shoulders.

I graduated with honors in English. My father didn't say anything to me, but my cousin told me that my dad was very proud. He took the commencement program for my mega state university to their house and pointed out where my name was set apart from the several hundred others who graduated the same day.

"She should be able to get a good job," he told them.

Encouraged by a college pastor to connect my writing gifts and my faith to my career choice, I placed self-expression, spiritual values, and creativity as priorities when I sought work. But first (and maybe still) I wrestled with the question of usefulness. Members of my family had almost always done things that were inherently useful: Raised grain and livestock, made drill bits and candy, cut lumber, built ships, drove trucks, balanced books, sewn clothes. Those before my generation who had sought higher education were schoolteachers, ministers, and a nurse.

It would be unfair and inaccurate to say that when economic conditions allowed them a choice in job my relatives made their choice on a purely utilitarian basis—that getting the bills paid and making a product was the only satisfaction they sought. For example, those of my relatives who were farmers—and owned their own land—loved that land, being outdoors, the growing of things, and self-sufficiency. They met practical aims and endured some drudgery, *and* they found meaning and pleasure in their work. But still, work that didn't somehow meet everyday needs would be seen as suspect. There was a bias toward the concrete.

So, I still sometimes ask the question, What good are words? I can find an answer, in part, in scripture: Through Word all was created. With words we tell the stories of where we are from and where we might go, and in this way help remake the world. I don't grow food, make tools, or heal the sick. But with words I try to further in practical ways the ends of justice (and mercy) and to communicate truth and beauty that might break hearts open and resurrect them one beat closer to the reign of God.

But the question of the "usefulness" or the purpose of work is increasingly pertinent in a time when "information" and services are the growth commodities. International corporate consolidation, restructuring, and the use of temporary employees in all types of work (from assembly lines to specialized professions) also undermine and fragment our understanding of who and what our work is for.

Neither virtual reality nor economic upheavals eliminate or replace a material world that has real needs; the faces of those we love or fear; the pull of faith; or the physical, spiritual, and emotional wounds of life. If our work primarily involves words or other information, we need an understanding of how that data are linked to concrete realities and experiences. If work structures or situations by design strain or negate our connection to coworkers or a sense of mission, then such structures need to be questioned. If we can't find the connections between data and people in our work, then either the other connections in our life need that much more attention or we need other work.

In "The Calling of Voices," an essay on vocation, Frederick Buechner writes:

> To Isaiah, the voice said, "Go," and for each of us there are many voices that say it, but the question is which one will we obey with our lives, which of the voices that call is to be the one that we answer. No one can say, of course, except each for himself [or herself], but I believe that it is possible to say at least this in general to all of us: we should go with our lives where we most need to go and where we are most needed.

Faith always calls us back into relationship with our God and a world that is beloved by God. Our vocation is to follow Jesus and to spread the gospel. He moved, preached, and taught in the ordinary, work-a-day world. Sometimes he called women and men away from their households, nets, and accounts;

discipleship meant leaving one's work and place. Sometimes he called women and men where they were; discipleship meant living differently in one's work and place.

Just as there was no single way to follow then, there is not now. God's call is on our whole lives, not specifically our career choice. What draws our heart, and where is our heart needed?

A person in their twenties now may have seven or eight jobs or careers in their lifetime. The upheavals caused by industry relocation, downsizing, and corporate consolidations are unnerving and damaging to people and communities, and reveal the facile lies rampant in much of the public debate over welfare. For the more comfortable, this same fragmentation may break up the idol that career can be. For some it may bring a needed reminder to work to live, not live to work. For others, it may turn them to look again at their work and its relationship to the world, and to see how they can offer justice and mercy in new and different ways—within or outside of paid employment.

Professor of ethics Donald Shriver describes how an ideology of "justification by work" is pervasive in our culture. He reminds us that this reverses the proper order of things as set out in Ephesians: "For by *grace* you have been saved through faith, and this is not your own doing; it is the gift of God. . . . For we are God's handiwork, created in Christ Jesus for good works . . ." (2:8–10).

If we can place our work in a balanced rhythm with worship (and rest and play), it will keep us rooted in the grace from which our whole life flows. Kathleen Norris writes of Benedictines that they "regard all time as holy and seek to use it well. . . . Moderation is essential, for, in the words of Amma Syncletica, a fourth-century desert nun, 'lack of proportion always corrupts.'"

A definition of liturgy is the celebration of the work of the people. We can be literal in this, holding up in recognition, litany, and prayer those in our congregations who volunteer and those who work for pay, those who are unemployed and those who have been promoted, those who care for young, elderly, or ill relatives, those who study, and those who are retired.

In the weekly worship I attend, we hold up in prayer a member of our congregation whose job requires him to work on Sunday mornings. In this brief moment we celebrate all of who he is—a child of God, who hungers to be at worship with his family and community, a father sacrificing to care for those he loves in the way that is possible at the moment, a brother missed from our circle. This, in the end, is what the people of God are to be about, in our worship and our work: to celebrate who and whose we are, people saved by grace and called by name.

Julie Polter was an assistant editor of *Sojourners* when this appeared in the January-February 1997 issue.

Mutual Aid's Radical Christian Roots

Isaac S. Villegas

From the book of Acts to Mennonite solidarity, mutual aid has long been a way to create networks of communal care.

In the early months of the pandemic, the "Care Bears" team of my local chapter of Southerners on New Ground (SONG), a Black, queer-led community of carceral abolitionists, reached out to members of the SONG family by phone. A small box arrived in the mail a few weeks later. The Care Bears had decided I'd benefit from a "a gift of love in a trying time"—tangerine tea, a candle, colored pencils, a notebook, and a tiny bottle of dandelion tincture made by the resident SONG herbalist.

I was drawn into the extended SONG family in 2017 when I joined the Black Mama's Bail Out Action campaign. For Mother's Day, SONG members paid the bail of mothers and caregivers held in the Durham, North Carolina county jail because, like tens of thousands of people imprisoned in the United States, they couldn't afford their release. As a minister familiar with the jail's protocols, I was called on to help obtain consent from the women being held. SONG raised the funds as part of a practice of mutual aid through paying off bail debt. "Money kept you in," Pat Hussain, a co-founder of SONG said. "Black love got you out."

My involvement with SONG has taught me the interconnections of Black feminism, prison abolitionism, and mutual aid—all as part of movements to create everyday institutions that nurture life. Abolitionism is about undoing the violence of incarceration, Angela Y. Davis writes in *Abolition Democracy*, "but it is also about building up, about creating new institutions." And abolitionist Ruth Wilson Gilmore asserts that "abolition is about presence, not absence."

Both Davis and Gilmore center the need for organized community to sustain life in a destructive world. They call for the creation of new institutions of mutual care while eroding the carceral system's grip on society. With exceptional clarity, organizer and educator Mariame Kaba recently reissued this call: "Our work isn't just a movement *against* cages and cops. It's a movement *for* different ways of living together." In this movement for a shared life where everyone can experience wholeness, "mutual aid exposes the failures of the current system and shows an alternative."

Nearly thirty years ago, Mab Segrest, a co-founder of SONG, named this reciprocal commitment "queer socialism"—" a politic that does not cut us off from other people, but unites us with them in the broadest possible movement." She expressed a shared need for "a less *lonely* society, where we think collectively about resources for the common good, rather than struggling individually against each other for material and psychic survival."

The SONG vision for queer socialism, rooted in Black feminism, is a kind of mutual aid that cares for the material and psychological well-being of each member of the community. This conception of "the common good" is not a collection of values or policies to impose upon the masses. Rather, the commitments are the building blocks for political institutions—beyond the state's policies and policing—based on the practices of mutual care.

Lives Bound Up

My introduction to mutual aid happened before I joined SONG's work—almost two decades prior when I became a member of a Mennonite congregation. On the Sunday I was presented for church membership, the gathered body pledged their commitment to sustain my life. "Sisters and brothers, do you accept your responsibility to care for the physical and spiritual needs of our new member?" the worship leader asked.

In the Mennonite tradition, mutual aid is intrinsic to an ecclesiology that understands the congregation as a body where the health of each member determines the health of the others. "Mennonite mutual aid is a reciprocal responsibility, based on biblical teaching, to provide material aid to other church members who face special economic and physical hardships," Donald B. Kraybill and Willard M. Swartley explain in *Building Communities of Compassion: Mennonite Mutual Aid in Theory and Practice*. We belong to Christ as we belong with one another. "If one member suffers, all suffer together with it," the apostle Paul told the church in Corinth. "If one member is honored, all rejoice together with it" (1 Corinthians 12:26).

Some churches take up an offering for a specific need in the community. Others, like the one I now pastor, include such funds as a line in our budget. In years when we expend more than we expect, the congregation is asked to replenish the fund. The deacons make the distributions, as one sixteenth-century Anabaptist congregation recommended, "so that the giver shall remain unknown as Christ teaches." Our deacons also welcome requests from church members to give money to those outside the church body whose lives are bound up with ours. If money remains in the fund at the end of the fiscal year, our congregation selects a few organizations and gives it away as a modest act of economic redistribution.

Once, in the early years of my pastorate, a longtime member of the church requested a meeting to discuss her concerns about a candidate seeking membership. I expected that she would divulge a community secret or perhaps an unaddressed moral indiscretion and advise that the prospective member be held accountable before we could, in good conscience, accept him. My speculations were very wrong. "I don't think he has health insurance," she said. "If he doesn't, we need to figure out how to make sure he's got coverage." She recognized the meaning of saying "yes" to his membership—the responsibility for us, as a congregation, to be responsible for his care, including his physical health.

Radical Roots

Our work as Mennonites is not without precedent. In the early part of the sixteenth century, as the Radical Reformation spread within peasant Christianity in Europe, Anabaptists returned to the biblical vision in Acts for guidance on church life. "No one claimed private ownership of any possessions, but everything they owned was held in common," Luke the Evangelist documents (Acts 4:32). *Omnia sunt communia*, meaning "all things in common," was the rallying cry of Anabaptist communities—a slogan they borrowed from the Latin translation of the verse from Acts.

The ruling classes considered this way of life a threat to theirs and teamed up with theologians to squelch the movement. In 1525, Martin Luther did his best to protect the reformation from the rebellious "hordes of peasants" whose economic revolution he considered violent. "Let everyone who can, smite, slay, and stab, secretly or openly, remembering that nothing can be more poisonous, hurtful, or devilish than a rebel," Luther wrote in a widely circulated pamphlet. "It is just as when one must kill a mad dog."

The monied rulers doubled down on their investment in Luther's theological ruthlessness with leaders legislating the persecution of Anabaptists to preserve the structures that governed society. Swiss cantons condemned adherents to Anabaptist faith and practice. "They [Anabaptists] hold and say that no Christian may either give or receive interest or income on capital, and that all temporal goods are free and common and everyone can have full property rights to them," read a 1527 decree. In 1571, when the Church of England affirmed their Thirty-nine Articles of Religion (still included in the *Book of Common Prayer*), they denounced Anabaptists: "The riches and goods of Christians are not common as certain Anabaptists do falsely boast," the thirty-eighth article declares.

Anabaptists didn't invent Christian communitarianism. In the *Didache*, an early church catechism, we read that a network of first-century congregations upheld a discipline of mutual aid. "Never turn away the needy; share all your possessions with your brother [and sister], and do not claim that anything is your own." However, in sixteenth-century Europe, Christian rulers feared that a revival of this gospel command would level their hierarchies of wealth and power. In *The Revolution of 1525*, historian Peter Blickle named these two, irreconcilable social visions as "the communal Reformation" and "the ruler's Reformation." Anabaptist communities "sought to save the remnant of the communal Reformation by withdrawing from the realm of this world, but the rulers mercilessly exterminated them."

Not quite all were killed off, however. Scattered enclaves survived persecution and passed their version of the Christian faith from one remnant community to another—an invitation to mutual care in a violent world. Those Anabaptist groups would later come together as Mennonites, Hutterites, Amish, and Brethren. Mennonites in North America in the early twentieth century would expand their mutual aid organizing to include relief work.

Benevolence within congregations overflowed into institutions for people beyond church membership rolls: health care services, famine and disaster relief, assistance for survivors of war, humanitarian work at home and abroad, and aid to neighbors across the street and around the world. These Christian commitments developed into various organizations: Mennonite Mutual Aid (renamed Everence in 2010), Mennonite Disaster Service, Mennonite Voluntary Service, Mennonite Central Committee, and Mennonite Health Services.

Embodying the Vision

I write from what I've experienced as a Mennonite and as part of SONG's extended family while also recognizing that there are other traditions of mutual aid. Through our SONG campaign to abolish money bail, I learned about the Believers Bail Out, an organization formed within Muslim communities in Chicago to collect their annual charitable contributions known as *zakat* to ransom people from ICE detention and the county jail. Masjid al-Rabia, a mosque and Islamic community center in Chicago, redistributed nearly seventy thousand dollars during the first year of the pandemic.

"As our communities respond and persevere amidst COVID-19, health crises, and financial implications of missing or losing work, we also enter the eve of Ramadan," the leaders wrote in a statement titled, "Radical Muslim Mutual Aid." "This time reminds us of the importance of *zakat*, the Islamic mutual aid practice around redistribution of wealth."

In the Christian faith, mutual aid is how we embody the vision St. Irenaeus of Smyrna preached in the second century: "The glory of God is the human being fully alive." To live into the fullness of our humanity requires mutual dependence and a love enfleshed through our material lives. We do so not to replace the provisions of society or to make the state's resources redundant, but to prefigure a world without the economic violence of the everyday, a way of life that doesn't deem some of us disposable. *None* of us are fully alive until *all* of us are fully alive. Mutual aid is our transformation from glory to glory into the fullness of God's life for us. It is the incarnation of divine care.

A commitment to mutual aid asks the Mennonite membership question to each of us: "Do you accept your responsibility to care for the physical and spiritual needs of the members of our community?" We answer by forming ordinary institutions in our neighborhoods, workplaces, and churches. Together, we become the kind of community we want for the rest of society: a peoplehood in which we find ourselves fully alive.

Mutual aid institutions such as SONG are invested in a common good that is noncoercive, a way of life that doesn't rely on the violence of law enforcement to guarantee political reforms. To give and receive mutual aid is an invitation to hold in common a commitment to the well-being and the wholeness of everyone within a community. As Suzanne Pharr, a SONG co-founder, explains: "How you treat each other should mirror what you're demanding of society."

Mutual aid is a style of collective living that enacts a faith in God's care for all of us. To hoard wealth is to disbelieve in God's benevolence, to refuse the governance of grace in our economic decisions. Through our mutuality we entrust ourselves to God's providence, not to our culture of greed. To develop communal institutions of sharing is to plant a seed in the lonely wastelands of our world and hope for the growth of a different society—or at least to nurture a sociality among ourselves while we wait for wholescale transformation, the transfiguration of all things.

Mutual aid is a prayer we offer with our lives, a petition for "this earthly life to swing up into heaven," as the sixteenth-century reformer Thomas Müntzer wrote. Collectives of mutual aid and care inspire hope in us as we flesh out alternative political imaginations. As Mariame Kaba more recently framed it, "As an abolitionist, I'm trying to prefigure the world in which I want to live."

Isaac S. Villegas was pastor of Chapel Hill (N.C.) Mennonite Fellowship and president of the governing board of the North Carolina Council of Churches when this appeared in the May 2022 issue of *Sojourners*.

Holy Economics

Rabbi Arthur Waskow

A rhythm of worthy work and reflective rest.

Because the Hebrew Scriptures are rooted in a landed community that had to deal with the everyday issues of food and money, they describe in considerable detail what might be called a path of "holy economics." At one level, there is the transformational vision of Leviticus 25 and Deuteronomy 15: Every seventh year, debtors were released from their debts and the land itself was released from human control, so that it could make its own Sabbath rest for an entire year.

And in the fiftieth year (seven times seven plus one), a Jubilee was to be proclaimed: The land should lie restful for yet another year, while every family returned to the equal share of the land it had been assigned when the people of Israel first came into the Promised Land. Thus the rich were to be released from the extra land they had acquired, the poor were to be released from their landless status, even indentured servants, no matter where they stood in their own seven-year term of service or a life-long obligation, were to be released to return to their original family landholding. (This "release"—in Hebrew, *dror*—is what is encoded on the Liberty Bell: "Proclaim liberty [*dror*] throughout the land to all the inhabitants thereof.")

But what about the time between transformations, between sabbatical years and Jubilees? As we lead our "ordinary" lives today, we certainly need to look at the Bible's notion of ordinary economic history as well as the times of transformation.

At first glance, it seems like six years of free enterprise. For six years at a stretch, the land could be worked and the land could be bought. Some could get poor enough to need to borrow money, some could get rich enough to lend it. For forty-nine years at a time, some could get rich enough to hold a great deal of land and to supervise a large number of indentured workers.

Even during these ordinary years, there were two socio-economic requirements that set limits to poverty and wealth: Everyone was entitled to work, and everyone was both entitled and obligated to rest.

Honoring Work, Promoting Equality

How did the Bible provide that everyone was entitled to work? Says Leviticus 19:9–10: "When you reap the harvest of your land, you shall not complete the harvest in the corners of your field, nor shall you gather the gleaning of your harvest . . . or of your vineyard. . . . You shall leave them for the poor and the foreigner; I am YHWH your God!"

And indeed in the book of Ruth we find this command carried out. Two penniless widows, one a foreigner from a despised community—the Moabites—arrived in Israelite society. The foreigner, Ruth, was welcomed onto the fields of Boaz, where she gleaned what the regular harvesters had left behind. Boaz knew that even this despised foreigner was entitled to a decent job at decent pay. And the work she did was not menial or undignified; it was exactly the kind of work that most people did in the world of ancient Israel.

Boaz acted with great generosity, but he was not free to act ungenerously. It was the law of his society, not his private generosity alone, that guaranteed Ruth a place in gleaning his crops. Everyone—not only one extraordinary woman—had the right simply to walk onto a field and begin to work for a decent income, begin to use the means of production of that era.

Notice that Boaz could not order his regular workers to be economically "efficient." They could not harvest everything, not what grew in the corners of the field, not what they missed on the first time around. Social compassion was more important than efficiency. No downsizing allowed.

When Ruth went one night to the barn where the barley crop was being threshed, Boaz spent the night with her and decided to marry her. With him the penniless foreigner became the great-great-great-grandmother of King David, and therefore (in both Jewish and Christian traditions) the ancestor of the Messiah.

If Ruth came to America today, what would happen? Would she be admitted at the border? Would she have to show a "green card" before she could get a job gleaning at any farm, restaurant, or hospital? Would she face contempt because she spent a night with Boaz on the threshing floor?

Through the book of Ruth, the Bible affirms that in a decent society everyone is entitled to decent work for a decent income. Everyone—even, or especially, a despised immigrant. Everyone—not just 95 percent of the people.

Ruth was entitled not only to a job, but to respect. Boaz reminded his workers: No name-calling, no sexual harassment.

And she, as well as Boaz, was entitled to Sabbath: time off for rest, reflection, celebration, love. She was entitled to "be" as well as to "do."

How do we know that Ruth was entitled to rest, as well as to work at a living wage? In both the places where the Ten Commandments of Sinai are recited (Exodus 20:8–11 and Deuteronomy 5:12–15), it is made clear that the whole family, all servants, and "the foreigner within your gates" are all to rest one day of every seven. In the second recitation, the Bible explicitly says that the reason for this Sabbath rest is to remember what it was like to be a slave in *Mitzraiim* (the Hebrew word for Egypt means, more generally, "the tight and narrow place"), where it was never possible to rest.

Yet America today sneers at immigrants; blames the poor for their poverty; keeps at least 5 percent of its people officially unemployed, and in fact far more (prisoners and those who have given up on ever finding a job, for example); dumps many, many more from jobs long held into jobs far beneath their abilities for the sake of "efficient" management; subjects others to exhausting overwork that leaves no time for rest, reflection, celebration, family, love, community—and drives them to alcohol or television to relax. In that America—this America—what is the obligation of those who, like Boaz, are well-off?

Because Ruth and Boaz, the outcast and the solid citizen, got together, they could bring Messiah into the world—the transformation that brings peace and justice. What does that teach us today?

It teaches us to make sure that every human being can find decent work and be decently paid for it. To make sure that every human being has time for calm and reflective rest, time to live in the midst of a loving family and community. Only through a rhythm of worthy work and reflective rest do human beings grow into moral and ethical people.

For individuals to be ethically responsible, their society as a whole must be ethically responsible. We create an irresponsible society if we tell individuals they are responsible for themselves—and then deny them the jobs, the decent incomes, and the time for rest and renewal that we all need in order to be responsible human beings.

No one offered Ruth a pile of food, free for the taking. She was both entitled and obligated to glean the food, even though she did not own the land on which it grew. That was responsibility.

Restful renewal is also an aspect of responsibility. Ruth, like every other citizen or foreigner, like every worker, even the earth itself and all its life forms, was entitled and obligated to rest on the Sabbath. Time to repose and reflect, time for family, community, and citizenship.

But today we keep millions of our people unemployed, and force others to be overworked. For millions, no gleaning. For millions, no Sabbath.

The point is not to go back to the failed policy of a "welfare" system focused on preventing the poor from either working or resting. That system failed because there were no jobs and no support for the places where people can rest and reflect on their lives and themselves—neighborhoods, families, religious congregations, grassroots politics, picnics, folk festivals, forests.

How do we provide jobs and rest for all? There is a great deal of honorable work that American society needs to get done, but has committed few resources for the doing:

- The physical work of replacing rotting sewers, creating effective mass transit, cleaning up chemical dumps, and replacing factory-size, alienating schools with schools built on a human scale for human interconnection.
- The person-to-person work of human interchange and learning done by teachers and teachers' aides, child-care workers, paramedics, and recreation leaders.

Universal employment can be achieved without creating swollen bureaucracies. For instance, new grassroots enterprises can lend investment capital and supply expert advice to new businesses owned and operated by the poor.

Increasing the number of jobs is only half the task, for the sharing of rest by everyone is just as crucial as the sharing of jobs. A reduction of work hours could be accomplished in several different ways:

- Set as a new standard, for example, a thirty-hour work week with little or no reduction in pay (a proposal put forth by Jeremy Rifkin).
- Require that employers provide all workers with a certain number of paid leave hours every week to invest in community service and family support, just as many businesses now provide their executives with paid leave time to serve on university or museum boards and the like.
- Pay large numbers of workers to spend years in self-enrichment through education, as America did in the 1940s when it had far less wealth, by providing millions of veterans with the GI Bill.
- Allow (or even require) everyone to take a paid nonwork true sabbatical year, supported by Social Security pension funds, sometime between their fortieth and fiftieth birthdays.
- Shut down the entire "work economy" for perhaps one day a month, one week a year, or for the official holidays that are now venues for frenzied sales and purchases. Instead, for that period of time, strongly encourage neighborhood festivals, local family outings, and similar celebrations. (The shutdown should include gasoline stations, airlines, television; life support services would of course be exempt.)
- Require all businesses to provide time for teams of workers to reassess the role of their work in their company's production, and the role of their company and its products in the world at large.
- Provide college scholarships in amounts and numbers proportional to those in the post–World War II GI Bill.
- Give tax rebates to people who give volunteer time to civic organizations (another Rifkin proposal).

- Require periodic "rest periods" (moratoria) on the introduction of new products that may have a massive impact on the environment, setting aside time for environmental impact assessments to be made and published.
- Require periodic "rest periods" (moratoria) on technological research and development, except that focused directly on the cure of lethal diseases, while scientists and engineers join in an examination of the ethical and environmental impact of various technologies and reassess which directions are likely to be the most nurturing and the least damaging.
- Set aside each year a focused week of reflective discussion in town meetings and in all media of one major institutional structure of American society, to assess the impact of that structure on the well-being of individuals, society, and the Earth.
- Put the sabbatical year itself into full observance, going the whole biblical distance (as Michael Lerner has suggested).

If we did all this, Ruth the Moabite could make a decent life in America. And then, who knows? She and Boaz, and all of us together, might be able to give birth to a Messianic era.

Rabbi Arthur Waskow, a leader of the movement for Jewish renewal and founder of The Shalom Center (theshalomcenter.org) in Philadelphia, traveled widely with his wife, Phyllis Berman, to speak, lead religious services, and offer Bible-based storytelling. This appeared in the September-October 1997 issue of *Sojourners*.

My Church Came Together to Pay Off Each Member's Debt

Joshua Grace

We moved together from bondage into mutuality.

Credit card debt plagues our communities. The average U.S. household carries a balance of $6,929 at the end of the month. And if you miss a payment, interest may jump from 15 percent to more than 20 percent.

Credit cards are part of a predatory industry with a history of racial bias. Many people can afford only the minimum monthly payment, barely making a dent in the principal—just as the system was designed.

About ten years ago at Circle of Hope, my church in Philadelphia, we began experimenting with "credit card debt annihilation." Our team's motto came from Romans 13, where the apostle Paul urged believers to "owe no one anything," except love.

We identified church members with credit card debt and an income. We established three cohorts with a half dozen participants in each. Each member covenanted to 100-percent financial transparency within their cohort, to meet monthly with the group and with their financial coach, and to stop using credit cards. Each cohort started with seed money and a three-year payoff plan to bring the whole cohort out of credit card debt.

We discerned an order of debt annihilation. Usually the card with the highest interest rate, among all the cohort members, was paid off first. We paid off one line of credit at a time, working down the list.

The biggest impact was made on the first day, when the seed money paid off the most problematic cards. As we worked down the list, each participant made their own minimum payment, if they still had a balance, and also paid $50 to $100 more to the credit card of focus, regardless of who had that card. Members actually wrote checks to someone else's lender with that person's name and account number in the memo line.

After someone's credit debt was annihilated, they kept paying in the same order. The amount that formerly went to their own minimum got added to their third-party check each month and sent to the specific lender. And thus, the snowball grew. The size of the concentrated payments increased as each card got paid off. When, together, we paid off all the balances, the seed money was replenished and passed on to the next group.

We decided to focus on credit card debt because of its fluctuating interest rates and relatively smaller amounts, compared to home mortgages or student debt—and because of the shame carried by people with this kind of debt.

Members of our cohorts had used their cards for temporary financial relief. When they needed money, they had turned to a lending corporation rather than to community. Their debt stories—how their debts grew—ranged from impulsive shopping to medical debt to a housing crisis.

As a church, we are practicing putting limits on oppression from the dominant corporation culture, much in the way the Hebrews imagined and practiced during their formation in the wilderness. The sabbatical year (or *shmita*), the traditional Hebrew agricultural sabbath year practiced every seven years, culminated in the vision of the Jubilee year. This redistribution of land and release from debt bondage socialized the Hebrew people away from intergenerational poverty and wealth. Just as Sabbath teaches rest as resistance, setting a limit to oppressive working conditions, so freedom from credit card debt sets mutuality, trust, and simplicity as limits to our economic oppression.

We've completed three cohorts using this strategy, eliminating more than $100,000 in principal debt, and we probably have saved as much in interest. Inspired by good stories of resistance in scripture, we're trying to embody new possibilities, moving together from shame into trust and from bondage into mutuality.

Joshua Grace, a Polish American settler, was living with his family in Philadelphia, traditional land of the Lenni Lenape, when this appeared in the July 2019 issue of *Sojourners*.

When Your Nation Is Stuck in a Spiritual Desert

Adam Russell Taylor

Facing political and spiritual deserts requires surrender to God.

Lent is a season of introspection and reflection as we prepare for Easter. By observing the forty days of Lent, we replicate Jesus' sacrifice and withdrawal into the desert for forty days.

When I was sixteen, my mom accepted a new job at the University of Arizona, and my parents made the untimely decision to uproot our family and move from the Pacific Northwest to the Arizona desert just before my last year in high school. As a result, I know something about deserts.

Deserts are not simply physical places—they are also spiritual and emotional seasons in our lives. What the physical desert does to the body, the spiritual desert does to our soul, making us feel drained and depleted. In moments of spiritual desert, we can feel disoriented and alienated from God. St. John of the Cross referred to these as dark nights of the soul—times when "we feel a spiritual drought and estrangement from God."

Nations can also go through what feel like periods of desert. America seems stuck in a dire one now. The current political crisis represents a test of our democracy and of the witness of the church. U.S. Christianity is also facing desert times as younger Christians abandon the church in record numbers.

Jesus knew something about deserts. He spent forty trying and formative days fasting and wandering in the desert, just before he faced and overcame the devil's three temptations of instant gratification, power, and control, which helped prepare him for his three years of public ministry. Time in the desert can be essential to prepare us for and sustain the long, hard work of seeking justice and advancing God's reign.

First, the desert provides time for preparation through deeper discernment. Time in the desert gives us the space to think more deeply, listen more carefully, and see more clearly. Solitude and silence must be learned and practiced. In the context of pursuing justice, discernment sharpens our analysis and enables us to see possibility in the impossible and hope in seemingly hopeless situations.

Second, time in the desert provides a time for purification. Many justice leaders burn out because their starting point is righteous indignation rather than steadfast love. Our soul yearns for the purification and renewal that real and regular contemplation provides. Contemplation grounds and sustains faith-inspired activism. As Christian leaders and activists, we must constantly resist the dangers of self-righteousness, absolutism, and, at worst, demonizing and hating our opponents and enemies, which has become all too common in American politics. We must overcome the evil that is external but also the evil that lies within each of us.

Third, the desert provides a time for total surrender. All genuine spirituality requires letting go. Letting go of illusion, ego, and sin. In the desert, we must be willing to give everything to God—our past regrets and hurts, our present problems and doubts, our future fears and dreams. In the desert, we are reminded that there is no burden that God cannot carry, there is no yoke that is too heavy for God.

Our communities, nation, and world may be in a harsh and difficult time—but if we engage in deeper discernment, purify ourselves, and surrender to God, we will be better equipped to lead out of the desert, transforming ourselves, our nation, and our world.

Adam Russell Taylor, an ordained Baptist minister and author of *A More Perfect Union: A New Vision for Building the Beloved Community,* was president of Sojourners when this appeared in the March 2020 issue.

Longing for Incarnation

Jim Wallis

The shots rang out at two o'clock Sunday afternoon—broad daylight on the Sabbath. The shooting victim was making a call at a sidewalk phone when somebody pumped seven rounds into him from an automatic weapon.

The murder occurred right outside the Sojourners intern house. Our newest group of interns had been here just two weeks. All but one of the seven interns were home, and they were among the first witnesses to one more senseless act of violence in our neighborhood. It was a baptism by fire for these men and women newly arrived in the city, and it prompted deep questions of faith.

The police went through their now common routine and, eventually, took the body away. Afterward, long-time Sojourners Community member George Gentsch came out with a pail of water and scrubbed the blood off the sidewalk. His simple act was one of both courage and faithfulness.

We know the causes of such violence only too well in the addictions to drugs and money, the root economic injustice, the culture of violence, the disintegration of families, the structures of racism, the lack of political will, and more. Underneath it all is the palpable presence of evil—in our institutions, our values, and deep within the human heart.

The following Sunday we celebrated the Feast of St. Francis, one of Sojourners' patron saints. Marie Dennis, a member of the Assisi Community here in Washington, D.C., reflected that

Francis was "attuned to the suffering and pain of the world and yet embodied both hope and joy." That is both the mystery and power of the incarnation that we will all soon celebrate once more.

To celebrate the incarnation in these days is to do so in the face of great evil and the virtual unraveling of our social fabric. That is precisely why it is so important. To embody the incarnation is the most concrete form of hope that can be offered in our time. To demonstrate the belief that the way of Christ is the ultimate reality is to radically assert that present realities are not ultimate. To steadfastly put our trust in the gospel is to boldly proclaim that violence, oppression, and chaos will not have the last word.

It is a much deeper kind of hope than that of placing our confidence in different political policies or new social movements. We should continue to work hard for both, but neither will ever remove the pain and suffering of the world or finally overcome the evil in our human condition, social institutions, and cultural habits. We need so much more than the promises of social reform and even political liberation. In the midst of such very human efforts, the presence of evil always will reassert itself.

What we long for is nothing less than the concrete inbreaking of the reign of God—incarnation. Whenever the Word is made flesh, incarnation occurs and history opens up again, revealing new possibilities for human life. That is why *Sojourners* has kept the tradition, each December, of telling the stories of those brothers and sisters among us whose lives have taught us the meaning of the incarnation. In their stories, we see the true hope of the world.

This, indeed, is the primary Christian responsibility—to make the gospel a reality in the face of the world's realities. Nothing else is more important, and no other priorities should distract us from this most central vocation.

This Advent season is a good time to reassess our priorities and decide what is most important to us. Advent means new beginnings and announces the birth of hope in a world that longs for those new possibilities. Never has that longing been greater.

There has been a lot of late-night conversation at the intern house, struggling to make sense of the events of that bloody Sunday. Why are we here? Are we safe? What good does our presence do? What difference do we make? One intern said it well when she testified that her ideals and commitments were not enough to answer the questions. To live with such evil at the front door asks us how much faith we really have.

You don't have to be on the front lines of urban violence to recognize that the evil is at all of our front doors now, and the question for all of us is one of faith. Do we believe in the incarnation and are we willing to become signs of that Word made flesh in a world whose aching moan is a desperate cry for hope?

Jim Wallis, a founding member of Sojourners, was editor-in-chief of *Sojourners* when this appeared in the December 1992 issue.

Radical Hospitality

Rosemarie Freeney Harding and Rachel Elizabeth Harding

How kitchen-table lessons in welcome and respect helped sustain the Black freedom movement.

Hospitality has been a central model for activism in my life. Starting before my children were born, I have been what some people would call an activist—working in political campaigns; organizing alternative schools; training, mobilizing, and reconciling in the Black freedom movement, the women's movement, and the peace and justice movement. I've worked with some magnificent people, deeply committed to spiritually engaged, compassionate social change. People like Bob Moses, Anne Braden, Prathia Hall, Gwendolyn Zoharah Simmons, Clarence Jordan, Bernice Johnson Reagon, Marion King, Grace Lee Boggs, Julia Esquivel, Ndugu T'Ofori-Atta, and Staughton and Alice Lynd. I've learned a great deal from these marvelous women and men, and many others like them.

But as I think about my own movement work and its deepest inspirations, I am continually drawn back to the model of my family—especially my mother, Ella Lee ("Mama Freeney"), and great-grandmother, Moriah ("Mama Rye"). Mama Rye, born in Africa, was a slave in Virginia and died in 1930 at the age of 107. Both Mama Freeney and Mama Rye cultivated a profound mystic spirituality and deep hospitality that they passed to their descendants.

In the years when I was growing up, people visited back and forth at each other's homes more regularly than folks do now. Our house was an especially popular destination for neighbors and relatives. We had a large family, and my older brothers and sisters had lots of friends. Also, my mother and father made the house welcoming. Sometimes it seemed "too" welcoming—all kinds of people came through, not just relatives and neighborhood friends, but peddlers, professional gamblers, petty thieves, prostitutes, and people we would probably refer to today as homeless. Mom set out beautiful china dishes and slices of her homemade pound cake for all of them—especially for the most transient-looking people, it seemed sometimes. It was as if she knew they needed the extra attention and acknowledgement, and she genuinely enjoyed their conversation and wisdom.

An itinerant bookseller would come to visit Mom now and then. The two of them would sit down in the dining room with Mom's best dishes and talk for hours about the events of the world and the world of books. The man was not always very clean and sometimes, especially in the winter when the heat was on full blast in our house, we could smell the mustiness of his old, ragged clothes and the heavy, acrid sweat of his body. He talked funny too, and we children were occasionally tempted to laugh—as much from discomfort as anything else. But if we let out the tiniest snicker, Mom would cut her eyes at us and we immediately changed our minds—and the expressions on our faces.

Hospitality was a foundation of my family's spirituality, as it had been for so many Southern Blacks. The efforts my parents made to be neighborly and to reserve judgment against those who society viewed as outcasts served as important examples for their children and grandchildren as we grew into adulthood. One of my first projects as a young activist in the Southern freedom movement was developing an interracial social service project and community center called Mennonite House in Atlanta during the early 1960s. In addition to our work of placing volunteers with various movement organizations, training young movement activists, and coordinating early efforts at interracial dialogue and reconciliation, Mennonite House became an important place of retreat for many who were struggling and sacrificing so much to transform the South and the nation. Because of my mother's example, I understood very clearly how important it was to have spaces of refuge in the midst of struggle—spaces of joy and laughter, good food and kind words. This kind of compassionate care is a transformative force in itself. As Cape Breton novelist Alistair MacLeod writes, "We are all better when we're loved."

One important way we expressed love, in family life and in the movement, was a certain formality of relations, rooted in Southern and African traditions. Respect was shown through the courteous use of forms of address when talking to strangers, persons of authority, and anyone in an age group higher than one's own. Women were always Miss or Mrs. so-and-so, men were called Mr. (unless they were relatives, and then they were called Aunt, Uncle, or Cousin). As children our responses of "ma'am" and "sir" indicated the good "home-training" we had received from the adults who raised us. Even among adults of comparable age and status, who had known each other for many years, there was often a kind of quasi-ceremonial care in the way they interacted with each other. In some respects, this must have been an antidote to the indignities these men and women regularly suffered from a discriminatory white society. But this practice of almost exaggerated mutual deference and politeness also was an important element of interpersonal relations in many of the West and Central African communities from which the majority of North American Blacks originated, and it was a common feature in slave communities throughout the Americas.

For those of us who lived and worked in the small towns of the rural South during the freedom movement, these relational dynamics became an integral part of the organizing model we developed. Gwendolyn Zoharah Simmons, the SNCC (Student Nonviolent Coordinating Committee) project leader in Laurel, Mississippi, in 1964, describes how she and her teenage and young-adult colleagues in Freedom Summer interacted with older community members with whom they were working to mobilize political and educational reform in the area. Simmons says, "We were seen as 'leaders,' people who brought a vision, people who brought resources, ideas, and materials that they wanted. At the same time, because of our youth we were also children to them."

Living with local community leaders, Simmons and other young activists were expected to replicate time-honored African American forms of intergenerational association. Euberta Sphinks, a long-standing local activist in the Laurel community, opened her home and her heart to Simmons. The relationship the two women developed was generally indicative of the way younger organizers and the older local citizens engaged each other.

"I had to obey Mrs. Sphinks when it came to what time I could come in and where I was going," says Simmons. "I had to tell her where I was going and where I had been. If she said I had to go to church, I had to go. But at the same time, they were willing to follow me into the jaws of the jail. . . . It was a very interesting dynamic."

This "interesting dynamic" was a central element of the organizing strategy of the movement and a large part of the reason for the movement's resonance and success all over the region. The young people of SNCC, CORE (the Congress of Racial Equality), and other movement organizations probably sometimes felt constrained by the behavioral expectations of their elders. But those norms of comportment were practical measures ensuring the well-being of the youth who (even if Southerners by birth) were often not familiar with the local community they were assigned to and who benefited greatly from being integrated into family and church structures of connection. Obeying the elders was a way of showing respect and acknowledging organic leadership and home-ground authority. Furthermore, the closeness and familiarity created by relationships modeled on family interactions were important sources of comfort, stability, and support amid the extreme tensions, uncertainty, and terrorist violence that were constant threats to everyone in the rural Southern Black communities.

Another vital source of support was music, particularly the sacred music of the Black experience, which has long been an alchemical resource for struggle: a conjured strength. Bernice Johnson Reagon has told a story on many occasions about the alchemy of singing in the mass meetings, demonstrations, and marches of the Southern freedom movement. Reagon, an extraordinary musician, organizer, and scholar, describes marching out of a movement church into the streets of Albany, Georgia, and toward the particular store or public facility that was the object of the day's demonstration. Raising their voices with freedom songs, in the cadence and spirit of church, Reagon and her fellow marchers could feel the songs swell into the air around them and transform the space. The songs changed the atmosphere, becoming an almost palpable barrier between demonstrators and police, giving the marchers an internal girding that allowed them to move without fear.

As Reagon explained in an interview with the Veterans of Hope Project, there is actually something about the experience of traditional Black congregational singing that, over time, "does something to the material you're made of. . . . It really connects you up with a force in the universe that makes you different. It makes you capable of moving with a different kind of access. You're connected to something else, other than what people think you're connected to. And they can't get to you."

Ruby Sales, a SNCC member who was active in the movement in Alabama, says that in her moments of deepest terror and anguish she called on the power of Black singing. "[The] thing that got me through is what has always gotten me through, Black songs. Singing those songs and hearing those voices . . . I sang, 'Will the Circle Be Unbroken?,' 'Tell Me How Did You Feel When You Come Out the Wilderness?,' 'We've Come this Far by Faith.'" Calling on these old songs, Sales linked herself to a tradition of sustenance in trauma much older than herself. In fact, she says that as she sang she felt connected to her grandmother and to all that her grandmother's generation had witnessed and survived. "It is in that moment, through song, that I am able to feel something other than myself," Sales says. "I become part of a community. I become part of a struggle."

The pervasiveness of spirit, the healing and transformative power of Black cultural and religious resources and practices, and a recognition of God's accompaniment in even the greatest of dangers sustained the movement—and continue to sustain so many of us still on the journey. "You know," Mama Freeney once said, "everything else passes, everything else will be destroyed, but the only thing that is going to be left is love. So, when you die, don't worry. The insignificant things will all go away, but that most significant thing will stand the test."

Rosemarie Freeney Harding was co-founder and co-chair of the Veterans of Hope Project—a center for religion and democratic renewal at the Iliff School of Theology in Denver—and **Rachel Elizabeth Harding**, Rosemarie's daughter, was the project's executive director. This appeared in the July-August 2003 issue of *Sojourners*.

The Howard Thurman Question That Changed My Faith

José Humphreys III

How the theologian and mystic called the American church back to Jesus.

Seventy-four years ago, scholar, mystic, and pastor Howard Thurman gave a lecture series at Samuel Huston College (now Huston-Tillotson University) in Austin, Texas. The series would become the basis for his seminal book *Jesus and the Disinherited*. One of Thurman's students, Martin Luther King Jr., reportedly traveled with a copy of Thurman's book. Through his writings and teachings, Thurman was a mentor and chaplain for many activists during the civil rights movement.

Jesus and the Disinherited continues to inspire many contemplatives and activists and has profoundly shaped my own approach to ministry. The main inspiration comes through a question Thurman posed to American Christianity: "What, then, is the word of the religion of Jesus to those who stand with their backs against the wall?" Thurman's question confronted the fact that American Christianity was, as historian Vincent Harding put it, a "strange mutation" away from the teachings and ethics of Jesus. Jesus, who was raised in the poor village of Nazareth out of the mainstream of Roman culture. Jesus, who was Galilean, which meant that even among the Jews, Jesus and his people were considered outcasts. Jesus, who spent many of his days moving from town to town touching lepers, transgressing boundaries, befriending Samaritans, and turning over the tables on corrupt economic practices in the temple. In light of Jesus' ministry, Thurman was challenging an American Christianity that was rampantly materialistic and segregationist, looming above the daily experiences of the disinherited. Thurman's writings demonstrated how a path-altering question can help inoculate our faith from harmful (American) mutations and point us back to the integrity of Jesus' Way.

For my East Harlem church, this has meant slowly moving beyond just holding space for middle-class comfort while challenging our preaching to be more rooted in the perspective of women and others in the Bible who have been overlooked. Our church is also participating in an interfaith Bible study with Central Synagogue and Exodus Transitional Community (ETC). ETC is an organization working with people impacted by the criminal justice system. Recently, participants in the Bible study became stuck on the question: "How do we discern hope through the looming shadows of our times?" Many in the group provided good responses, but the most profound came from Gary Brown, a director at ETC. Gary spoke about his arrest during the Clinton administration, which adopted punitive measures in the so-called war on drugs. He was sentenced to life without parole and said, "I reached my lowest moment" when viewing the sentencing document and seeing his release date, which read: "Deceased." From this hopeless place, Gary kept faith. He used his time at the Florence Correctional Facility in Colorado to mentor young people; he didn't want them to repeat his same mistakes. He also led anger management classes, rescripting his story even while in the valley of the shadow of death. After serving twenty-six years, against all odds, Gary was granted clemency. After his release, Gary would find ETC and work his way into management, living a powerful story of liberation and resilience.

At our Bible study that day, Gary's testimony breathed life into our constricted perspectives. He was the embodied response to what the religion of Jesus has to offer those whose backs are against the wall. Even today, Thurman's question continues to change my faith, while for many it continues to illuminate the path to faithful justice-seeking.

José Humphreys III was author of *Seeing Jesus in East Harlem: What Happens When Churches Show Up and Stay Put* and coauthor of *Ecosystems of Jubilee: Economic Ethics for the Neighborhood* (Zondervan) when this appeared in the May 2022 issue of *Sojourners.*

What About the Meek?

Margaret Atwood

On the most difficult beatitude.

This is surely the most difficult beatitude. First, it's hard to interpret. Does "meek" mean a Uriah Heep–like unctuous humbleness? Does it mean softness or gentleness or weakness? Are "the meek" the powerless, or perhaps the poor? Is their meekness to be displayed toward God, but not toward people? How meek is meek, and do you always have to let bullies kick sand in your face at the beach?

Next, what about "inherit"? That's a legalistic term; who's going to die so someone else gets an inheritance? Will the non-meek be pushed over a cliff so that only the meek are left? Or will the non-meek be lowered in status and the meek become rulers, thereby shedding their meekness?

And what about "the earth"? Another beatitude refers to the kingdom of heaven—the poor in spirit have it already, it seems—but "the meek" will instead inherit "the earth." The material world.

Being Canadian, I memorized the beatitudes at school. But I wondered whether "the meek" had to be *people*. Could they be some other life form? Scottish physiologist J. S. Haldane felt God shows an inordinate fondness for beetles—having created so many—and my own father speculated that, if humankind destroyed itself by nuclear bombs or otherwise, the earth would be inherited by cockroaches. That would explain everything!

But the opposite of "meek" is surely "proud," and pride goeth before a fall. Perhaps the meek will inherit when the proud become top-heavy and topple over, as in the reversals of fortune that accompany revolutions. Many of the beatitudes propose place-changing: Those who are up will be down, and vice versa. Is this a warning to the one percent to stop hoarding and start sharing?

What would meekness really be like in action? The three books of my MaddAddam Trilogy contain the Crakers, who lack aggression. To make this plausible, I had to give them some other characteristics. One reason for aggression is sexual competitiveness, so my new Crakers mate seasonally, communally, and without violence. Another reason is greed for *stuff*—those who go to war hope to acquire land, money, slaves, riches, and so forth—so my Crakers aren't interested in stuff. They don't wear clothes, farm land (they can eat leaves), or have social hierarchies.

This is not a virtue in them: They don't choose their meekness; they're just made that way. It follows that they would have to be protected from beings of our sort, because they would quickly be killed by us.

In the same trilogy there's a group that makes consciously meek choices. These are the God's Gardeners, who attempt a green vegetable-raising lifestyle on flat rooftops in a slum. They've opted out from the sinister hierarchies that surround them and are trying to live in a nonviolent manner that is not harmful to other life forms or to the planet. That's ultra-meek! It's much more difficult to live this way than you might think at first. (Toilet paper, yes or no? What about the trees? Every small item must be considered.)

Inevitably the moment of decision arrives for the God's Gardeners: What should they do when they're threatened physically? Should they defend themselves or not? If not—if they persist in their ultra-meekness—their chances of inheriting anything so concrete as "the earth" will rapidly vanish.

Matthew 5:5 is a paradoxical beatitude, and fraught with pitfalls and perils, once you start considering it. But Jesus was speaking at the time of the Roman Empire, and paradox is a useful tool when you're surrounded by the double-plus-unmeek.

Margaret Atwood, author of *Dearly: New Poems* and *The Handmaid's Tale,* is an award-winning Canadian poet and novelist. This appeared in the January 2015 issue of *Sojourners.*

Chapter 5

Green Confessions

Creatureliness

The advent of artificial intelligence makes current the question of our human "creatureliness." We are cousins to our earth and all its intricate communities because we are gifts of the same Creator. Our unstable climate is forcing together the branches of our family long separated, requiring that we live together in new ways. Spiritual imagination encourages experimentation in times of great change. Potawatomi Christian Kaitlin Curtice embodies new ways of understanding God working in history. Irish priest Seán McDonagh explores why trees should be part of Christian core curriculum. Dianne D. Glave opens the rich and varied roots of Black mysticism and the natural world. At Sojourners we ask, how do our daily actions impact creation and those most vulnerable?

The Sacredness of the Earth as She Is

Kaitlin Curtice

When I first joined my partner, Travis, for long hikes with our family, I always had a particular goal in the back of my mind. I'd search the ground as we walked, looking for something that might catch my eye, something meaningful that I could take home with me. It would remind me of that space, an Ebenezer to mark that I had seen and experienced God. Wondering if those rocks had been there for generations, or how many people that dirt felt walk on her dusty skin over the years, I was searching.

Now I realize that while this is a meaningful thing to do, it is the wrong idea. In a way, it's selfish. I enter the home of the land and the creatures there, and I expect something from them, something that will give *me* pleasure, fill *my* cup. It is about taking, not giving; it is about demanding, not receiving.

Recently I went out to Stone Mountain, a state park in our city, Muskogee Creek and Cherokee land that, over time, has been taken over by a confederate carving in the side of the granite mountain. When I go there, I sit by the water. I gently touch and greet the trees. And this day, I asked the water for permission, greeting her, giving thanks.

I realized that I was not there to demand and take whatever I wanted. If a gift came to me (in words or as inspiration), I would receive it with gratitude. I simply wanted the trees, the ants, the dirt, the water, and the wind to know that I was grateful to be among them, grateful that they might want a relationship with me.

We've been trained to think on an individualistic level in the United States. When European peoples colonized Turtle Island, they replaced our Indigenous ideas of communal living and identity with individualism, with *every man/woman for themselves* ideas that eventually became the rallying cry of the United States, a land that prides itself on the American Dream. *If you work hard enough, you'll succeed. Don't show weakness. Masculinity is the key, and patriarchy is the rule of the land.*

As we continue to enter deeper into the crisis of climate change, into the reality of human rights abuses and eruptions of violence happening not just here but all over the world, perhaps we need to take a different approach in our relationship to one another and our creature-relatives all over the earth.

Perhaps we need to remember that being a recipient of a gift is different than demanding a gift be given to us in the first place.

Perhaps being aware of the sacredness of the Earth as she is, is more important than worrying only about how we will be affected as humans when she is hurting and reacting to *our mistakes.*

Perhaps if we returned to loving the land, waters, and all beings that live and breathe around us, we might learn how to love our human relatives again.

We are, after all, *dust to dust*. No one can escape that reality.

In this process we must break apart systems that have been created in this country (and across the world through colonization) of patriarchy, which is a culture of *taking*.

Patriarchy takes the autonomy of women and tells us we are voiceless.

Patriarchy takes the lives of immigrants and refuses to enact gun control. Patriarchy takes away voter's rights and puts oppressors in power.

Patriarchy takes away the inherent and sacred rights of *Segmekwe*, Mother Earth, and tells her that she, too, is voiceless.

We can no longer be people who take.

We must return to being people who ask, who greet, who extend gratitude, who, when we receive, pass that gift on to the next who are in need, practicing reciprocity in this world.

Kaitlin Curtice is a Native American Christian author and speaker. As an enrolled member of the Potawatomi Citizen Band and someone who has grown up in the Christian faith, Kaitlin wrote on the intersection of Indigenous spirituality, faith in everyday life, and the church when this appeared on sojo.net on August 12, 2019.

Healing Grounds for the Earth—and for Christianity

Liz Cooledge Jenkins

> If we're serious about fighting climate change by rebuilding soil carbon, we have to address the colonialist systems in which we live.

When I speak on the phone with Anne Symens-Bucher, she tells me about the end of St. Francis of Assisi's life. Francis "was losing sight, suffering from the pain of the stigmata, and on the margins of the community that had grown up to follow him," Symens-Bucher explains. "This is the moment he writes the 'Canticle of Creation.'" Symens-Bucher is one of the founders of Canticle Farm in Oakland, California, a community of eight households where the fences are taken down, giving access to a large garden in the middle. Canticle Farm is made up of people who, in Symens-Bucher's words, are "experimenting at the intersections of faith-based, social justice-based, and Earth-based nonviolent activism." In his canticle, after which this community is named, Francis praises God from a deep sense of kinship with all creation. He sings of "brother fire," "sister water," "brother wind," "mother earth." Birthed as Francis approaches his own death, it is a vivid, sober-minded song of the interconnectedness of all life.

Western colonialist people have often failed—or refused—to recognize this interconnectedness. Earth, animals, plants, and people suffer from our (and I say "our" because I speak as a white U.S. citizen) denial of this oneness. Soils are depleted, waters and air are poisoned, and sea levels rise and temperatures warm, threatening the most vulnerable among us immediately, and all of us eventually. Perhaps in this time of environmental crisis, we might find a "canticle" moment, one that renews our kinship with creation.

Liz Carlisle explores these questions in *Healing Grounds: Climate, Justice, and the Deep Roots of Regenerative Farming.* As an environmental scientist looking for healthy soil, Carlisle interviews experts who are Black, Indigenous, and people of color—scientists and farmers engaged in work ranging from bringing buffalo back to the prairie ecosystems of Montana to growing mushrooms on ancestral forest land in North Carolina. Through the process, she realizes that if we're serious about fighting climate change by rebuilding soil carbon, we're going to have to address the very roots of the colonialist systems in which we live.

How Do Soil Depleters Repent?

Carlisle does not directly address the Christian faith tradition, but I wonder about the possibilities for connection. Are there ways Christianity could inspire a transformative vision similar to Carlisle's—or is Christianity always and only the religion of the colonizers, the depleters of soils, the displacers of peoples? What does it look like to repent—to really repent, in a way that includes reparations—and learn to live in a different way? Are there healing grounds for Christianity?

The Bible is full of vivid images of land and people flourishing together. In the language of the psalms, seas lift up their voice (93:3) and all the trees of the forest sing (96:12). Earth is a gift from God, and all her beings return praise to God. Perhaps

God is inviting Christians to think more deeply about the land beneath our feet—land that was not meant to be exploited and degraded but to rest and heal every seven years (Leviticus 25:1–7). Land that was not intended to be hoarded by a few but to be redistributed to every family once every generation (Leviticus 25:8–13). God blesses people by making "grass grow for cattle, and plants for people to cultivate" (Psalm 104:14) and by promising that "the trees will yield their fruit and the ground will yield its crops; the people will be secure in their land" (Ezekiel 34:27). This is also the vision of Carlisle and her interviewees: Land security. Abundance. Health and holistic well-being.

Perhaps the connection between right worship and abundant produce is not so metaphorical as those of us steeped in Western Christian traditions might imagine. We might read God's promises of blessing and think, *If we praise Jesus' name, then God will supernaturally make our crops productive in answer to our prayers.* This might happen. But what if, more often, the idea is that whole-bodied, whole-community worship builds and reinforces a sense of collective identity and connection to place? Maybe this care for Earth and for one another is where the blessings lie.

Perhaps right worship is less about saying the right things and more about learning to live in ways of interdependence. Ways that "see plants and animals as gifts, and indeed as teachers," as Carlisle puts it, and that "let go of the idea of domination." Ways that, as Jesus taught, consider the lilies and pay attention to the birds (Matthew 6:25–34). Ways that, as Aboriginal scholar Tyson Yunkaporta puts it in *Sand Talk: How Indigenous Thinking Can Save the World*, help us "start working with the land, rather than against it." When we work with the land and with each other, as Yunkaporta continues, diverse communities can "share knowledge with one another while maintaining their own unique systems grounded in the diverse landscapes they care for."

A Vision of Abundance

We see the devastation of colonialism in land and ecosystems, and we see it just as surely in human communities and relationships as well. Theologian Willie James Jennings reflects on this in *After Whiteness: An Education in Belonging*: "[T]he goal of the colonialist . . . was to reduce the many to the one as a point of negotiation, management, conversion, and profit . . . to move people slowly but clearly from any kind of group thinking about their wants and needs to thinking like an individual." To restore the land, then, is to restore interconnectedness among humans. To refuse to reduce everything to profit. To choose to live in community rather than by a myth of independence.

Symens-Bucher has seen this at Canticle Farm. As her community takes down fences between houses, they are finding new ways to exist together. They are living into the reality that, as Symens-Bucher says, "we are not separate from Earth." They are cleansing the water in their well, which then flows back out into the broader Oakland community. As a diverse community—in age, race, class, and nationality—they are learning to heal trauma, to live in shared love and commitment. "Our security is in relationships," Symens-Bucher tells me. "We invest in relationships and put our trust and security there."

We live in a time of deep imbalance. As Indigenous ethnobotanist Stephanie Morningstar tells Carlisle in *Healing Grounds*, "climate change signals a profound imbalance . . . rooted in the violent restructuring of relationships between people and land that lies at the very heart of this continent's history." Healing this imbalance will be difficult but not impossible. We can join God in rebuilding the kind of interconnected communities that colonialists sought to destroy. We can grow our own food in regenerative ways or support those who are. We can get involved in movements to restore land to Black people, Indigenous people, and people of color.

With visions of healing—like those of *Healing Grounds* and of Canticle Farm—and with faith the size of a mustard seed (Luke 17:6), we can collectively uproot the exploitative colonialist systems that keep us all from the abundant life Jesus promised. We can build something better in their place.

Liz Cooledge Jenkins was the Seattle-based author of *Nice Churchy Patriarchy* when this appeared in the April 2023 issue of *Sojourners.*

The Problem of Big and Small

Bill McKibben

> Hunkering down is deeply attractive, but we have work to do first.

It's reasonably clear to me that the natural tendency of our society at this moment is toward smallness, localness, and intimacy. After several centuries of constantly extending our supply lines around the world so that our food and our energy and our capital came from every corner of the planet, we find it increasingly pleasing and increasingly necessary to hunker down.

Local food is the best example. Our best restaurants and our sharpest cooks are no longer concerned with copying French recipes; for a generation now it's been all about what's close to home. Farmers' markets have been the fastest growing part of our food economy, and suddenly there are more breweries than there were before Prohibition. It tastes good; it feels neighborly.

Next on the agenda: local energy. All of a sudden it seems weird to be piping stuff in from Saudi Arabia, or even Texas, when there's plenty of good sunshine to be had close to home, when the wind blows over your house more days than not. In the wake of the financial crisis, there's even a move toward Slow Money and local banking. It's possible to imagine how it might all fit together into something quite beautiful—a new/old world that actually kind of works, instead of the careening one we're used to.

But there's one small problem. Actually, one large problem—the largest we've ever faced. The devastation from climate change threatens to undo every one of these sweet trends (if it doesn't rain for a month, it doesn't matter how organic your farm is; ditto if it rains every day). And climate change, given the time that we have, can only be solved on very large scales. Say the United States—greatest of carbon sinners—somehow decided to sober up and get its house in order. Even in that dream world, you'd still need to persuade the developing world to go along.

So, in some other sense, we've never needed our largest scale institutions more: the United Nations, the World Bank, all those semi-corrupt agencies that seem mostly to talk the talk while the corporations and governments simply walk right over them. I wish it weren't so: I wish I could just concentrate on Vermont, where I live. But Vermont can't be Vermont unless we can get the world moving in the right direction. And it isn't fair anyway, since the last hundred years of American history is a big reason others are suffering.

The best test, then, of the world's seriousness going forward may well be what it does about financing the rest of the world's conversion to renewable energy. In Copenhagen in 2009, then–Secretary of State Hillary Clinton promised that the rich nations would come up with $100 billion annually in "public, private, and other" funding to help with this transition. It's the bare minimum required, but since then there's been no solid plan about where it will come from or who will pay.

Hunkering down is deeply attractive and deeply useful. It should be a far more local world (with the wildcard of the internet to keep it from getting too provincial). But before we go about our own business, there's the outstanding problem of global warming to take care of. We need to somehow get big enough to deal with it before we get pleasantly small.

Bill McKibben, founder of 350.org, was the author of *Oil and Honey: The Education of an Unlikely Activist* and a *Sojourners* contributing editor when this appeared in the November 2014 issue.

Eye on the Sparrow

Beth Norcross

> Howard Thurman was "one of the greatest spiritual resources of this nation" and a pioneer in environmental theology.

When I read about the dire impacts of global warming, I think about Howard Thurman. This might be perplexing to those more familiar with Thurman as the author of *Jesus and the Disinherited*, a book Martin Luther King Jr. was said to carry with him wherever he went.

While Thurman is well-known as a theologian, prolific writer, mystic, seminary professor, and religious leader, few realize that—well before environmentalism became mainstream—Thurman articulated a complex theology of the "original harmony of creation," a harmony that human action had significantly disturbed. As he lamented in 1971, "Our atmosphere is polluted, our streams are poisoned, our hills are denuded, wildlife is increasingly exterminated, while more and more [humanity] becomes an alien on the earth and a fouler of [our] own nest."

From the early years of his life at the start of the twentieth century, Thurman's faith was formed in intimate connection with the natural world—specifically, the Halifax River and northeast Florida woods and coastline, where he wandered and played as a boy. Thurman's relationship with nature deepened when a heartbreaking event estranged him from organized religion. When he was seven, his beloved father died quite suddenly. The family pastor refused to conduct a funeral because his father was not a regular churchgoer, and a traveling minister who officiated at the service took the opportunity to expound on the dangers of dying "out of Christ"—to the small boy's wonderment and rage, "preach[ing] my father into hell," as he later recalled.

In contrast, the young Thurman found solace and comfort in nature's seasons and cycles:

> Here I found, alone, a special benediction. The ocean and the night together surrounded my little life with a reassurance that could not be affronted by the behavior of human beings. The ocean at night gave me a sense of timelessness, of existing beyond the reach of the ebb and flow of circumstances.

Sitting against an oak tree, he would "reach down in the quiet places" of his spirit, take out his "bruises and . . . joys, unfold them, and talk about them . . . know[ing] that I was understood." As an adult, Thurman began to understand that it was God that had been stirring there; when "the boundaries of my life spilled over into the mystery of the ocean and the wonder of the dark nights," it was a "cosmic religious experience." In young Thurman's sense of intimate belonging to something deeply personal and intuitive as well as grand and external, he experienced both the immanent and transcendent God. He found the quiet space necessary for his spirit to meet the Spirit.

Throughout his career, Thurman would return to nature as a means of expressing his personal theology. In his meditation "Surrounded by the Love of God"—published in 1953, but first developed as part of his ministry at the pioneering interracial Church for the Fellowship of All Peoples in San Francisco, which he began to co-pastor in 1944—he wrote:

> The earth beneath my feet is the great womb out of which the life upon which my body depends comes in utter abundance. There is at work in the soil a mystery by which the death of one seed is reborn a thousandfold in newness of life . . . it is order, and more than order—there is a brooding tenderness out of which it all comes. In the contemplation of the earth, I know that I am surrounded by the love of God.

While Thurman was decidedly not a pantheist (one who believes that God *is* nature), he did see God's spirit, God's very breath, in each and every one of God's creatures. As he wrote in his 1963 book *Disciplines of the Spirit*, Jesus saw and taught that:

> God breathed through all that is: the sparrow overcome by sudden death in its flight; the lily blossoming on the rocky hillside; the grass of the field and the clouds, light and burdenless or weighted down with unshed waters; the madman in chains or wandering among the barren rocks in the wastelands; the little baby in his mother's arms . . .

As his reputation as a theologian and religious leader grew, Howard Thurman carried with him his deep connections to the earth community.

Although he did not link the oppression of African Americans to the oppression of nature as explicitly as do present-day figures such as James Cone, in *Disciplines of the Spirit* Thurman drew a connection between the way the dominant culture treated nature and the manner in which that culture treated other humans. He explored that connection in a passage in which, inspired by South African writer Olive Schreiner, he affirmed that Christianity has misunderstood Jesus' teaching in Matthew 10 that a sparrow does not fall to the ground "apart from your Father." While this passage is certainly meant to be reassuring to humans, Thurman, like Schreiner, believed that

Christians too often forget its literal premise: God cares deeply for the sparrow.

"Christianity as it has developed since the time of its founder wrongly limits the ethical concept of reverence for life to human personality," Thurman wrote, where "personality" means that which culture defines as fully human. This limitation, he pointed out, leaves the door open for the mistreatment of *both* the nonhuman creature and of the person to whom the dominant race does not ascribe full humanity: "Deny personality to [certain] human beings and the ethical demand no longer obtains . . . People who are victimized by injustices must be defined as being, in Kipling's phrase, 'the lesser breeds without the law.'"

To illustrate his point, Thurman told the story of a young white girl for whose family he worked when he was growing up in Florida. One day, as she kept re-scattering the leaves he was raking, he threatened to report her to her father. In retaliation, she pricked young Thurman with a pin. When he drew back in obvious pain, the little girl was taken aback, saying, "That didn't hurt you really! You can't feel." By denying Thurman's full humanity, the girl gave herself permission to do him violence.

In a meditation published in 1951, Thurman articulated the connection between the oppression of nature and that of humans in the evolution of human power. In early times, Thurman wrote (in the gendered-language convention of the day), "man learned how to use a club in self-defense and thus to extend his control over an area farther than his arm unaided could reach. When he learned to throw this club with precision and power, it meant that the control of his environment was farther extended." Thurman then traced the increasing sophistication of human power over the earth from club to "bow and arrow, gunpowder, gasoline engine, through various kinds of vehicles and machines up to . . . the atomic bomb." The challenge then to "modern man is to match spiritual and moral maturity with the amazing power created by . . . mastery over nature. He has learned a part of the secret of energy by unlocking the door of the atom, yet he continues to be moved by prejudice, greed, and lust!" The use of power began as a means of controlling one's own environment and quickly expanded to the violent domination of other peoples.

Howard Thurman could not have foreseen the extent to which humans have used their power to unravel the original harmony of creation, most notably by significantly altering the climate of the planet. However, his most famous book—*Jesus and the Disinherited*, published in 1949—offers poignant insights as Christianity attempts to come to grips with the impacts of climate change on the earth's most vulnerable. In this work, Thurman made the compelling case that, despite Christianity's historical use by dominant powers to affirm their dominance, "the basic fact is that Christianity as it was born in the mind of this Jewish teacher and thinker appears as a technique of survival for the oppressed." Jesus stands, side by side, with those who have "their backs against the wall."

As I reread this book today, it is hard not to think of the farmers of Bangladesh, struggling to grow rice on flooded fields, or the villagers of Shishmaref, Alaska, an Indigenous community being forced to relocate from its ancestral lands due to the melting permafrost. It's hard not to think of the nearly ten million people in the Horn of Africa who face a severe food crisis, brought on by a prolonged drought. It's hard not to think of the "climate gap" in the mainland United States, where the poor are bearing a disproportionate burden of climate change impacts. As temperatures soar and sea levels rise, Thurman offers hope to the oppressed, as well as a distinct challenge to those of us who, by our own actions and inaction, have become the oppressors. Thurman reminds us that Jesus was, first and foremost, a poor Jew who suffered the indignities of the mighty

Roman Empire, not to mention from the religious authorities of his time. As such, he speaks, always, on behalf of those who are afflicted, on behalf of those who suffer at the hands of the powerful.

While he boldly confronted the dominating powers of his time, Howard Thurman also was an unwavering believer in the potential of humankind to alter the course of history when we are open to the leading of the Spirit. More than sixty years ago, Thurman wrote the following words in *Jesus and the Disinherited*, in the face of the pernicious racism of the mid-twentieth century: "The disinherited will know for themselves that there is a Spirit at work in life and in the hearts of [humans] which is committed to overcoming the world . . . For the privileged and underprivileged alike, if the individual puts at the disposal of the Spirit the needful dedication and discipline," he or she "can live effectively in the chaos of the present the high destiny of a [child] of God." Today, Thurman's words offer renewed hope as we confront the seemingly overwhelming challenges of our overheating Earth home.

Howard Thurman's understanding of God, and the human relationship with God, was molded in large measure by his intimate connection with the natural world. It was here that he saw the Creator's original intent for creation—harmony and unity. It was here that he found the divine in the complex entanglement between all creatures, human and non-human. That unified, loving community, which binds us all together, holds our primary hope for redemption and renewal.

Beth Norcross was founding director of the Center for Spirituality in Nature in Arlington, Virginia, and adjunct faculty at Wesley Theological Seminary in Washington, D.C., when this appeared in the August 2012 issue of *Sojourners*.

Existing Intentionally with the Land

Kat Armas

Growing up as a daughter of Cuban immigrants in Miami meant that much of my childhood was spent learning how life was lived *en el campo* or the countryside of the island that birthed my ancestors. Some of my most powerful memories include digging, planting, and learning how to tend the earth with my *abuelita*. I'd spend hours with her, picking the best mangos from the trees for our afternoon snack while listening to her stories of life before the revolution. Abuela always reminded me that *Cuba es la isla más bella del mundo* ("Cuba is the most beautiful island in the world").

It was during these moments, with our fingers in the dirt, that my abuelita deepened my understanding of her life and our history. She loved her garden, and that is the place where I saw her come to life, where she reconnected with the earth and found restoration and wholeness. For her, gardening was a way of living out her own form of embodied resistance after being forced from her land only a couple of decades before.

Abuela taught me that we can live lives of resistance simply by existing intentionally.

In *Sabbath as Resistance*, Walter Brueggemann argues that even rest can be seen as an act of resistance because "it is a visible insistence that our lives are not defined by the production and consumption of commodity goods."

All of us have witnessed the detrimental effects of mass production and consumption that Brueggemann talks about, not only in the anxiety that fills our daily lives, but in the destruction of the very earth that sustains us. Because of this, we understand that not only tending the earth but connecting to nature around us can also be a form of resistance, similar to that of rest.

In *The Christian Imagination: Theology and the Origins of Race*, Willie Jennings argues that when we talk about earth and land, we cannot do so without talking about body and soul. He references his mother and how she taught him to respect the dirt because like many Black women from the South, "she knew the earth like she knew her own soul."

Jennings reminds us that from the beginning of creation, human beings were commissioned to watch over the earth, take care of it, and receive nourishment from it. The connection among God's creation—land, animals, and humans—in the narrative is beautiful, divine, "*very good*."

This human connection to the land and to animals isn't just something we see in the creation narrative, it continues to play out across time and across communities. In fact, much of Israel's story is deeply rooted in land—their displacement from it and their longing to be restored in it.

Throughout history, coming across a people also meant coming across the land they were connected to and the animals that were a part of their family. It's a divine sense of "creaturely entanglement," Jennings explains. "We've always lived in an enmeshed world where our lives are intertwined and continuously interweaving."

Paul affirms this connection in Romans 8 when he addresses the issue of suffering through the perspective of creation. Paul personifies creation as sharing in the decay that characterizes this present age. Like humans, it is groaning to be set free. As we lament for a better reality, so do the mountains.

When talking about race, Jennings recognizes that what colonization essentially did was rip peoples from their land and animal-kin. What was once a holistic identity, one that mirrored the goodness of creation, now became a distorted identity. Because of this, resistance and decolonizing work must involve restoring these broken and distorted identities. While this is a lifelong task in which we all engage in continuously and communally, I often find myself going back to those moments in the garden with my *abuelita*. These moments of reconnection with the land offer me respite for the journey ahead.

As I seek for ways to live in an embodied state of resistance and decolonization, I remember the divinely sanctioned relationship between humans, animals, and the earth in which we coexist. And as I spend time feeling the earth in between my fingertips and listening to the birds above me, I remember that gardening can be not only an act of worship, but my own personal act of resistance. Jennings reminds us, "We are of the dirt. The dirt is our kin. We are creatures of the dirt, bound together."

Kat Armas, a Cuban-American writer and podcaster from Miami, was the author of *Abuelita Faith: What Women on the Margins Teach Us About Wisdom, Persistence and Strength* when this appeared on sojo.net on April 26, 2019.

Forty Shades of Green

Seán McDonagh

> The oldest known redwood in the United States was a sapling during the Babylonian exile: Why trees should be part of Christian core curriculum.

I grew up in rural Ireland in the 1950s in a world surrounded by trees.

Close to my home, a ribbon of horse chestnuts lined both sides of the road. Each summer their intertwining canopies shut out the light, which gave the road its name—the dark road. In the fields around our house there were stands of oak, birch, elm, and sycamore. About forty yards to the south and west, my father planted a shelter belt of Leylandii. We had different varieties of apple trees in the orchard, and two pear trees.

In 1962, just as the Second Vatican Council was beginning, I entered St. Columban's seminary to be a priest. The seminary was located on a large estate called Dowdstown in County Meath. More than 150 acres were covered in woodlands full of indigenous trees such as oak, hazel, holly, ash, Scotch pine, willow, elm, and rowan. There were also exotic species, including a number of the sturdy cedars of Lebanon, a variety of cherry trees, and even a few California redwoods. The folklore in the area was that the trees had been planted in the 1820s by Gen. Robert Taylor, who had fought alongside Wellington at the Battle of Waterloo.

Trees are the dominant life form on land—and the longest-lived creatures on earth. During my seven years in seminary, while studying philosophy, theology, spirituality, and scripture, we never once looked to the natural world or trees for insight into our relationship with God, other human beings, or other species. And there is so much to learn! Sadly, theology and scripture presentations were isolated almost exclusively to the divine-human relationship, with little consideration given to the rest of creation.

This is due in part to the legacy of the early church fathers, who elaborated their theology of creation in the context of the prevailing teaching of Gnosticism and Manichaeism, both of which tended to despise the material world and basic bodily functions. As a result, at seminary in County Meath in the early 1960s, the woodlands were out of bounds for the students. We were not encouraged to give trees the basic respect of learning their names. (Little has changed in the intervening four decades in churches, seminaries, or divinity schools.)

Vines, Branches, and Superstorms

The Bible, on the other hand, is replete with a theology of trees and the environment. In chapter 15 of his gospel, John presents Jesus as the true vine: "I am the true vine, and my Abba is the vine grower" (John 15:1). The believers are the branches, but they cannot bear fruit unless they are joined to and sustained by the vine tree. "Just as the branch cannot bear fruit by itself unless it abides in the vine, neither can you unless you abide in me. I am the vine, you are the branches" (John 15:4–5). The author of John's gospel makes it very clear that the dynamic relationship between the trunk and the branches is an apt metaphor for the active, engaging relationship between Christ and the believer.

The vine and branches also instruct us on the dynamic relationships in our world. There is no good fruit if the vine and roots are damaged or severed. The devastating, interconnected effects of climate change reveal this in the most catastrophic ways.

In 2012 and 2013, the Philippines was hit by two super typhoons—Bopha and Haiyan. More than seven thousand people died. Homes, schools, roads, and other vital infrastructures were destroyed. What is forgotten is the long-term damage that typhoons do to the environment when tree cover is removed. A study carried out in Central America in the 1980s showed that a single rainstorm can dislodge up to 150 thousand kilograms (331 thousand pounds) of topsoil from one hectare (2-1/2 acres) of hillside once the trees have been cut. The comparable figure from a forested hillside is a mere forty-four kilograms. Intact forests regulate water run-off and thus mitigate the risks of flooding and droughts. Conversely, the destruction of forests also impacts rainfall. Cutting trees leads to a reduction in evaporation and transpiration that in turn leads to less rainfall. On hydrological grounds alone, protecting forests is essential for the future of food production.

Cedars of Lebanon and California Redwoods

In scripture, trees set the moral and religious context for the lives of both the individual believer and the community. For example, many of the majestic cedars of Lebanon grew to a height of 120 feet and often lived for more than one thousand years. The long life and erect stance of cedars represented a symbolic challenge for humans. For the psalmist, "the righteous flourish like the palm tree, and grow like a cedar of Lebanon. They are planted in the house of the Lord; they flourish in the courts of our God. In old age, they still produce fruit; they are always green and full of sap showing that the Lord is upright" (Psalm 92:12–15).

In North America, the equivalent of the cedar of Lebanon is the California redwood. Redwoods are the tallest trees found on the planet. Some have reached heights of 360 feet. Redwoods are also among the longest-lived trees on earth. Unless disturbed, a redwood can live between five hundred to one thousand years. In 2013, researchers discovered a 2,520-year-old redwood, which beats the previous record-holder by three hundred years. No wonder the Latin name for redwood, *Sequoia sempervirens*, means "green forever."

During the Cretaceous period, more than 100 million years ago, redwoods were among the predominant trees found in the forests of a much more moist and tropical North America. As the climate became drier and colder, the redwoods retreated to a narrow strip along the Pacific coast of northern California, where summer fog and mild winters contrast with harsher inland climates.

Unlike their tree cousins in the tropical forests, which are devastated by climate change–related superstorms, recent research seems to confirm that the old-growth redwood forests along the California coast and in the Sierra Nevada are in a "growth spurt the likes of which has never been seen before." The director of science for Save the Redwood League believes that this unprecedented growth is due to global warming. So, while climate change is wreaking havoc on other creatures and ecosystems, from polar bears to coral reefs, it is spurring growth in the redwood forests in California. The trunks are adding girth, report the scientists, and storing large amounts of carbon dioxide. Our sequoia elders are compensating for extremely high atmospheric carbon levels, but they are also preparing for a long, hot, dry millennium that will be climactically adverse to fostering seedlings, laying in now as much growth as possible.

A Community of Trees

What do the trees know that we have yet to learn? Trees stand at the hub of communities. Community is at the heart of the

Christian message, from our belief in the nature of a Trinitarian God to our understanding of the communal dimension of human flourishing, and to our current understanding that all life on earth is connected and interdependent. The oak trees here at St. Columban's support about three hundred other forms of life. The numbers in the tropical forests are beyond our wildest dreams. Harvard entomologist Edward O. Wilson described "a single leguminous tree" in the Tambopata Reserve in Peru that had forty-three species of ants belonging to twenty-six genera.

During the past decade, redwood researchers from Humboldt State University in northern California have made some remarkable discoveries about the community of life in the stands of old-growth forests. Climbing more than three hundred feet up into the canopy of ancient redwood forests, the researchers have found a complete ecosystem of birds, bugs, salamanders, ferns, shrubs, and whole trees, growing high up in and above the fog belt. These upper-forest "epiphytes" include many fern species, and such trees and shrubs as tanbark oak, California bay, cascara buckthorn, Sitka spruce, Douglas fir, and Western hemlock. A whole ecosystem lives in the tree canopy! My understanding of the nature of the church and of Christian community would have been enhanced if my teachers, and I, had paid more attention to the world of trees during our discussions.

Building Great Houses

Talk of trees and plants almost always involves politics and economics. Visitors to Ireland from across the world comment on the greenness and beauty of the country, the Emerald Isle. There was even a popular Johnny Cash song celebrating the "40 shades of green," reflecting the range of Irish grass species. Over the past few decades, however, intensive agriculture has been on the rise. Ireland's "40 shades" have been dwindling down to one: the shiny dark green of perennial ryegrass. Farmers use it because livestock find it palatable, but it requires high nitrogen levels from fossil-fuel based fertilizers for it to achieve maximum productivity.

The demise of the Irish forests is intimately related to the political and economic issues of the time. According to pollen analysis, the first tree to reach Ireland, after the last glacial period, was the juniper. It was followed quickly by pine, hazel, and rowan trees. By 8,500 BCE, Ireland had established oak and elm forests. Humans arrived in Ireland about one thousand years later as hunter-gatherers who made little enough impact on the landscape. With the rise of agriculture, however, they cut the trees to open up pasture land.

In the seventeenth and eighteenth centuries, much of the oak was shipped abroad to build the great houses of Britain (not unlike King Solomon clear-cutting the cedars of Lebanon for his temple). Ireland's trees were used to make charcoal for the burgeoning industrial revolution in England. By the time of the Act of Union in 1800 (forming the United Kingdom), only 2 percent of Ireland was covered by woodlands, despite the fact that Ireland has the best growing conditions for trees of almost any country in Europe. Since achieving independence in 1921, successive Irish governments have promoted forest projects. As a result, in 2014, nearly 10 percent of Ireland is forested again. Unfortunately, priority has been given to planting Sitka spruce, a North American import, rather than to native species such as ash and oak.

Pope Francis and the New World Coming

If contemporary Christian communities could see ourselves as part of the wider community of life, then it would help shape our ethical, political, and economic consensus to guide human interaction with trees, forests, and the wider natural world, which would lead to a mutually enhancing relationship between humans and the rest of creation, instead of the predatory relationship that is now in place.

Various Christian churches are only now beginning to take the global environmental crisis more seriously. During the 1980s, the World Council of Churches adopted the Justice, Peace, and Integrity of Creation (JPIC) ministry. Meetings were held in a variety of countries and continents culminating in the March 1990 meeting in Seoul, Korea. The Catholic Church has been somewhat slower in responding to the crisis. Even though the environment is mentioned in a number of social encyclicals such as *Sollicitudo Rei Socialis* ("The Concern of the Church for the Social Order," 1987), the first document devoted exclusively to addressing the ecological issue was announced by Pope John Paul II on World Peace Day in January 1990, titled "Peace with God the Creator, Peace with All Creation."

It is obvious that Pope Francis is very concerned about the deteriorating ecological situation right across the globe. In his inaugural homily in March 2013, he appealed to all who have positions of responsibility in economic, political, and social life, and all people of goodwill: "Let us be 'protectors' of creation, protectors of God's plan inscribed in nature, protectors of one another and of the environment. Let us not allow omens of destruction and death to accompany the advance of this world!"

In *Evangelii Gaudium* ("The Joy of the Gospel"), which many people see as the blueprint for Pope Francis' ministry, he makes his own "the touching and prophetic lament voiced some years ago by the bishops of the Philippines: 'An incredible variety of insects lived in the forests and were busy with all kinds of tasks. . . . Birds flew through the air, their bright plumes and varying calls adding color and song to the green of the forests. . . . God intended this land for us, [God's] special creatures, but not so that we might destroy it and turn it into a wasteland. . . . After a single night's rain, look at the chocolate brown rivers in your locality and remember that they are carrying the life blood of the land into the sea. . . . How can fish swim in running sewers like the Pasig [in Manila] and so many more rivers that we have polluted? Who has turned the wonderworld of the seas into underwater cemeteries bereft of color and life?'"

Many commentators believe that Pope Francis soon will issue an encyclical on God's creation, climate change, and the role of the human in the sanctity of creation. Hopefully, such a document will help the Christian community around the world see itself as part of the wider community of life, encouraging us to celebrate the beauty and wonders of forests and trees with poets, musicians, and other artists. Only then will Christians develop mutually enhancing relationships between humanity and the rest of creation.

Seán McDonagh, SSC, is an Irish Columban missionary priest who worked for more than two decades in the Philippines. His book *To Care for the Earth* (1986) was one of the first theological books to address the ecological crisis. Pope Francis issued *Laudato Si'* on creation care in 2015. This appeared in the November 2014 issue of *Sojourners.*

The Green Confessions of Nat Turner

Dianne D. Glave

> The rich and varied roots of Black environmental liberation theology.

When one thinks of Black environmental liberation theology, the name of slave-rebellion leader Nat Turner might not immediately spring to mind. Perhaps it should.

A biopic on the life of Turner, called *The Birth of a Nation*, releases this year. Based on early reviews, I expect the film by director Nate Parker (*Red Tails, Arbitrage*) to deliver a powerful recounting of Turner's life.

In 1831, Turner led enslaved and free African Americans in a rebellion against slaveholders in Southampton County, Virginia. The uprising was swift, violent, and bloody. At least two hundred African Americans and more than fifty whites died. After whites quelled the rebellion, Turner hid in the woods for several weeks. He was eventually captured and executed.

Turner's time alone in the woods offers surprising insights. He is an African-American man familiar with nature. He is a Christian preacher given to visions. From that arises a deep environmental wisdom.

The original report of the slave rebellion is found in *The Confessions of Nat Turner, The Leader of the Late Insurrection in Southampton VA*, as told by Turner to a white lawyer in Richmond, Virginia. "The blood of Christ [that] had been shed on this earth, and had ascended to heaven for the salvation of sinners," Turner says in the book, "was now returning to earth again in the form of dew."

Turner's visions were based on his understanding of the Bible. He was literate (that in itself was unusual for one enslaved) and worshipped God. Turner was a prophet of God, in the context of nature and revolt.

In *The Confessions*, he says, "I then found on the leaves in the woods hieroglyphic characters, and numbers, with the forms of men in different attitudes, portrayed in blood, and representing the figures I had seen before in the heavens. And now the Holy Ghost had revealed itself to me, and made plain the miracles it had shown me."

His theology—an analysis of scripture, faith, and practice—galvanized him to rebel against white slavers. He incited rebellion out of his faith in a Christian God. As an enslaved man, he fought for African Americans.

Turner's ideas and experiences are part of the history of an eco-theology based on Black liberation theology. It is forged out of the history of environmental justice and activism rooted in Christian experience, worship, and theology by and of African Americans. This theology seeks transformed practices that shield African Americans from exposure to toxins, pollution, and the general effects of environmental racism.

In recent times, we have witnessed inspiring examples of faith-rooted resistance by people of African descent through Black eco-theology. In 1977, Wangari Maathai organized the Green Belt Movement, which planted trees in Kenya in response to deforestation and soil erosion. Maathai recounted how Western missionaries rushed to cut down trees, counter to the experience of Maathai's community, which saw the trees as sacred. Her great act of rebellion, as an African who embraced both her Christianity and African spirituality, was to fight for the trees to be replanted as a prayer to the earth through action.

Another example can be found in the work of Lennox Yearwood. On the tenth anniversary of Hurricane Katrina, in 2015, Yearwood, an African-American pastor and head of the Hip Hop Caucus, advocated for environmental equity for many African Americans in Louisiana who have not seen their neighborhoods, homes, and lives restored in the same way white people have. Among many other efforts, Yearwood has led marches against companies that profit from the damage done by fossil fuels to the environment.

Nat Turner, Wangari Maathai, and Lennox Yearwood are just a few of the many encouraging practitioners of ecological resistance, actions led by people of African descent and Christian faith that carry on the rich tradition of Black environmental liberation theology.

Dianne D. Glave, author of *Rooted in the Earth*, was coordinator of diversity development for the Western Pennsylvania United Methodist Conference Center when this article appeared in the May 2016 issue of *Sojourners*. A version is also included in *Black Eco-Theology Through History: The African American Experience* (Routledge: Taylor & Francis Group).

The Spiritual Satisfaction of Freely Gardening

Josina Guess

"Do you make any money from it?" a visitor asked as we walked behind my house, where goats, chickens, fruits, and vegetables grow among the weeds. I shook my head and laughed.

We entered the garden where my seventy-four-year-old father knelt, breaking up soil with an old cultivating fork. He was planting spindly tomato plants I had started from seed and almost abandoned.

We don't make money from it, but the garden is the place where my father cultivates joy. When I was a child, he poured water on rows of collards to wash away stressful days working for a Washington, D.C., nonprofit. Gardening restores his soul. These days, Dad splits his time between my parents' home in Ohio and my home in rural Georgia, planting gardens in both places.

We don't weigh the bushels of okra, cantaloupe, peppers, watermelon, and beans to see if they equal or surpass expenditures of time or money spent on Dad's trips down South. Some work can't be measured in dollars.

In her poem "Photosynthesis," Ashley M. Jones, the poet laureate of Alabama, remembers her father's garden: "The difference, now: my father is not a slave, / not a sharecropper. This land is his and so is this garden, / so is this work. The difference is that he owns this labor."

There must be another phrase than "hobby farmer" to express the spiritual satisfaction of freely gardening, especially for people carrying centuries of trauma connected to the land. African American farmers make up less than 2 percent of farmers in the United States. Places like Soul Fire Farm in New York, or Earthseed Farm in California, use methods rooted in African and Indigenous ways to repair centuries of harm. Practices like heavy mulching, planting cover crops, and growing a variety of plants help soil to recover from heavy tilling and monoculture. The slow, small-scale farming my father does isn't even included in the "2 percent." Yet, our little farm joins other plots of liberation, places of healing for people and the land itself.

From my desk window, I watch my dad wade through the green. Though I try to hide it with nail polish, my fingers are cracked, with an earth-brown patina staining the grooves of my fingerprints. I walk out to join him. Other work pulls at me: deadlines, emails, and writing. But I stop to pull weeds. An hour later, I'm more at peace, ready to face the work waiting at my desk.

"What you call waste, / I call power. What you call work I make beautiful again," Jones writes in "Photosynthesis." I probably earn less money because of the time I spend in the garden. But my dad is teaching me that living a life you love is a way to make a good living.

Josina Guess was a *Sojourners* columnist and contributor to *Bigger Than Bravery: Black Resilience and Reclamation in a Time of Pandemic*, when this appeared in the August 2023 issue.

Consider the Turtles of the Field

Brian McLaren

Many evangelicals find themselves in an emerging theological habitat, where care of creation is central to mission.

Right now, I'm thigh-deep in muck. Clad in hip waders, I'm slogging through a spring-fed bog in northern Maryland. I'm surrounded by tussock sedge, alder, jewelweed, skunk cabbage, and swamp rose. And I'm having a great time.

I've done this for a couple of days almost every spring for the last dozen years. I'm out here as a volunteer to do wildlife surveys. In particular, we're looking for the rarest turtle in North America, *Glyptemys muhlenbergii*, the little four-inch bog turtle. In the 1970s, they were found in more than four hundred sites in our little state. In the 1990s, we could only find them in about half those sites. The other sites had been ditched, drained, bulldozed, polluted, invaded by non-native plants, bisected by roads for turtle-smashing cars, depleted by collectors, or otherwise made uninhabitable for these little creatures.

When I meet professional wildlife biologists and other volunteers, they're surprised that an evangelical (or post-evangelical, or "younger evangelical," or whatever) pastor would be out here doing this sort of thing. They're not used to seeing mud-smeared pastors who aren't afraid to grope around in bog muck for turtles or who keep track of chorus frogs and Baltimore checkerspots and Indian paintbrush. I know what they're thinking: Christians, especially ones associated with the term "evangelical," are part of the problem, not part of the

solution. They listen to James Dobson and Pat Robertson and James Kennedy, not Wendell Berry and Herman Daly; they focus on the family and the military, not the environment.

The surface causes of environmental carelessness among conservative Protestants are legion, including subcontracting the evangelical mind out to right-wing politicians and greedy business interests . . . putting the gospel of Jesus through the strainer of consumerist-capitalism and retaining only the thin broth that this modern-day Caesar lets pass through . . . a tendency to be against whatever "liberals" are for. Even more important, though, are the deeper theological roots of environmental disinterest—and the emerging theological values that many of us are embracing instead.

People who are sensitive to creation know that creation is in constant flux. Continents drift, climates change, magnetic poles flip-flop, and bogs like this one gradually give way to wet meadows and then various kinds of forests. There's a natural succession out here under the sun, and I think there's a kind of natural succession going on theologically for many Christians as well. Let me mention three of these elements.

First, increased concern for the poor and oppressed leads to increased concern for all of creation. The same forces that hurt widows and orphans, minorities and women, children and the elderly also hurt the songbirds and trout, the ferns and old growth forests: greed, impatience, selfishness, arrogance, hurry, anger, competition, irreverence—plus a spirituality that cares for souls but neglects bodies, that prepares for eternity in heaven but abandons history on earth.

When greed and consumerism are exposed, when arrogance and irreverence are unplugged, when hurry and selfishness are named and repented of, the world and all it contains (widows, orphans, trees, soil) are revalued (or re-deemed) and made sacred again. No, in this emerging view, these little bog turtles we're looking for today are a priceless treasure, an original

creation of the greatest Artist in (and beyond) history—even though they are deemed precisely worthless to someone who would want to build an interstate highway through this bog.

Second, the eschatology of abandonment is being replaced by an engaging gospel of the kingdom. The phenomenon of evangelical-dispensational eschatology (doctrine of last things or end times) makes perfect sense in the modern world. Understandably, Christians in the power centers of modernity (England in the 1800s, the United States in the 1900s) saw nothing ahead in the story of modernity—nothing but destruction. Their only hope? A skyhook Second Coming, wrapping up the whole of creation like an empty candy wrapper and throwing it in the trash can, and the sooner the better, so God could bring us all to heaven, beyond time, beyond matter, beyond this creation entirely. In this model, virtually no continuity exists between this creation and the new heavenly creation; this creation is discarded like a non-recyclable milk carton. Why get sentimental about a cheap container destined for the cosmic dumpster of nothingness?

This pop-evangelical eschatology made one understandable but serious mistake: It assumed that modernity was all there was or ever would be. Just as the early Christians could not imagine the gospel outlasting the Roman Empire (unless they got the point of the Apocalypse of John), nineteenth- and twentieth-century evangelicals couldn't imagine the gospel outlasting modernity, the empire of reason, consumerism, and individualism. For pop-evangelical eschatology to proliferate and maintain hegemony, it had to reinterpret the Hebrew prophets. Their prophetic visions of reconciliation and shalom within history (metaphorically conveyed via lions and lambs, children and serpents, swords and plowshares, spears and pruning hooks) had to be pushed beyond history, either into a spiritualized heaven or a millennial middle ground—between history and eternity, so to speak.

The eschatology of abandonment also had to marginalize Jesus (which they did, to a degree, by letting Jesus remain as savior but promoting Paul to master-teacher). But now, as more and more of us rediscover Jesus as master-teacher, we are struck by the centrality of "the kingdom of God" in Jesus' message (and Paul's too). And it is clear to us that this kingdom is not just about heaven after we die: It's about God's will (or wish) being "done on earth" now, in history.

In this kingdom, Jesus said, sparrows matter. Lilies of the field matter. Yes, people matter even more, but it's not a matter of either/or; it's a matter of degree in a world where everything that is good matters—where everything God made matters. God sent Jesus into the world with a saving love, and Jesus sends us with a similar saving love—love for the orphans and widows, the prostitutes and lepers, the poor and forgotten to be sure, but also for the little creatures who suffer from the same selfish greed and arrogance that oppress vulnerable humans.

Third, the hallowed concept of private ownership is being confronted by the biblical concept of stewardship. If liberal Christianity was tempted in the last century to become the civil religion of socialism that reverences state ownership, then certainly conservative Christianity has since become the happy mistress of capitalism that enshrines private ownership. No wonder then that private ownership and private enterprise are defended by many conservative Christians as vigorously as the doctrine of the Trinity or salvation by grace.

For increasing numbers of us who consider ourselves post-liberal and post-conservative, words like private (meaning personal and individual), ownership (meaning autonomous personal and individual control), and enterprise (meaning autonomous, personal, individual control over projects that use God's world for our purposes) seem to fly in the face of kingdom values. Values such as community (meaning seeing beyond the individual to the communal), fellowship (which

means sharing, holding in common with the community, not grasping as "mine!"), and mission (meaning our participation in God's projects in God's world for God's purposes).

Can there be some alternative to the extremes that either deny or enshrine private ownership? Could a biblical stewardship that celebrates God's ultimate ownership someday fuel a new grace-based economy—just as private ownership currently fuels our greed-based consumerist economy (or as government ownership fuels a control-based socialist economy)?

A stewardship economy doesn't see every majestic mountain as a potential site for strip-mining operations, nor does it see forests as board-feet of marketable lumber, nor does it see this spring-fed emergent wetland (drained and bulldozed) as a lucrative site for a "housing development" (an unfitting term if there ever was one, since bulldozers and pavement un-develop in hours what it took God's creation centuries to develop). Rather, whatever we "own" (including the molecules and cells that constitute our bodies) is really lent and entrusted to us by God, received by us and reverently used for a time, after which we must let go one way or another—either through giving and voluntary sharing, or through dying and involuntary relinquishing.

So, what do we do differently in this emerging theological habitat, this new stage in the spiritual forest succession? That remains to be seen. But for starters, we see differently, and we care differently, and we value differently—and if those differences catch on, with Christianity being the largest religion in the world, there are bound to be good effects in our world.

Ultimately, those effects will have to go beyond the important but limited conservation actions of individuals (recycling, reusing, abstaining, etc.).

The effects of caring will have to change our systems—transportation systems that depend on fossil fuels and that divide and devastate our nonhuman neighbors' habitats,

housing systems that maximize human impact through suburban sprawl, farming systems that violate rather than steward land, advertising systems that make us want more stuff that we don't need and that will soon fill even more square miles with trash. Even our family systems will need reconsideration. For example, we may realize that nuclear family (of so much Christian focus) and "subatomic family" (i.e., the nuclear family further split by divorce) both require (and waste) more resources than the truly traditional family—the extended or "molecular" one. Could extended families and intentional households ever make a comeback? If they do, it will be good news for all of creation—including humans.

Okay. Enough talk. I need to continue my survey. It's one little way as a member of my watershed (one's watershed being one's most important creational address, by the way—more important than nation, state, or zip code) that I can express my care for creation. A care that flows from my identity: a creature who wants to care for other creatures, because I am made in the image of a Creator who cares for us all. I hope you'll find your own ways to express care too, wherever your creational address.

Brian McLaren was founding pastor of Cedar Ridge Community Church in Spencerville, Maryland, and coauthor of *Adventures in Missing the Point: How the Culture-Controlled Church Neutered the Gospel* when this article appeared in the March 2004 issue of *Sojourners.*

Chapter 6

"Led Out in Joy"

Communal Resilience

Our ancient stories are religious—as are the lives we are living now. The word "religion" means "rebinding," putting body and soul together again, remembering that God knows and loves us intimately. As Daniel Berrigan writes, God wants to clear away "the forest of idols"—producers of loneliness, nihilism, and despair—that keep us captive. Deep wisdom is secreted within authentic cultures (not the manufactured ones), the cultures of our ancestors—a wisdom handed down in families, art, and sacred stories to teach us to live *buen vivir*, a good life. God wants to lead us out together, rejoicing. Community, as Christian mystic Cynthia Bourgeault says is "the threshold for the oneness in the collective body of Christ." At Sojourners we ask, where are God's people pulsating with joy?

Working Through to the Early Hours

Sandra Ovalle

> Is this the price we must pay for entrance into delight, rest, or relationships?

"*Hay más tiempo que vida*" was my dad's refrain every time I was stressed and weary. "There is more time than life." His simple words had profound implications.

Being present to life is difficult. Life demands that we "rise and grind." Reward comes to those who make the most of the time they've been given. Time is money. Time is a commodity we trade. The promise of life is the goal of all this grinding—or retirement, if we are privileged.

During the pandemic, I've pushed against beliefs that commodify time. I've cooked the foods that nourished my ancestors: tamales verdes, atole de tamarindo, and nopalitos. My senses have been awakened through mixing the nixtamalized corn flour with water and fat until it reached the right texture, peeling and deseeding each tamarind pod, cutting the nopal (cactus) and cooking it with a few tomatillo husks to remove the slime.

The preparation of these foods forces me to notice the rough spots on the cacti where thorns still make their home, to smell the acid scent of tamarind in the pulp clinging to my fingers; it invites me to play with the unruly dough that believes its place is on top of the corn husk and not inside. If death shows up in separation, life sprouts in connection.

But on most mornings, I check my email as soon as I wake; on some nights, I work through to the early hours of the morning. This grind separates me from life. Is this the price we must pay for entrance into delight, rest, or relationships?

Jesus knows this dilemma and offers a way forward: "The thief comes only to steal and kill and destroy. I came that they may have life and have it abundantly" (John 10:10). The life Jesus presents is abundant, flourishing, overflowing. He notices the widow bringing her two cents to the Temple treasury; his gaze is on the woman who had been bent over for eighteen years; he feels the person who touched his garments. Jesus made space to be present, to notice.

The voracious hunger of the rich, the "thieves" who take more than they need, speaks death over our souls. Economic "efficiencies" in an industrialized production process too often serve to move money to the top while stealing the life out of life. It's hard for us to know how even our food was produced. For example, the most accessible masa for tamales in the United States is made with genetically modified corn from the United States that is sold to a global company in Mexico (the birthplace of corn) for branding and processing in U.S.-based factories, then placed in local U.S. grocery stores and sold as a Mexican product. Too often we are blocked from the lives of those people and environments who give life to our food before it reaches us. We are separated from their stories.

Life longs to have a relationship with us. Reconnecting with the people involved in the web of production is one way of moving toward life. I say a simple prayer before dinner: "*Te pedimos por todos los que colaboraron en esta mesa que tengan trabajos y descansos justos, mesas abudantes y alegres.*" A reminder of those along the way that brought this food to our table. I ask that they have full and joyful tables, fair wages, and abundant rest.

My dad's *sabiduría* (wisdom) offers me a prophetic invitation to something he did not experience. While reminding me to be present to my life, his life was one of intense labor—as if he was preparing the way for my rest, joy, and abundant life. *Hay más tiempo que vida.*

Sandra Ovalle, a native of Mexico City, was director of campaigns and mobilizing at Sojourners when this appeared in the November 2021 issue.

The Marvelous Design
Reflection on Isaiah 25

Daniel Berrigan

You are my God,
I extol you, I praise your name;
for you have carried out your excellent design,
long planned, trustworthy, true.
A mighty people gives you glory,
for you are a refuge for the poor,
a refuge for the needy in distress,
a shelter from the storm,
a shade from the heat.
—Isaiah 25:1, 3

Isaiah offers a prayer of thanksgiving in chapter 25, a prayer on an exalted but extremely realistic and concrete note. "Thanks for what has been and is." Thanks also for what will be. A strange sort of thanksgiving! It takes into account and includes most awful events that touch—with a finger of death—on Isaiah's life.

"You are my God" (verse 1). A revolutionary word indeed, the clearing away of a dense forest of idols. The toppling of false gods, who are in many lives, and as a plain matter of conduct, "my gods."

The verse sings with reasoned clear-sighted ecstasy. The true God has put into the mouth of the prophet a flame of truth. The prophet cries out, knowing Someone is attending.

For most of us, this is a leap in the dark. We neither see nor hear nor touch nor taste; the sense of God is neutral on our tongue and in our mind. It does not touch the heart; the emotional life is not so much drained away as directed elsewhere. We give our hearts, hardly blamefully, to those we know and love—because we see and hear and touch and kiss. So, we plod along, hoping against hope that one day we may pass "from shadows and images into the truth."

Still, here and now, God strikes fire in our mouth also—though muted, invisible even. And if not, why not then borrow the flame of Isaiah? And as debtors of the flame, why not be assured that the God we invoke, the God we claim even, is the God who once stood by our great ancestry and stands by us, and the children as well?

Then the clearing away of the forest of idols proceeds. Insofar as God is invoked, the toppling of the idols is the work not of benighted spirits like ourselves—who often cannot tell an idol from a burning bush—but the work of the true God. The God who knows and loves. The God who is truth and love, immeasurable, and who clears a way in the underbrush—a clear way between our faltering and waywardness and the holy sanctuary of the *Shekinah*, the divine presence.

"You are my God." A child can say it; children do say it and sing it, content, the simple words on their lips. Adults too, in the measure we are unbesotted by the world, are offered a monosyllabic volume in one phrase, a triumph, a gift from the One invoked. When many say it, heartfelt, "there I am in the midst."

How sad that the words, and the joy and confidence implied, are not as close to our affective life as a hand or an eye in motion are to our physical makeup. To look on a lovely sky or tree or the sea and say it. To touch the face of a child and say it. In consequence of such beauty, touching it, touched by it, understanding (in the sense of standing under). Knowing the source of such beauty, the Resource.

And the return. The One who waits, and who comes. The One who is. And all in the deepest here and now.

I do not know if we can say this verse with a full heart, meaning it. Mostly we founder about with religious language, trying not to sound utterly absurd to ourselves—and not always succeeding. What we are left with is something else: the language of lapsed humans, the hiatus and stammering in a world that is too much with us. And a God who is afar, the Unknown and unknowable (as we conclude in a kind of functional despair), not after all counting for much.

But this is not all. In dire need of instructors, we have an instructor at hand, one whose counsel has endured. And, as we ruefully reflect, even a borrowed language is better than none. So we borrow and beg from the wise, if we are wise.

We borrow from Isaiah. The God we invoke grants us a tongue to invoke, a reminder, a mind. God is the builder and healer of the vacant and vapid and wounded mind, which left to its own devices is dumb, blind, and deaf in the world. We are, left to our own devices, what we have made of that world. There remains the task of putting on the language of the great, the "seers"—like dwarfs in the armor of giants.

Thus verse 1 offers the plenary shocking force of a tradition brought to bear, bearing down and yet strangely freeing as well. What need we have of such a prayer! We, left to our little or great stockpiles of destruction, our "securities," our vain scrambling about the world. What a monstrous mockery of the "great design" saluted, celebrated, offered by Isaiah!

Does there exist a "marvelous design" of things, as stated? A design sovereignly outside our wrecking will? We doubt it with all our hearts. And with doubt for a wrecking weapon, we set about proving it is not so. Or proving that the design is in our own hands, no one else's—which is the same thing, only worse.

Wreckage. Doubt. The doubt that becomes a habit of the mind, and the wreckage—of truth, of community, of the world itself—that follows close on. A bull rampaging about in a moral twilight.

I long to pay tribute to the "design," to master the doubt. I long to enter that stream of life and holiness, that "plan formed long ago," to which I am called, beyond any doubt, beyond any wreckage of mine, beyond a culture of doubt and wreckage.

The grand design exists, no matter what the world makes of it (or resolves to unmake). The design of reality is nobly conceived here. It is a web, whispering and weaving its pattern of moral beauty and fidelity. It summons us, but it does not require us. It stands firm, inviolate, without us. Thus the sorry tale of a wounded freedom.

We are free to stand outside the design, in a pitiful charade of the superhuman. We are free to be American, to be silent, to be complicit, to consume with ardor, to embrace violence like an iron bridegroom whose embrace crushes.

And yet, the design of God, we are reminded, is "perfectly faithful." It perdures, no matter what, no matter the infidelity on our part. A majestic steadfastness reigns, an unstained love, despite all the stains of a venomous and adventuring generation—our own.

"For the citadel of the arrogant is a city no longer; it will never be rebuilt" (verse 2). What a gauntlet is hereby cast down! The statement is abrupt, it admits of no intervention, softening, or repair. What can it mean?

The overthrow of the proud, moreover, is adduced as the cause and occasion of holy praise. "I will exalt your holy name, for you have worked wonders . . ." and "you have reduced the city to a heap of stones." Such a strange juxtaposition of divine works! And it is equally strange that the second statement evokes praise, as does the first.

The "report on the city" (verse 2) is first of all a moral statement, a judgment of the state of affairs, here and now. It is the "glance within," the calm conclusion of the one who pierces through semblances to the heart of the matter. Judgment is mine, says God.

There is something about the "last word." Who utters that word, and with what authority? According to Isaiah, the outcome of moral crisis rests in other hands than the powers of this world. Those manicured hands, their thumbs down! They, too, will be judged.

For such reasons as precede and are to follow (Isaiah is a great one for logic that defies all human logic), therefore the nations too will revere God (verse 3). What a statement, what a claim—then or now!

Nonetheless, they shall one day see; pride and chariots and spears and all their hardware and claptrap go exactly nowhere. A salutary lesson; perhaps the beginning of the end? In any case, we take note of the vision of Revelation, that the nations will stream into the gates of heavenly Jerusalem.

These redoubtable nations may see, to their confusion, two occurrences that strike them blind. The first, as above, is a disaster to their unchecked ego. And then they see that God is the God not of the big achievers and puny believers, but of the helpless, the needy, the victimized, and the distressed (verses 4 and 5.) God is shelter and shadow; such this God is, for those who have no chariots to trust in.

On the other hand, we are offered wonderful images of the powerful, reduced and rendered. Like rain against a wall, like (more intense) heat in a time of drought. God brings their power to nothing, like a cloud tempering a hot spot.

What do we make of all this? It appears that such worldly power as is excoriated here, held up to scorn, is literally stuck, without hope or compassion. It never learns.

Newly offered, and always available, is the biblical analysis of, first, the desperate measures of the "old way," and, second, the possibility of a "new way."

Verse 6, the grand feast, "for all people." This is the universal theme so dear to Isaiah and the other prophets. God is host of the banquet. Then her role changes; she becomes the Comforter.

The feast is ready. The menu is dwelt upon, with pride, with anticipation. A menu for all! What people love, what awakens and satiates appetite, this will be served. "On this mountain" refers to Zion, understood as pivot of the universe, a place of gathering and departure both.

The end of things is a celebration. This is something beyond fantasy or dream wish. It is the substance of hope. The imagery also is exorcising; it liberates us from images of nuclear Armageddon. God so loves creation as to celebrate, and not for its mere perdurance or survival—let alone its utter destruction, as some have claimed, making Armageddon an idea whose time, so to speak, will never come.

Another outcome is indicated by the image of the universal banquet. God, together with all people, will celebrate.

Celebrate what? Humanness vindicated, in the right order and cherishing of all creation. What was true in the beginning remains true through all the tormented path of history, and is true to the end. God's love, our love, God-community, we in community; sweet creation, no longer "groaning" or "in travail"; itself in us. A dance of creation to follow the banquet. Christ calling the tune.

The tone changes in verses 7 and 8. It is as though the feast were proceeding as planned, in all its splendor and pomp—and the overarching tent had become strangely oppressive. A realization dawns; we are not yet altogether liberated. There are empty places at the table. More, sorrow is in the air, a sense of loss, the absence of loved ones. At this late hour, when our liberation is both announced and celebrated, is death in command?

We can perhaps pursue the tent image as apropos. Suppose the tent were to collapse; not catastrophically (this after all is post-catastrophe). But it wafts down slowly over the guests. It is silken, not suffocating, light as down. Still, it darkens the scene, interferes with free movement, gets in the way of gesture and dance. It has become a kind of "veil of mourning," it lies upon "all people." Now it encompasses them more closely. It veils their faces, one from another.

Are we the living? Are we the dead? We gaze at one another through this veil. Death has dared to make an appearance, even at the feast of life; it is an ancient and terrible tale.

Something further must be done. The guests cannot of themselves lift the veil of death, that tegument which has become a kind of second skin. A claim that says, "You do not know one another; but I know you. You may celebrate life as you please, but death owns you. Multitudes of you have died. You will all die. Eat, drink, and be merry."

This is intolerable. The feast of life, arrogantly becoming a feast of death!

The guests are helpless. Who shall lift the central pole, and with it that huge adhesive burden? God must act.

God acts. Death is banished forever.

And then a further ritual of tenderness. We see the Host passing among the guests. They are again breathing free, their beloved restored to them. All are weeping in joy and relief. And God passes among them in spontaneous tenderness and wipes the tears from faces.

"God will remove the reproach from his people, over all the earth" (verse 8). In light of the preceding, the reproach, the opprobrium, includes all the ways in which death has laid claim to people in the terror of our history. To me, that terrible word "control" sums it up. The iron will to own others is the will to magnify and justify the spirit of death.

Appalled we have heard with monotonous regularity of "new attacks by the contras; civilian deaths high." Likewise in the Philippines, in Northern Ireland, in South Africa, in so many other tormented regions of our world. At whose door will these crimes be laid? Who will pay for the blood of the innocent?

These are very old questions, alas. But they must be raised again and again, though the heavens be turned to adamant and the skies rain blood. "For God has spoken."

"And it will be said on that day . . ." (verse 9). Surely it is helpful to reflect on the strange, incongruent tenses: the Lord having once spoken, and then the echo, "on that day, it will be said."

We are to echo that holy Word, on a given day. Not yet. And why not yet? Why not now? If not now, when? If not now, never? What is this delay we are so tolerant of, so afraid of?

We can at least say, in our humiliation and scorn, "I will not be a party to the delay," which is a matter not to be laid to God, but to cowardice, fear, and ennui—to ourselves, in other words.

But let us look at the word that "will be spoken," and yet is not spoken. And yet, "God has spoken it."

This is the awaited One, present in hope. Thus meaning is bestowed on things, above all on those things that seemed to have no meaning, that escaped and evaded and even mocked any possible meaning—such as present political "realities," the most unreal phenomena of our lifetime. A politics of murder, condemning us to a polis where murder is the ordinary tactic.

We have clear instruction in verse 9 concerning the character of this God who saves, his moral physiognomy. The instruction is offered in the Sermon on the Mount and is verified on the mount of Calvary. The message is so clear it blinds. And in blindness, we place our hope elsewhere, in almost anyone—except God. Ultimately, in anything, since the hope embodied in those we grant our hope to—the "hope" of our leaders—is in the bomb. Thus hope is demonized, lodged in dead gods, gods of death. These, it is debasedly hoped, will save us.

Thus our hope is that death, more properly murder, will save us from death. This is the knot we have twisted about our own throats.

We die of it before we die.

Always intriguing, those words "save" and "salvation." There is of course a hyperspiritualized translation, intensely concerned with self, fermenting, to all appearances, in the head only, a kind of pseudo-ecstasy, without cost or outlay of pain. It operates in a closed circuit of the like-minded, borrows a closed language.

So understood, "salvation" also welcomes, without critique or second thought, a large assimilation of the culture: attitudes about women, money, success, ego. It is purportedly apolitical, but in fact acknowledges little or no difficulty with wars, hot or cold, with racism, violence, foreign incursions.

Implied in this view is a quite clear conviction, a cultural one to be sure. There is nothing seriously wrong with America. America is, in fact, God's finest triumph. Let us wage wars, let us be racist and sexist and rampage on the earth; it is all blessed, all according to His (*sic*) will.

To be "saved" in this sense, in the final analysis, is to have America justified by a god of the culture. And as to the Christians—for many of them, their Christianity is qualified; it dangles from the chief noun, "American"—these are justified in the same swath of benignity.

An image suggests itself. In Acts 10:9 and following, we are told how Peter, at prayer, is rewarded with the vision of a great napkin descending from heaven, teeming with the fauna of the world. It is as though all creation were offered to him for blessing and nourishment. And he understands that the law of clean and unclean is, to say the least, put in question.

All to the good. But it occurs to me that, for large numbers of Christian Americans (*sic*), the "napkin from heaven" is in fact an American flag. This magical talisman descends from a questionable realm of political authority, beyond accountability, a mount of Olympus.

The flag unfolds. The teeming "goods and services" that tumble out are all marked "made in America." They are for the most part weapons. They are meant to mollify and glorify the "complete American," including of course the Christian Americans heretofore referred to, including also those abroad who seek to emulate mother country and her mother church and the "salvation" offered jointly by the twin powers.

There is another more modest, thoughtful, and critical understanding of the word. This "other" Christian is burdened, at times overwhelmed, by a sense of the sins of his people, and by implication his own sins. This one confesses, and seeks reconciliation; crosses lines and enters forbidden territories to declare the presence of the God of life in the midst of the lurking apparatus of death. Wherefore pays up.

The faith of such a one has a dark and poverty-stricken look. This one hears from his betters, the mystics, that "all will be well," if only because God has spoken—not (God knows!) because things are anything but grievously unwell.

If God has spoken, it must be so. Though how and when and whence? She raises eyes to the heavens, weary but unquenched. Even at times, now and then, not often, she "rejoices, is jubilant" (if you can believe that!). Sometimes, one is tempted to say, the good humor of believers is itself a kind of salvation, a kind of saving.

From ill humor, rancor, dwelling perversely in the underside of things, deliver us, O God!

"For the hand of God rests on this mountain (Zion)" (verse 10). The hand of God makes the mountain the very center of earth, a pivot, a lyre in the winds, a sounding board, a point and end of pilgrimage and worship. All these. Whereunto we are summoned and therefore go. And arrive. An image of eternal life.

While the adversary (Moab) is dealt with otherwise, to say the least. A series of striking images of subjugation: "trodden down like straw on a manure pile." And though he "stretches out his hands, like a swimmer entering the waters," it will all come to nothing. An image of pride and control and skill, daring the plunge into an unfamiliar element, and he sinks. The "trickery, magic of his hands" goes nowhere.

Moab is addressed directly in verse 12 for the first time. Isaiah has become the direct oracle of the divine will. This is of course a kind of holy folly: to look on these "unassailable ramparts and wills," and announce in a dead calm, "It will all come down."

And more, the present tense. The downfall, rack and ruin, are even now under way. We mourn, we rejoice, we endure.

Daniel Berrigan, SJ, priest, poet, and peace activist, was a *Sojourners* contributing editor. This appeared in the December 1989 issue of *Sojourners*.

I'm Agnostic. Here's Why I Went Back to Church

Oisín Rowe

Over the past five years, I've deconverted from Christianity. The decision felt comfortable following multiple rounds of reckonings in pews, parks, Burger King, and the comfort of my bed. My supportive husband, Jonathan, still identifies as a Christian. But throughout it all, he encouraged me to find out what I believed and affirmed that he would stand by me when I found out what it was. So, comfortable in the mystery, I began letting go of religious fear and discovered that I doubted the legitimacy of Christianity.

It began with a disillusionment of church. Throughout my childhood, I was a part of high churches and low churches. I received my first Holy Communion and told the priest in penance how I killed a spider in the garden. I visited congregations that marketed themselves as simple and positive Christian communities, but secretly were homophobic Southern Baptist church plants. My family joined an authoritarian, fundamentalist Baptist church for ten years where my siblings and I made enough waves as teenagers that the pastor sat us down and poured out his wrath on us.

In my adult life, I thought that if I found a church I morally aligned with I would feel at home and Christianity would make sense. Overall in the United States, church attendance has been declining. A recent Gallup poll revealed that only three in ten adults in the United States attend a weekly religious service.

The frequency of those who do attend services varies among religions and denominations. Thirty percent of Protestants and 23 percent of Catholics said they attend every week.

As my husband and I evolved, our choice of church did too. We started with a church that said their focus was on racial justice. But we were both suspicious of that claim, considering they typically sang Hillsong and Bethel worship music (both Bethel and Hillsong leaders were then-President Donald Trump's guests in the White House). Nonetheless, we tried to settle in and joined a small group. But after each service, I continued to feel unconvinced. Eventually, we left because the church failed to adequately care for and empower queer, infertile, and disabled communities. However, I knew that there was more to why I left.

Even today, it feels cruel to refer to the height of the COVID-19 pandemic as a time of learning and reflection. We were surrounded by mass death. Each of us carried the fear that our disabled or vulnerable family and friends could be next. However, amid the horror and fear, everything paused. In so many ways, this pause was a thing to grieve, especially for the ways it impacted the mental health of kids and teenagers. But, for me, the break from in-person church felt like a weight had been removed. At first, I attributed this feeling to simply being able to sleep in one more day. But then, as time passed, I realized I still did not miss church. We attended virtual services infrequently.

Once it was safe to return in person, we attended sporadically for a year and then stopped going altogether. Jonathan prompted us to reflect on why each of us no longer wanted to be at church. The first thing that came to my mind was how the story of Noah's Ark is often painted in children's Sunday school classrooms and nurseries. The cute animal heads poke out of the boat, viewing the rainbow with Noah, who always seems both cautiously optimistic and faithfully smug. The water is always an opaque, dark blue, and never depicts what has happened to those who didn't make it onto the boat: drowning. In her *Sojourners* article, writer and podcaster Patty Krawec offers this reflection: "I've wondered if this story that celebrates obedience immunizes us to the suffering of others—if it teaches us to see suffering as proof of God's judgment." This is not the only time God condones or commits genocide in the Bible.

Slowly, then quickly, my thoughts turned from deconstruction to deconversion, and I felt a peace. If I had to pick a label today, agnostic feels comfortable. Jonathan had a different path. While his beliefs and spiritual practices shifted, he still felt strongly that his Christian faith was an important lens through which he saw the world and himself.

After the birth of our miracle son following our years-long battle with infertility, we started discussing church again. Jonathan, forever loving and supportive of where I am spiritually, asked me what I thought about occasionally bringing our child to church. We both agreed that we did not want him to feel the same pressure under religious education that we had. Still, I also wanted to honor Jonathan's desire to be involved in a religious community again.

As we spoke, we looked out of our apartment windows toward the cars below, lined up for a local church's food pantry. We walked into the same church several months later with our four-month-old.

The first thing I noticed was the smell. They used the same polish on the pews as the fundamentalist Baptist church my family had attended for a decade. It was something I never expected to be triggering, but I felt myself start to sweat and my head spun. I was anxious and fidgeted throughout the service. The pastor stood up to preach in jeans and a hoodie and gave a message about liberation. I resonated with the message but when she mentioned Jesus as a liberator, I didn't believe it. I was still thinking about the people God killed in the flood.

Previously, when I would be in church settings and have these thoughts, it felt jarring. But now, it felt affirming to recognize my disbelief even while sitting in the pew. Jonathan felt at peace after the first service, and the baby loved the music, so we went back twice more.

One warm Thursday morning in early spring, I woke up after a night of little sleep between myself and my son. I was drained physically, mentally, and spiritually, so I got us ready for the day, put the baby in a carrier, and set off on a walk. We wandered into a local coffee shop where I bumped into the pastor. Being seen and known and met with a smile was glorious. We sat and chatted with another member of the congregation and the pastor even held the baby so I could finish my coffee. As we left the cafe, the pastor assured me that I was not the only agnostic in the community and the church had no expectations of conversion or shared doctrine.

This small moment reminded me of church-thrown baby showers and potlucks. Even in the depths of high-control religion, there were moments of being fed and cared for that I did not know I missed until I did. I knew that this was what Jonathan had been missing too and I craved more.

If more churches turned away from pushing doctrinal expectations on their congregants, perhaps more people would stay. They would feel safe enough to deconstruct or deconvert in community rather than leave to find out what they believe in isolation. According to a 2024 Pew Research survey, most religious "nones" believe in God or a different higher power. The majority also believe that while religion can be harmful, it can also do good. As the United States shifts away from a Christian majority, it could also be moving toward a stronger doctrinally diverse community that embraces the "nones."

Personally, deconversion has healed my soul, which had been long battered by religious trauma and control. I have returned to church, but not strictly or forcibly or out of guilt.

Jonathan and I returned for community. What a glorious thing it is to have community without it being contingent on conversion or how well I follow the pastor's rules. We still are introducing ourselves to this small church body but each smile and hello, each acknowledgment that we house precious thoughts and souls, is a welcome gift.

Oisín Rowe (formerly Elisa Rowe), a writer and poet, was living in Boston when this appeared on sojo.net on August 8, 2024.

My Métis People Blended Christianity with Their Beliefs. I Cannot

Chris La Tray

To the left of a buffalo photograph on my wall, a rosary hangs from a thumbtack. Frequently, my eyes linger there. It came to me a couple of years ago on my birthday as part of a gift from my mother—looped through the ribbon of a wrapped box that contained a tea set. When I held the rosary before my face, I found it curious. My mother explained that it had been my late father's, and that it was one of his most prized possessions. I was a little stunned because I had never seen it before. It was a gift, my mom continued, made by his grandmother who died two years before I was born. Now, it had come to me.

My great-grandmother's parents were part of a group of twenty-five Red River Métis families who settled on Spring Creek in central Montana in 1879, an area now known as Lewistown. They, like all the tribes of the region, were pursuing the final dwindling herds of buffalo. It was a tumultuous time to be Indigenous, with settlers flooding the landscape from all points east and gobbling up land, whether it had been promised to Indians or not.

The origins of my Métis people can be found in the late 1600s, and likely earlier, when the first European traders first began establishing trading posts in the Red River Valley. This region, named for the mighty Red River of the North, is centered at what is now Winnipeg, Manitoba, and extends into today's Minnesota and North Dakota. These early Europeans, mostly from France—with some coming from Scotland, Wales, and England—married into the Indigenous people already inhabiting the region: Cree people and Ojibwe people. From these unions sprang descendants who created their own unique, mixed-culture people—the Métis.

The Border Crossed Us

We Métis are a distinct cultural and Indigenous people recognized as such in Canada but not in the United States. The difference between me and my Canadian relatives? Our respective addresses relative to the forty-ninth parallel north on this continent, otherwise known as the border that separates the United States from Canada—the Medicine Line. We are the same people; we didn't cross the border, the border crossed us.

From the early 1800s until the buffalo nearly went extinct in the 1880s, the people from the Red River ventured out onto the plains in convoys of two-wheeled Red River carts—a Métis invention largely considered to be the first use of the wheel on the Northern Plains—to hunt buffalo. These enterprises contained anywhere from a few dozen carts to more than one thousand essentially moving entire towns' worth of people out to practice their traditional economy. It wasn't just subsistence hunting, it was trading: buffalo hides and, most importantly, pemmican—a food product made of dried meat, fat, and usually some kind of berry (like the high cranberry, or *pembina*, from which the Pembina Band of Chippewa Indians earned their name) that was highly valued not just for its caloric wallop but also its accompanying portability.

Beginning around 1820, these ventures out onto the plains often included a Catholic priest; priests had begun arriving just a few years before. It was an uneasy alliance at first. The Métis had developed their own unique blend of Catholicism before the priests came, taking the lay teachings of the first-arriving Europeans and blending them with Anishinaabe cosmology to create what Canadian scholar Dr. Émilie Pigeon called a "lived" Catholicism. It wasn't a conversion to Christianity; it was an inclusion. Life was hard in the region, and Indigenous people were happy to take whatever spiritual power they could. Spirituality and prayer were as much a part of life as breathing. There was no reason not to include these new ideas with what they already had.

This began to change when missionaries arrived in the Red River Settlement from the other side of the Great Lakes region. The missionaries didn't like the way the Indigenous worshippers played fast and loose with church doctrine. They didn't like that there were couples calling themselves married who had done so outside the auspices of the church—and with heathen children the result of these unions. But the problem was, they didn't initially have the strength to enforce any change to the Indigenous way of doing things. Then, as more settlers arrived—to the dismay of the people already living there—and built schools, and began to establish and enforce rules, the balance of power shifted. A couple of decades preaching out on the prairie during the buffalo hunts, and the spiritual lives of a growing number of Métis people began to reflect a more European practice of Catholicism.

Exploring the Mystery

Growing up, my family was not a religious one. I don't recall my father ever attending church, though now, with the revelation of his prized rosary, I wonder about my own Catholic baptism. I always assumed it was to please my grandparents, though they never exerted any kind of spiritual pressure on my family that I am aware of. Now I wonder if it was something my dad saw as important. My mom, who today remains a spiritual person but would never claim to be religious, was not raised Catholic. Instead, she was in and out of various churches, mostly Lutheran, during my adolescence. I too attended off and on for a couple of years during my elementary-age years, both with her and as a guest of another family whose daughter was a friend of mine. Even so, I would be surprised if I attended more than a score of services, or even a dozen, and to this day I wonder why I ever did.

As an adult, I've dabbled in other spiritual traditions. Most recently, I have spent more than a little time reading Buddhist writers and contemplating Zen. As relevant as many of the ideas I have encountered are to my animist, nature-based, tree-hugging-dirt-worshiping proclivities, it hasn't seemed quite right for me. So much still feels dogmatic and hierarchical, even misogynistic. As I struggled with the language—the names, the lineages, the terminology—I also wondered what use it was to learn the tongue of another faith when I did not even know mine?

I became curious about Catholicism because of a decade of research into the history of my Métis people, and the blend of European faith with that of the Anishinaabe. It was a hint of the "lived" Catholicism of my Métis ancestors that I hoped to find on Christmas Eve when I decided to see if my local church in Frenchtown, Montana, would be holding a midnight Mass. This was as good a chance for Catholicism to welcome me back into the fold as it would ever get. I was interested in exploring the mystery, to see if this particular brand of spirit would reveal any fresh insights into the spiritual lives of my ancestors. Also, if I had a community church, St. John the Baptist was the closest thing to it, even sharing the building with the Lutheran congregation of my youth until the Lutherans built their own small church not far from where the valley's first Catholic church was constructed of hewn logs to serve the Red

River Métis worshipers. My high school choir performed Handel's *Messiah* from the balcony there one afternoon in the early 1980s. I'm fairly certain that was the last time I ever set foot inside it.

I found the church website and scanned for a midnight Mass on the schedule. There wasn't one listed. I started clicking around. At that point, I wasn't looking for anything in particular but immediately was struck by what I *didn't* find. There was nothing mentioned about Indigenous boarding schools. It had only been a few months since the remains of thousands of children had been found in unmarked graves in Canada and the United States, a heartbreaking story the Catholic Church played a huge role in. And while there was an 800 number on the website to call if you "know of or have cause to suspect an incident of child abuse or neglect," there was nothing related to conciliatory remarks about the church's own sad history of abuse.

Returning to the church's website a few days after the Supreme Court cast aside the half-century-old Roe v. Wade decision, I find links to celebratory posts in favor of this cruel decision. I find links to websites for "ex-gays" that amount to little more than "pray the gay away" propaganda. I find these attitudes hateful. I am reminded how I felt on Christmas Eve, like a man standing in the doorway of a church my ancestors had found some peace in during very troubled times, only to find the door slammed in my face.

I won't cast my shadow there again.

Hard to Reconcile

The pale, lingering twilight of early summer is settling outside the window of my home office. My eyes linger on the view of the western horizon, then drift back to the wall just above my computer monitor. An old black-and-white 8 × 10 photograph hangs there in a cheap, black plastic frame. The image is of a small herd of *mashkode-bizhikiwag*—Ojibwe for "buffalo"—spread across a grassy plain. In the shadowy light, they are little more than dark spots against a gray landscape. There is nothing special about the photograph, but I stare at it often. It brings me peace of mind.

Beyond the status as the U.S. national mammal, *bizhiki* is a sacred animal to many people of North America, including mine. In the tradition of the Seven Grandfathers' Teachings of my Anishinaabe people, bizhiki represents *mnaadendimowin*, or respect: Respect for the self, for others, for all life. Bizhiki can be said to be a representative of what so many of us might better understand as the Golden Rule: Treat others as you would want to be treated.

These seven teachings of the ancestral grandfathers—humility, bravery, honesty, wisdom, truth, respect, and love—provide all the guidance I need to live an Anishinaabe life. On my best days, I hope "every footstep becomes a prayer" as the life is described by the late Ojibwe elder Edward Benton-Banai. But like so many people who strive to live a spiritual life, I am not always living one of my "best" days. It is only recently that I have even dedicated myself fully to trying to live an Anishinaabe life. Along the way, my feet have grown dusty and dry in making footsteps to this spiritual place. They are ready to linger awhile.

It is hard to reconcile the world I live in today with the decisions my ancestors were forced into. They chose to incorporate elements of Catholicism into their daily lives for some reason that I can't uncover. I know too much now about how the long game played out, and I struggle with my encounters with Indigenous Christians because it feels like the ultimate betrayal. That is a struggle I will face for the rest of my life, I think. It is a lonely undertaking too, because where I live isn't exactly an Anishinaabe stronghold. To immerse myself in that spiritual life, I will likely have to relocate to the other side of the Medicine Line, to Manitoba, or perhaps Saskatchewan.

But I have buffalo, my magnificent mashkode-bizhikiwag, near me. I can be in their presence in minutes. They are living, breathing reminders of a different kind of spirit that my people pursued for centuries. Among them, at a safe distance, I find some solace.

They are not extinct. Neither are we.

Chris La Tray is a Métis storyteller, a descendent of the Pembina Band of the mighty Red River of the North, and an enrolled member of the Little Shell Tribe of Chippewa Indians. He was author of the Substack newsletter "An Irritable Métis" when this appeared in the December 2022 issue of *Sojourners*.

Embracing a Millennia-Old Cosmovision

Néstor Medina

Indigenous communities honor relationships with all life. Will European descendants learn to do the same?

I grew up in Guatemala, a country where the Indigenous people make up more than 50 percent of the population. I was told growing up that my ancestors were Europeans (Spaniards and Italians). Even though I was identified as *ladino* (not Indigenous) by Guatemalan official nomenclature, I was attracted to Mayan languages and communities (K'iche', Kaqchikel, and Q'eqchi', among others).

I felt a resonance with their orientation toward the earth, their deep sense of communal cohesion, and their mystical world of ancestral spirits. After doing some genealogical work, I learned that one of my grandfathers was Mayan.

I began to notice practices and attitudes in my family that I was certain were of Indigenous origins: my dad's idiosyncratic disregard for manufactured material goods in favor of plants; my uncle's pouring of alcohol on the floor before serving a drink; my mom's smoking of cigars as an invitation to the spirits and San Simón to be with us in our gatherings. All have an Indigenous provenance.

As I learned more, I recognized those familial practices as part of a millennia-old cosmovision and mindset, a way of viewing the cosmic order of a civilization through which

Indigenous peoples organize everyday activities, even today. Each is a theo-ethical gesture for safeguarding their relationship with life itself, in all life's diversity.

My travels around other Latin American nations have allowed me to interact with other Indigenous peoples and learn from their traditions and wisdom. As a scholar, I have also encountered similar patterns of life among First Nations in Canada and Native Americans in the United States.

Through the large expanse of the Americas, these ethnic groups and communities share common views of the origins of the world. They share an understanding of the earth as teeming with life; all of them operate within a mystical-spiritual relationship that weaves together the earth, the spirits of their ancestors, celestial bodies, other forms of life, and humans.

In these cosmovisions, humans are not the most important agents, but are also not neutral bystanders. For example, Berta Cáceres' activism for the protection of Honduran ecosystems against transnational mining corporations was not only the work of an "environmentalist." Her work was deeply rooted in an Indigenous cosmovision that gives priority to protecting the sustaining life force of the earth and understands humans as key agents in that effort.

Buen Vivir

These approaches to life remind me of what Indigenous peoples in South America have dubbed *buen vivir* (literally, good living). Buen vivir emphasizes a holistic approach to life that requires rethinking the social structures and dynamics that shape people in community and how those structures directly impact the environment. Buen vivir refers to a qualitative measure of the relationships between people, others in their community, and their surrounding environment. It envisions a different way to build society.

Those communities that subscribe to buen vivir are built on the principle of profound interrelationship—individuals are linked to a larger diverse communal whole, which includes nature and the spirits of the ancestors and animals. Ideas like "life, liberty, and the pursuit of happiness," for example, are understood in a collective sense, not in terms of individual rights and privileges. Individualist focus disrupts the communal equilibrium based on coexistence and the survival of the community. The consumption of natural resources and concepts such as "absolute" ownership of property are measured in relation to the survival of the members of the community and how those concepts protect existing natural resources for generations to come.

At its heart, buen vivir presupposes the collective ethical imperative to protect life in all its forms. Unlimited extraction and exploitation of natural resources, individual accumulation of wealth, and forced cultural assimilation are fundamentally antithetical to buen vivir. What these communities seek to build are "plurivocal" societies where many voices are heard, and the central axis of existence is not humanity but the larger structures and forces that sustain life on the planet. In buen vivir, the values of interrelationship and interdependence, the survival of each other, and the preservation of natural ecosystems are all preconditions for the survival of the community.

Buen vivir provides a framework for understanding life, people, community, and the divine from the vantage point of mutual coexistence. In the mythical cosmovisions of Indigenous peoples, humans are understood to be part of the larger vortex of life that connects all living things. Respect for life in its richly diverse expressions requires unique interactions with each living thing. Diverse peoples are celebrated as heirs to diverse forms of knowledges and life experiences. They are not catalogued according to prejudiced ethnoracial differences. Nature is not seen as a material repository of potential products for consumption. Instead, the earth is properly appreciated as the "mother," the life source that sustains all. If something happens to nature, the entire structure of life falls out of balance and the future of life itself is at risk.

Across the Continent

Buen vivir is not unique to the Indigenous communities of South America. I've also encountered it among the Zapatistas, as they continue to reclaim self-government in Chiapas, Mexico. Two main features of the Zapatista social structure are an affirmation of the bonds of mutuality and a refusal to adopt punitive approaches to policing and fighting crime. To safeguard the community, they've chosen a model of "transformative justice," an approach that focuses on the restorative nature of justice, not punishment. In Guatemala, the Mayan phrase "*Utz' K'aslimaal*" (good life or a life in balance) is another example. The concept conveys a similar proposal as buen vivir.

Cognate terms from other ethnic groups in Latin America describe similar realities. Orlando Fals Borda and Arturo Escobar remind us that among Afro-Colombians from the North Cauca river communities, the governing idea is *sentipensar* (literally translated as to think-feel). Sentipensar focuses on communities' attitudes in carrying out their daily activities—as they consider the effect of each choice and action on the water and the fish in the river from which they draw their sustenance and on the land that feeds them.

The first *Encuentro del Buen Vivir* held in Mexico in 2012 and the seventh *Encuentro Internacional por el Buen Vivir* held in Peru in 2020 are examples of the wide range of Indigenous and non-Indigenous communities that resonate with the principles of buen vivir across the continent.

Some refer to buen vivir as if it were a recent development. But women's rights activist and Guatemalan Indigenous leader Aura Lolita Chávez Ixcaquic reminds us that these cosmovisions are part of the long-standing legacy of generations of Indigenous ancestors who have lived this way. The crucial teaching of buen vivir is that the Indigenous communities of the Americas are offering us a *proyecto de vida*—a "life project"—that runs on a different path from the pervasive structures of capitalism, commodification of life, and extraction of natural resources.

Buen vivir is informed by a logic that views the multifaceted and multiform expressions of life as sacred, therefore it resists reducing life to the lowest common denominator of capital. The value of human labor is in its responsibility to actively strive to preserve the fragile balance between humans, other forms of life, the earth, and the ancestral spirits—not in amassing wealth or producing material goods.

A Project of Death

Among Latin Americans, when an individual has great financial resources, they are said to *vivir bien* (to live well). But such a mode of living focuses on ideas of individual abundance and affluence with little consideration of the impact such wealth has on the environment and the community. The Indigenous concept of buen vivir highlights the importance of consuming only what one needs. The goal is not unfettered economic growth but sustenance for all. In other words, it goes beyond the horizon of normative economics through capital. The more I think about these dynamics, the more I am convinced that buen vivir stands on a different path than the pervasive structures of the Doctrine of Discovery—and the colonization and capitalism that accompany it.

The Doctrine of Discovery—a series of edicts that established a theological, political, and legal justification for European colonization and seizure of lands that were not inhabited by Christians—developed over time. By the middle of the fifteenth century, such edicts had become a legal mechanism that the Portuguese, who sought to invade the Canary Islands and North Africa around 1436, used to justify enslaving Africans. The Portuguese colonizers received "full and free permission" from Pope Nicholas V through the papal bull *Dum Diversas* (1452) to "invade, capture, and subjugate" the non-Christian inhabitants. Shaped by notions of European ethnoracial, civilizational, cultural, and religious superiority, the doctrine became the catalyst for the Western European military, genocidal, and colonizing project, through which Western Europeans (and eventually Americans) invaded and took possession of Indigenous lands around the world.

From a Western European perspective, the logic seemed flawless.

But from the perspective of what theologian Enrique Dussel calls "the underside of modernity," the Doctrine of Discovery paved the way for globalized market capitalism in its multiple expressions. Ideas of the commodification of bodies and of life itself—as well as the adoption of a racialized social evolutionary construction of societies—all stem from that doctrine.

The "imperial gaze," which saw the earth as the repository of quantifiable wealth (in capitalist terms) and was pervasive in European conquests, has contributed to rapacious attitudes today that view natural resources as freely available to provide and serve the needs of humans. The extraction of natural resources—such as minerals, oil, and precious stones—is the extreme manifestation of the doctrine's logic of the commodification of nature and epitomizes the radical qualitative separation between humanity and the rest of creation. This worldview runs counter to everything for which buen vivir stands. Capitalism enshrines the doctrine's attitudes of despoliation of nature behind a facade of progress, advancement, and modernity.

A Project of Life

In 1615, Quechua Peruvian Felipe Guaman Poma de Ayala wrote *El Primer Nueva Corónica y Buen Gobierno* (*The First New Chronicle and Good Government*), which he sent as a handwritten manuscript to King Philip III of Spain. After thirty years of research across South America, Guaman Poma concluded that the Incan empire and society were all-around *better* than the colonial rule imposed by the Spaniards, who had arrived in the Incan region in the 1530s. He bolstered his conclusions by identifying the ways Indigenous peoples were maltreated, and he detailed the hypocrisy of Europeans who did not live up to the standards of their own proclaimed religion—one that valued love of neighbor, peace, hospitality, and deep reverence for their creator God.

I would posit that not much has changed since then. Indigenous origin stories and cosmovisions continue to articulate their peoples' relationship with the existing world in similar ways—and continue to believe those understandings to be "better." Be they Guaraní, Quechua, Aymara, or Maya, among others, their understanding of the world and society are diametrically different from those the Europeans brought to the Americas.

Through the notion of buen vivir, these Indigenous communities challenge all of us to reconsider our attitudes toward each other, ancestral spirits, other peoples, and the world. They offer a radically alternative "life project" that stands against oppressive European-rooted systems steeped in the heritage of colonialism and capitalism (including racialized discrimination, hyper individualism, and unfettered contamination of the environment).

It could be said that the Doctrine of Discovery is actually part of a "death project" that perpetuates the radical disconnect between human groups and between humans and other living things and the earth. This death project requires military activity, violence against the environment, and the exploitation of other human groups to subsidize the extravagance of the few. Many refer to this "end of the world" time as the Anthropocene—a geologic era not only of human modification of the natural world, but one in which humans have the power to eradicate human life altogether.

In contrast, buen vivir emphasizes the radical interconnectedness and interdependence between all living things, as well as between human groups. The endgame is to work together and coexist to ensure the survival of the human community today and for seven generations to come. Attention to the logic of buen vivir enables the diagnosis of root causes for the impending doom, of which global warming is only a symptom.

As Lolita Chávez teaches, "We draw strength from many principles, including reciprocity ('you are me and I am you'). That gives us strength as women and this connection with life and the network that we all form. . . . So, as part of that mesh, we declare that we must have territories free of companies and free of violence against women, and that empowers us so that we can say that we are moving toward the full meaning of life." That's buen vivir.

Néstor Medina, a Pentecostal minister, taught at Emmanuel College of Victoria University in the University of Toronto when this appeared in the January 2021 issue of *Sojourners*.

Recentering Spirituality for People of Color
An Interview with Teresa P. Mateus

Da'Shawn Mosley

How the Mystic Soul Project is creating a space for activism, mysticism, and healing for people on the margins.

When Teresa P. Mateus attended gatherings on Christian contemplative spirituality, she often didn't see herself reflected in the spiritual practices "centered in whiteness" that she found emphasized there. She yearned for spiritual resources that drew on the experiences of people of color—and out of that yearning, the Mystic Soul Project was born.

Mateus is a graduate of the New York University School of Clinical Social Work and the Living School at the Center for Action and Contemplation and author (under the name Teresa B. Pasquale) of two books on recovery after trauma, including Sacred Wounds: A Path to Healing from Spiritual Trauma. *Da'Shawn Mosley, assistant editor of* Sojourners, *spoke with Mateus about how the Mystic Soul Project brings healing and spiritual nourishment to people on the margins.*—The Editors

SOJOURNERS: Tell us about the Mystic Soul Project.

TERESA MATEUS: Our basic mission is activism, mysticism, and healing centered around the life experiences of people of color. We create space for conversations, relationship building, practices, and other programming that have a people-of-color perspective and allow many to reclaim ancestral practices that have been abandoned or erased by Western traditions.

SOJOURNERS: How did the project get started?

MATEUS: The Mystic Soul Project was born from my deep yearning for a contemplative life into which I could integrate my identity as a person of color. I wondered how healing is inherent in our spirituality and how the action and activism that people of color do is grounded in their spirituality and healing, and I wanted space to explore those questions.

But gatherings on Christian contemplative spirituality are dominated by white, wealthy people who are baby boomers or older. That doesn't represent all the people yearning for contemplative spirituality. In speaking with other people of color, I realized that my deep yearning was more universal than I thought, because it's difficult to worship in dominant white spaces with spiritual practices centered in whiteness.

I thought about what people of color need from a conference. I realized that we go to a lot of places that help us with our brand, give us information, and train us and equip us to do things. But what would it be like to go to a conference that is mostly about nurturing and pouring into our soul? I thought about this and got to work with others to make the vision a reality. Since we have few examples of what it looks like to decolonize and deconstruct societal paradigms that overlook people of color, I spent a long time trying to figure out how to do that.

SOJOURNERS: What shaped your vision for these gatherings?

MATEUS: Some of the inspiration and permission to be focused on people of color and Indigenous traditions—in all of the meanings of "Indigenous"—came from the week I spent doing trauma care at Standing Rock. That environment was so crafted and curated as being unapologetically Lakota, unapologetically Indigenous, and adamant that marginalized voices would be heard and the call on people who weren't marginalized was to be quiet.

I had never been in a space where people did that firmly, but with love. And so, for me, that became something I wanted to do at our gatherings.

So, everyone who facilitated any piece of programming was a person of color. We had both a person-of-color and a non-person-of-color spirit-care team to provide attendees spiritual direction. We had a creative arts space that was all about projects that allowed people to express themselves, their identity, and their wholeness, and we also had programming, from morning to night each day, that focused on embodied healing: acupuncture, Reiki, and massage.

For our workshops, we had a rule of life, a tenet of co-teaching and co-learning. We believe there's not one person who has all the wisdom, but rather we're all carrying individual wisdom: How do we combine that knowledge and share it with each other?

At the conference, we also had a contemplative practice space, in which we did guided meditations and allowed time for people to just sit and be. We also held conversations, for people who are external processors and wanted that space.

But most of the conference was dedicated to nurturing the parts of ourselves—this especially pertains to people of color—that we forget to take care of.

SOJOURNERS: How were the attendees chosen?

MATEUS: We had a six-month application process, wanting to make sure that we were inviting people who were ready for what we wanted to do, because we intentionally wanted to deconstruct and decolonize paradigms of power and reorganize them to prioritize people of color.

We received 425 applications. I read every single one and realized that the application itself was having a profound effect on people, many of them saying things like, "Just finding this website and knowing that this conference is going to happen is the thing I've been waiting for my whole life." Even people as far away as New Zealand and Canada expressed that sentiment.

At the conference, elders—elders of color—said to me, "I have wanted a space like this to exist for so long." That was amazing to hear, that we were providing space for people to allow all the parts of their self to come together and not be suppressed.

SOJOURNERS: What obstacles have stood in the way of the Mystic Soul Project's growth?

MATEUS: Because of our focus on spirituality, activism, and healing, rather than just one of those areas, we connect to a multitude of spaces, but don't fit into any one of their quintessential boxes. That makes funding more difficult than if we were of a specific denomination, faith practice, or kind of activism.

Healing fits in the funding box for mental health, but because we're not providing exact, in-person counseling services, we don't necessarily fit into that box. And grants for activism are usually given based on what your campaign is, what your target is. There's not a widespread awareness yet that healing in movements is just as necessary as what the movements themselves are doing.

Also, the idea of reconnecting to traditions of your ancestry and letting go of Western traditions is fairly new. Many people are unaware that Western Christianity's initial function was demonizing practices that were ancestral to people of color—colonizing faith. They don't know that sometimes when they talk about decolonizing spaces and deconstructing white supremacy in the context of their Christian faith, their language is still language of colonization and still demonizes ancestral practices. Revealing that to people, so they will want to invest in deep examination of ancestral practices, is a lot of work.

SOJOURNERS: How does the Mystic Soul Project address intersectionality?

MATEUS: Trying to center the lives and ancestry of people who have been decentered and marginalized in multiple ways is maybe the hardest thing I've ever tried to do. In attempting this, my fellow organizers and I didn't get everything right. When you're trying to lift, create space for, and have sensitivities around people's diverse identities, there's constantly room to improve.

When we asked people to attend the conference, we made it clear that, besides being centered on people of color, we are also spiritually inclusive. We recognize the abundance of spiritual identities and encouraged attendees to not make assumptions that everyone else was Christian just because several Christians they recognized were in attendance. Whenever I mentioned God, I said, "The divine force that *I* call God," because that may not be indicative of other people's spirituality. The balance is being authentic to each of our specific traditions while also being invitational.

In addition to being multireligious, the Mystic Soul Project is also queer- and trans-inclusive and inclusive of the disability community. Before anyone arrived at the [January] conference, we were intent on addressing accessibility issues and making the bathrooms gender-neutral.

There's no space I can think of that prioritizes and lifts all those identities. There are places that are people-of-color centered but aren't purposefully queer- and trans-inclusive, and there are spaces that are queer- and trans-inclusive but there are barely any people of color involved with the space.

At least half of our board is queer. At the conference, we gave queer and trans people the floor to speak. To make sure that conference attendees were sensitized to gender identity, the name badges we provided them allowed them to select the gendered or gender-neutral pronouns they identified with and write down an alternative designation.

But despite all that, we have farther to go in our inclusion. There are lots of parts we need to expand to make the space inherently and authentically intersectional, not just an idea of intersectionality but rather lived and breathed.

SOJOURNERS: What's ahead for the project?

MATEUS: We've started a podcast and a virtual teaching series—a web series of various teachings but also conversations. We also want to build smaller community groups around the country, creating space for people to have dialogues about different ways of healing, spiritual connection, and activism and bring those things together in a people-of-color-centered way. Our next conference, in June 2019, will be space for people to meet face-to-face—wisdom is in community, the history, personhood, and fullness of everyone who shows up.

The night before our January gathering, we had an advance party in a school we were using as space for the conference; we called it "Mystic Soul Prom." It was just everyone dancing, having the prom they never got to have as themselves, in all their fullness.

Watching all these people of color dancing, having a 100-percent moment of joy, I thought, "This is it. This community is born." The community always existed, but its members just needed to find each other.

Da'Shawn Mosley was a *Sojourners* associate editor living in the Washington, D.C., metro area when this appeared in the December 2018 issue.

Five Things Christianity Can Learn from Buddhism

Christian Piatt

Could Christianity's future lie in Buddhism's past? This is a possibility that's been haunting me lately, but in a good way, I think.

One big critique, understandably, of postmodern views on Christian spirituality is that there's too much time and energy spent deconstructing old systems and ways of thinking that need to be torn down or reimagined, while lacking the same effort to build up something more helpful—more Christlike—in its place.

This is true, and I'm as guilty of it as anyone. In my current spiritual practices as part of the current year I'm calling "My Jesus Project," I'm trying to more fully understand what we mean when we talk about following Jesus. So it might seem strange to some that I would look to Buddhism for help in rebuilding my daily walk along the path of Christ.

Author and monastic Thich Nhat Hanh wrote a book years ago called *Living Buddha, Living Christ*, that had a profound impact on me. At the time, I was "A-B-C," or "anything but Christian." I had been thrown out of my church of origin for asking too many questions, and up to that point, I assumed there was no way I could ever associate myself with Jesus or the Gospel again. Thankfully—if surprisingly—it was a Buddhist monk who reintroduced me to Jesus.

In his book, he draws many parallels between the life, teaching, and practices of Jesus and those of Siddhartha Gautama, later known as The Buddha after achieving enlightenment. For Jesus, I imagine a similar experience of enlightenment coming to him during his monastic retreat into the desert. And as I seek my own moments of illumination during My Jesus Project, it occurs to me that Buddhism has much to teach us about where we might take Christianity in the twenty-first century.

No Ego

One of the greatest weaknesses of modern Christianity has been the focus on the individual. This comes more from our individualistic culture than from Christianity itself. Though we focus on personal (often translated as sexual) sin, the idea of sin within the Hebrew Bible was more corporate. There was more of an interdependent, tribal culture, and as such, so were the shortcomings. We've also focused too much on personal salvation or a "personal relationship with Jesus Christ," which has also led to such bastardized interpretations as the false gospel of personal prosperity.

In Buddhist practices, one must learn to let the self die, in a manner of speaking, in order to create a deeper, more meaningful relationship and interdependence with others and the rest of creation. This is actually more consistent with ancient Jewish and Christian thought than our modern, egocentric version of Christianity.

Seeking Wisdom, Not Knowledge

If you were like me growing up, you were taught to be "armed with the Word," which basically meant knowing your Bible inside and out—or at least just memorizing it—so you'd be ready to argue with anyone who refuted it in any way.

Meanwhile we didn't spend much, if any, time actually experiencing the "real world." Though our present culture values amassing a wealth of knowledge, or expertise, it actually does very little to prepare us to live in a Christlike way beyond the church walls.

Wisdom, unlike knowledge, comes as a byproduct of lived experience. Something happens, and as often as not, we screw up. Then we reflect, learn and change our attitudes or behaviors moving forward. Christianity, however, too often teaches us to entrench ourselves in self-righteousness, seeking instead to change others to be more like us. (God forbid we would be changed by someone who isn't a Christian.) But true wisdom means we learn and are affected by all of our experiences, and use that wisdom as an opportunity to do and be better in the future.

Right-Heartedness Over Right Belief

When someone joins a Christian church, or before they get baptized or commit their lives to Christ, we inevitably ask them with three telltale words: "DO YOU BELIEVE. . ." But Jesus didn't ask people what they believed, or to recite some creed before following him or going and doing for others what he did for them. He was more concerned with the nature of their hearts than any claim of belief.

This is where a fundamental tenet of Buddhism serves us very well. We're taught that right hearts lead to right thoughts, and this, in turn, leads to right action. But it all begins with the orientation of our hearts, how we see, receive and respond to the world. We're not sent out into the world so much to coerce people into like-thought; rather, we're charged with going out and offering ourselves fully and sacrificially in humble service to others, regardless of who they are, what they believe or what the result might be for us.

Impermanence

We seem to become pretty fixated on some false correlation between our faithfulness and the lifespan of our churches and denominations. We know we're doing God's work if our churches are full, budgets are met, and we can hand off a healthy institutional legacy to those who come after us. But Jesus preached the destruction of the temple not just to freak people out; he was warning them not to cling too tightly to all the trappings of religion around them that would inevitably crumble and fail.

We can learn much from the Buddhist artistic discipline of creating mandalas. These elaborate sand-art designs sometimes take weeks or more to make, with several monks attending to them many hours each day. And though our instinct is generally to preserve and even defend something beautiful, the mandala is intentionally destroyed not long after it is finished. The sand is returned to the earth and the only remaining impression of the mandala is in our consciousness. It's a humbling exercise in letting go—one from which we can learn a great deal.

Care for All Creation

We Christians have been greatly affected by the industrial revolution in ways that have negatively impacted our relationship with the rest of creation. This, combined with an overemphasis of disdain for our own bodies and sexual identities, has created a sense of disembodiment that also causes us to feel less interdependent on each other and less dependent on all of nature. The notion of dominionism falsely teaches within some Christian circles that the planet is ours to use as we please. And some even go so far as to suggest that anything we can do to help hasten the end times gets us that much closer to heralding God's kingdom on earth.

Buddhism, however, teaches simplicity, humility and intentional care for all of creation. Practices of mindfulness and humility help us loosen our grasp on personal desire and avail ourselves to the excesses and insensitivity of our habits. When we regain a healthier sense of our own places within a much larger, very delicate ecosystem, we not only treat our surroundings with more care; we treat ourselves with greater care as well.

Christian Piatt was author of *postChristian*, *Blood Doctrine*, and the *Banned Questions* book series when this appeared on sojo.net on April 16, 2015.

In Pursuit of Wholeness
An Interview with Cynthia Bourgeault

Bob Sabath

Spiritual teacher Cynthia Bourgeault seeks not only wisdom but also wholeness in her work and practice. As a modern-day mystic, she teaches countless Christians how to mine the streams of contemplative Christianity to foster spiritual and social transformation. Bourgeault—an Episcopal priest, author, and leader for various "wisdom schools"—is cultivating a new generation of Christians who can deeply develop their faith and sustain their work in the world. Sojourners' resident contemplative and web technologist Bob Sabath spoke with Bourgeault about why it is vital to integrate spirituality and prophetic witness.—The Editors

SOJOURNERS: What need is your vocation responding to in the world today?

CYNTHIA BOURGEAULT: I would say that I'm creating a bridge between contemplative Christianity and action. I bring forth some of the skills in the contemplative path to help avoid the usual pitfalls of burnout, violence, judgment, and hypocrisy, and also to bring forth some of the prophetic and compassionate skills in the action traditions to help contemplatives move beyond the sense that the domain of their wisdom is "inner" work. There really is no inner and outer: There's one world.

SOJOURNERS: Some people talk about the church needing three energies to really be the church: an inner, an outer, and a together—or spirituality, mission, and community. In my experience, churches and individuals major in one of these energies, minor in a second, and have a blind spot on the third. How can individuals and churches do a better job of holding these energies together?

BOURGEAULT: The reason why that map flies apart is because those three divisions are all at the same level. What is missing in Christianity is the real understanding that practice doesn't just mean people going inward to do their own little spiritual trip. It is a way of repatterning the whole physical, neurological, emotional, devotional animal so that it understands what it's doing.

The real inner map that's classically used—the tri-part division—is the exoteric, the mesoteric, and the esoteric. The exoteric is the threshold, the door, where you invite people in through the liturgy, tradition, and sacramental worship. The mesoteric level is about practice. It's where you begin to really develop an understanding of the inner and more-sophisticated heart transformation that lies behind the external practice. And then there is the esoteric level, which really happens when the exoteric portals are taken deep into a heart that's been awakened through mesoteric practice.

Community, which is really the important point, is the threshold for the oneness in the collective body of Christ. It will almost inevitably be saturated and infected with lower agendas—clinging ego esteem, affection programs, power, control—until the mesoteric level has kicked in to help people see what they're doing because of unidentified emotional and spiritual needs. The mesoteric takes the questions deeper, and it begins to till the soil for a whole different level of understanding, in which you see that these three things are organically intertwined. They can't be separated.

SOJOURNERS: What would you say to Christian social justice activists who see themselves primarily concerned with faith and action, who perhaps have had a difficult time working with the inner journey and almost see it as getting in the way?

BOURGEAULT: I'd say come back and see me in fifteen years. I don't think anybody ever becomes a prophet thinking that they may be wrong and the rest of the world is right. There's this real sense that, by virtue of my mantle as a "prophet," I have the moral high ground. I see what's wrong. I have to take it on myself to speak up about the ills and the excesses. Along with that, from the point of view of that mesoteric level, is identification. I'm very bound up in the energy of my role. I'm actually using that role as a source of motivation and that creates identification, which is a violence in its own right. It also quickly lands a person in burnout and anger, which are the basic shadow sides of social action. It's very hard for people to understand how to work like a Gandhi, like a Dag Hammarskjöld, or even like Jesus. The very zeal that impels us toward action also fatally skews it.

The shadow side of contemplative practice can be a quietism and a spiritual narcissism, a kind of premature oneness with God. But that's not where it's intended to go. I would say that everybody needs to sit down on the cushion of practice, whether their initial temperament is toward the more activist side or the more contemplative side, and to understand how each of these pillars holds the space for one another and for something new to begin.

SOJOURNERS: The media have been talking about the "nones," the increasing segment of young people and others who are checking "none of the above" as their religious affiliation. What might you say to them?

BOURGEAULT: I'd say, stay your course. For the past one hundred years, churches have been so reactionary, self-preoccupied, and stuck that the younger generation has passed them by. It's also quite true that the level of morality, ethical responsibility, and inclusiveness that's being struck in the culture at large is far higher than in the churches. My grandkids and most people I know don't have a problem with ordaining women or gay marriage. It's live and let live. There's a fundamental current of civility there. But the church is so pumped up on its own agendas that it seems compelled to defend them at the cost of its life.

There is a new kind of consciousness that's beginning to arise in critical mass nowadays that allows a significant number of people to think from the whole to the part. The shorthand we often use for it is non-dual thinking, which basically includes the capacity to see from a higher collectivity that doesn't sacrifice the part but can move from whole to part in a spontaneous engendering rhythm. You give up autonomy at one level in order to realize majesty at a higher level of collectivity. Jesus and Paul talked about it. Paul said we are all parts of the body of Christ—an intimation of that higher collectivity.

Kids growing up today are far more steeped in that and think globally and interconnectedly. More and more are able to sustain the "one universe, higher collectivity" vision.

I'm not invested in keeping alive old dinosaurs. What will survive in all the traditions is exactly what's shaping up now—the understanding and the unanimity—which is reached through the mesoteric and into the esoteric groups. The trappings of old religion survive, but they will survive only to the extent that they purify themselves of these dinosaur elements.

SOJOURNERS: Tell me about the "wisdom schools" that you have been doing for more than a decade. What makes them unique?

BOURGEAULT: They're a hybrid between traditional contemplative practice and self-awareness retreats, as it's come to us through the esoteric tradition. We roughly and loosely adopt the rule of St. Benedict. We look at prayer alone and together and work alone and together as a rhythm for establishing balance and harmony in whatever place you are in your life. You don't have to go to a monastery to do it.

We take these Benedictine experiences as our form. But what makes ours a little different is that we take the inner traditions of the West to that quadrant of work. How do we become consciously alive? How do we use every moment in our life as a moment to awaken to this different possibility, to this consciousness that's emerging, and to the things that block it inside us? It really brings this whole element of presence, inner observation, and three-bodied awareness that's been maintained in Christian practice but often without that dimension of conscious awareness.

SOJOURNERS: Can you tell me more about the Living School and what you hope to accomplish?

BOURGEAULT: Richard Rohr's original idea was this deep sense that we have a need for an "underground seminary." What he means by that is really what I call that mesoteric level of development: hands-on formation that allows people to connect the dots in their Christianity to truly carry forward the pattern of its master—love and compassion, feeding the poor and hungry, caring for our world.

In general, many seminaries have gotten co-opted to the point where they serve the institution. It's not rocket science to say that the institutional agendas are in variance with the gospel. As the institution and its official functions turn inward and become impacted in serving its own needs, people who are attuned to and empowered to listen to the cry of the world and who have a solid grounding in the scripture and the mystical traditions are not being tended.

The goal of the Living School is to form people cognitively in a responsible and responsive, gospel-based, mystically interpreted, non-dual, wisdom-rooted understanding of their own Christian tradition. And to root them in it formationally as well, because it's through the practices—such as meditation, chanting, and Lectio Divina—that the heart opens and can hear the cry of the world and respond to it without violence or self-righteousness. We're not into "lifelong learning" in the sense that people just come and take seminars. The whole idea is to create people who can do deeply grounded work, and not just be in reactive mode.

SOJOURNERS: What other people or places are doing work that encourages you?

BOURGEAULT: I continue to be deeply rooted in and grateful to the witness that comes through the Christian Benedictine tradition, particularly as it's exercised in two contemplative branches: The Camaldolese Benedictines and the Trappists. I still find that the whole tradition holds a stability and a compassion that water me very deeply. I'm also grateful to the witness of places such as Taizé and Iona, which are experimenting with the interface between monastic practice, prophetic witness, and beauty. So, these are my first line of defense.

I still come back to Quakerism, which has always insisted that the social and prophetic witness not be forgotten. Having gone to Quaker schools as a kid, I simply can't separate contemplation and action, because they're one. That was imprinted in me from the start. In my immediate sphere of action, that's what is closest to my heart.

Bob Sabath is a founding member of Sojourners—one of the seminarians at Trinity Evangelical Divinity School that began Sojourners with Jim Wallis in 1971. Bob lived with his wife Jackie in Mt. Rainier, Maryland, when this appeared in the February 2014 issue of *Sojourners*.

Led Out in Joy, with Rainbow Cookies and Fresca

Mihee Kim-Kort

This year, my church joined a loose network of other open and LGBTQ+ affirming churches in the area to host an ecumenical Pride service. We had an Agape Feast of rainbow cookies and Fresca, a pop-up choir singing about a new world, and a beautiful preacher in drag. Many of the festivities and gatherings throughout the city are hosted by Annapolis PRIDE whose mission is to "advocate for, empower, and celebrate the LGBTQ+ community in Anne Arundel County, Maryland, to live fully and authentically."

"To live fully and authentically." It's a phrase that resonates for me as someone who came into their queerness later in life. For a long time, the possibility of living fully and authentically felt just beyond my reach; I felt I was skimming the surface of my being and longed to be fully immersed—soaked and drenched—in who I am. But I was afraid. What would living authentically mean for my place in the world? As a second-generation Korean American who has long struggled to be seen and accepted, I wondered if being queer would foreclose this possibility.

I remember when Darnell Moore, author of *No Ashes in the Fire* and host of the new podcast *Being Seen* said the following words on Trevor Noah's *The Daily Show*: "Queerness is magic." Yes. I remember when I finally let this magic into my life, I confided in a friend: "I think I'm queer." They responded:

"Of course you are." Those words cracked open the universe for me and I saw myself in the light of a completely different sun. Instead of feeling like I was walking on eggshells, I felt I could step anywhere, and I wasn't beholden to the expectations of the world. I was less constrained by standards around gender and sexuality; some days I let myself feel more masculine, and other days I embraced my femininity. I started to feel and be more free, and even more deeply committed to my life because every day, out of joy, I would choose my spouse, my children, my community.

Queerness created a way for me to live fully and authentically. The language of "being out" has never fully resonated for me, and these days it seems to contribute to a binary, either-or approach to identity instead of the reality that people hold multiple truths. But for me, living fully and authentically was less about being fully out and more about being deeply human. It meant being God's beloved creation. And embracing my queerness was a way to embrace the gift of humanity.

I felt at home in my own skin and my own body. Embracing queerness made joy possible in new ways. Of course, I previously experienced moments of happiness and contentment, delight and pleasure, but through queerness I found the kind of joy that seems to fall out of the sky catching me off guard with the beautiful and ordinary wonders of this life: Growing a garden. Marching in a parade. Singing about the beauty of all God's creation. Watching the boats come in. Sometimes joy is like a shield that we clutch to our bodies as we take one step forward at a time, or at least try to simply hold our position. Sometimes joy can be so entangled with sorrow that we don't know where our hearts begin or end when we look at the ones we love.

Our local network of LGBTQ+ affirming churches has hosted storytelling and networking gatherings for the Annapolis community. Inspired by Julie Rodgers' biographical account in *Outlove: A Queer Christian Survival Story*, we called our first event “Outlove.” From Julie and others in our community, we heard both the hard and the good, the trauma and the recovery in stories of queer people of faith; we held space for all those who showed up looking for the healing that comes from liturgy, music, and the presence of community in this city. We called our most recent gathering “Outjoy,” this time lifting up the flourishing of queer people in our midst, and their stories of joy. Outjoy. I love this neologism and say it to myself sometimes, like an incantation, a prayer, an amen.

Outjoy. Once more, for me, being queer is less about being fully out and more about going out—being led out into the world to live and love, work and build something brave and beautiful with others. A while ago I had the words of Isaiah 55:12 tattooed on my back: “For you shall go *out in joy*, and be led back in peace.” This verse spoke to me of my love of the mountains, of the wilderness, and now, it’s also claiming the promise of my creatureliness, my holy wildness, and thus, my humanity, and the joy of that humanity. It’s right in the middle of my back, and I like to imagine it is perhaps a spot where the hand of the Holy Spirit might nudge me forward. She keeps me going, reminding me of the goodness of this strange life, this stunning world.

Mihee Kim-Kort was co-pastor with her spouse of First Presbyterian Church in Annapolis, Maryland, author of *Making Paper Cranes* and *Outside the Lines*, and coauthor of *Yoked* when this appeared on sojo.net on June 23, 2023.

Afterword

I had the honor of becoming Sojourners' second president in 2021, just as the organization and publication celebrated fifty years of "articulating the biblical call to social justice, inspiring hope and faith-rooted action." After a deep and extended process of discernment and consultation, we produced a strategic plan for the future of Sojourners, which centered around the theme of "building a faithful future." At the heart of our strategy is a recognition that one of Sojourners' central charisms is our commitment to spiritual renewal as part and parcel to putting faith in action for justice and peace. Integral to spiritual renewal is a combination of sabbath rest, contemplation, solitude, simplicity, and communal resilience.

I thought of Sojourners' commitment to spiritual renewal as I sat down to write this reflection. By their nature, anthologies necessarily look backward. Yet this book is not an exercise in navel gazing—far from it. Reflecting on and learning from work already completed, struggles previously lived, and crises navigated are in fact critical disciplines that directly impact how we live into the future. With this anthology, we explore Sojourners' firm conviction that successful faith-inspired action and movements for change require an active inner life; that we must endeavor to embody the change that we seek in the broken systems and structures of this world; and that we co-labor with God to make our life on earth look more like the reign of God to come. The "light for the way" that we've sought to share in this anthology can sustain the spirits of both individuals and of communities amid even the most dire and demoralizing times.

We're deeply grateful for the depth and breadth of our roots. Five decades of ministry have equipped us to envision and plan for what Sojourners will be for the next five decades and beyond. I hope that in reading this anthology, you've gotten some sense from the writings and themes we've chosen of the future we are building for Sojourners. It is a future that remains faithful to our history and witness while also becoming what we're called to be for today and for the uncertain times to come. The increasing threats of Christian nationalism and authoritarianism in the United States and around the world require a more resilient faith that is able to resist powers and principalities and prophetically imagine and build alternatives that are centered in justice, righteousness, and steadfast love. To that end, we know that we are called to find even bolder ways to speak truth to power, while also, where possible, to build bridges of understanding that enable transformational dialogue. We will want to ensure that Christians, alongside people of conscience and other faiths, are on the front lines of protecting and transforming a truly just, inclusive, and multi-racial democracy in the United States—in solidarity and conversation with similar struggles around the world.

Ultimately, what we seek is nothing less than finally realizing the moral vision that animated the twentieth century's civil rights movement—the vision of the Beloved Community. In other words, we seek to build a society in which neither punishment nor privilege is tied to race, ethnicity, gender, ableness, gender identity, sexual orientation, or anything else that has been used to create or enforce a hierarchy of human value. In the Beloved Community, everyone is equally valued and everyone is able to thrive.

We're eternally grateful that so many of you have sojourned with us this far. We are profoundly grateful for the future that we're building together rooted in simplicity, connection, and a tireless commitment to repair a broken world. Come join us.

—Adam Russell Taylor
President, Sojourners
www.sojo.net

Contributors

Julia Alvarez was the author of many books, including *Afterlife, How the García Girls Lost Their Accents*, and a picture book for young readers, *Already a Butterfly: A Meditation Story* when "(Mis)understanding the Spiritual Practice of Centering Prayer" appeared in the June 2020 issue of *Sojourners.*

Hannah Keziah Agustin was an opinion writer for the Spring 2024 Sojourners Journalism Cohort when "How a Week with Benedictine Sisters Made Me a Better Radical" appeared on sojo.net on July 30, 2024.

Rachel Hope Anderson was a resident fellow at the Center for Public Justice and director of Families Valued when the article "We Need Sabbath. In the United States, We Don't Trust Each Other Enough to Take It" appeared in the January 2022 issue of *Sojourners.*

Kat Armas a Cuban-American writer and podcaster from Miami, was the author of *Abuelita Faith: What Women on the Margins Teach Us About Wisdom, Persistence and Strength* when the article "Existing Intentionally with the Land" appeared on sojo.net on April 26, 2019.

Mitchell Atencio was senior associate news editor of sojo.net when the article "A Black Christian Approach to Veganism" appeared on sojo.net on April 2, 2024.

Margaret Atwood, author of *Dearly: New Poems* and *The Handmaid's Tale*, is an award-winning Canadian poet and novelist. Her article "What About the Meek?" appeared in the January 2015 issue of *Sojourners.*

Rose Marie Berger, author of *Who Killed Donté Manning?* and *Bending the Arch: Poems*, was senior editor of *Sojourners* magazine when the article "You Can't (Fully) Blame Your Distraction on Your Phone" appeared in the February/March 2023 issue.

Daniel Berrigan, SJ, priest, poet, and peace activist, was a *Sojourners* contributing editor. The article "The Marvelous Design" appeared in the December 1989 issue of *Sojourners.* © 2025 Daniel Berrigan Literary Trust (www.danielberrigan.org).

Walter Brueggemann was professor emeritus at Columbia Theological Seminary in Decatur, Georgia, when the article "What Would Jesus Buy?" appeared in the November 2007 issue of *Sojourners.*

William T. Cavanaugh was associate professor of theology at the University of St. Thomas in St. Paul, Minnesota, and author of *Theopolitical Imagination* (T&T Clark) when the article "When Enough Is Enough" appeared in the May 2005 issue of *Sojourners.*

Kaitlin Curtice is a Native American Christian author and speaker. As an enrolled member of the Potawatomi Citizen Band and someone who has grown up in the Christian faith, Kaitlin wrote on the intersection of Indigenous spirituality, faith in everyday life, and the church when the article "The Sacredness of the Earth as She Is" appeared on sojo.net on August 12, 2019.

Dianne D. Glave, author of *Rooted in the Earth,* was coordinator of diversity development for the Western Pennsylvania United Methodist Conference Center when the article "The Green Confessions of Nat Turner" appeared in the May 2016 issue of *Sojourners.* A version is also included in *Black Eco-Theology Through History: The African American Experience* (Routledge: Taylor & Francis Group).

Joshua Grace, a Polish American settler, was living with his family in Philadelphia, traditional land of the Lenni Lenape, when the article "My Church Came Together to Pay Off Each Member's Debt" appeared in the July 2019 issue of *Sojourners.*

Josina Guess was a *Sojourners* columnist and contributor to *Bigger Than Bravery: Black Resilience and Reclamation in a Time of Pandemic,* when the article "The Spiritual Satisfaction of Freely Gardening" appeared in the August 2023 issue.

Rosemarie Freeney Harding was co-founder and co-chair of the Veterans of Hope Project—a center for religion and democratic renewal at the Iliff School of Theology in Denver—and **Rachel Elizabeth Harding**, Rosemarie's daughter, was the project's executive director.

Their article "Radical Hospitality" appeared in the July-August 2003 issue of *Sojourners.*

Joyce Hollyday was *Sojourners* managing editor when the interview with Joan Chittister appeared in the June 1987 issue.

José Humphreys III was author of *Seeing Jesus in East Harlem: What Happens When Churches Show Up and Stay Put* and coauthor of *Ecosystems of Jubilee: Economic Ethics for the Neighborhood* (Zondervan) when the article "The Howard Thurman Question That Changed My Faith" appeared in the May 2022 issue of *Sojourners.*

Liz Cooledge Jenkins was the Seattle-based author of *Nice Churchy Patriarchy* when the article "Healing Grounds for the Earth—and for Christianity" appeared in the April 2023 issue of *Sojourners.*

Alexander Jusdanis was a writer with work in *The Outline* and *Dissent* when the article "How to Be Alone" appeared on sojo.net on June 22, 2020.

Céire Kealty holds a doctorate in theology from Villanova University, where she studied fashion theory, spirituality, and ethics. Her article "The Demon, the Desert, and the Wardrobe" appeared in the August 2022 issue of *Sojourners.*

Mihee Kim-Kort was co-pastor with her spouse of First Presbyterian Church in Annapolis, Maryland, author of *Making Paper Cranes* and *Outside the Lines*, and coauthor of *Yoked* when the article "Led Out in Joy, with Rainbow Cookies and Fresca" appeared on sojo.net on June 23, 2023.

Timothy McMahan King was chief strategy officer for Sojourners when the article "Five Simple Living Tips for Millennial Christians" appeared on sojo.net on November 18, 2014.

Chris La Tray is a Métis storyteller, a descendent of the Pembina Band of the mighty Red River of the North, and an enrolled member of the Little Shell Tribe of Chippewa Indians. He was author of the Substack newsletter "An Irritable Métis" when the article "My Métis People Blended Christianity with Their Beliefs. I Cannot" appeared in the December 2022 issue of *Sojourners.*

Laurel Mathewson was pastor of St. Luke's Episcopal Church in San Diego when the article "My Spiritual Director Told Me I Needed a

Silent Retreat" appeared in the April 2024 issue of *Sojourners*. Her article is adapted from *An Intimate Good: A Skeptical Christian Mystic in Conversation with Teresa of Ávila* (Whitaker House, 2024).

Ann B. McClenahan spent twenty years as an advertising and marketing professional before entering Harvard Divinity School, where she completed the Master of Divinity program in June 1999. "Lives of Compassion and Meaning" appeared in the July-August 2000 issue of *Sojourners*.

Seán McDonagh, SSC, is an Irish Columban missionary priest who worked for more than two decades in the Philippines. His book *To Care for the Earth* (1986) was one of the first theological books to address the ecological crisis. The article "Forty Shades of Green" appeared in the November 2014 issue of *Sojourners*.

Bill McKibben, founder of 350.org, was the author of *Oil and Honey: The Education of an Unlikely Activist* and a *Sojourners* contributing editor when the article "The Problem of Big and Small" appeared in the November 2014 issue.

Brian McLaren was founding pastor of Cedar Ridge Community Church in Spencerville, Maryland, and coauthor of *Adventures in Missing the Point: How the Culture-Controlled Church Neutered the Gospel* when the article "Consider the Turtles of the Field" appeared in the March 2004 issue of *Sojourners*.

Néstor Medina, a Pentecostal minister, taught at Emmanuel College of Victoria University in the University of Toronto when the article "Embracing a Millennia-Old Cosmovision" appeared in the January 2021 issue of *Sojourners*.

Jeania Ree V. Moore, a writer and United Methodist deacon, was a doctoral student in religious studies and African American studies at Yale University when the article "Rest Is Resistance, Too" appeared in the January 2021 issue of *Sojourners*.

Da'Shawn Mosley was a *Sojourners* associate editor living in the Washington, D.C., metro area when the interview "Recentering Spirituality for People of Color" appeared in the December 2018 issue.

Ched Myers, an activist theologian, had worked in social change movements for more than twenty years when the article "Jesus'

New Economy of Grace" appeared in the July-August 1998 issue of *Sojourners*. Myers, author of *Healing Affluenza and Resisting Plutocracy: Luke's Jesus and Sabbath Economics* (Fortress), co-directs Bartimaeus Cooperative Ministries (www.bcm-net.org) with his partner Elaine Enns in the Ventura River watershed of southern California.

Beth Norcross was founding director of the Center for Spirituality in Nature in Arlington, Virginia, and adjunct faculty at Wesley Theological Seminary in Washington, D.C., when the article "Eye on the Sparrow" appeared in the August 2012 issue of *Sojourners*.

Sandra Ovalle, a native of Mexico City, was director of campaigns and mobilizing at Sojourners when the article "Working Through to the Early Hours" appeared in the November 2021 issue.

Katherine Paterson is author of more than thirty books for young readers and a two-time Newbery and National Book Award winner. She was named the National Ambassador for Young People's Literature by the Librarian of Congress and served as an elder in the First Presbyterian Church of Barre, Vermont. Her article "The Power of Story" appeared in the May 2010 issue of *Sojourners*.

Christian Piatt was author of *postChristian*, *Blood Doctrine*, and the *Banned Questions* book series when the article "Five Things Christianity Can Learn from Buddhism" appeared on sojo.net on April 16, 2015.

Julie Polter was senior associate editor of *Sojourners* when the article "Why We Must Honor the Worker, Not Just the Work" appeared in the January-February 1997 issue.

Julian Davis Reid, a Chicago-based artist-theologian, was the founder of Notes of Rest, a spiritual formation ministry grounded in scripture and Black music that invites the body of Christ to receive God's gift of rest, when the article "All Is Calm" appeared in the December 2023 issue of *Sojourners*.

Richard Rohr, OFM, a Franciscan priest of the New Mexico Province, was founder of the Center for Action and Contemplation in Albuquerque when the article "Finding God in the Depths of Silence" appeared in the March 2013 issue of *Sojourners*.

Oisín Rowe (formerly Elisa Rowe), a writer and poet, was living in Boston when the article "I'm Agnostic. Here's Why I Went Back to Church" appeared on sojo.net on August 8, 2024.

Bob Sabath is a founding member of Sojourners—one of the seminarians at Trinity Evangelical Divinity School that began Sojourners with Jim Wallis in 1971. Bob lived with his wife Jackie in Mt. Rainier, Maryland, when the interview "In Pursuit of Wholeness" appeared in the February 2014 issue of *Sojourners.*

Nancy Sleeth, author of *Almost Amish: One Woman's Quest for a Slower, Simpler, More Sustainable Life,* was co-founder of the faith-based environmental nonprofit Blessed Earth when the article "Ten Ways to Live 'Almost Amish'" appeared on sojo.net on August 2, 2012.

Adam Russell Taylor, an ordained Baptist minister and author of *A More Perfect Union: A New Vision for Building the Beloved Community,* was president of Sojourners when the article "When Your Nation Is Stuck in a Spiritual Desert" appeared in the March 2020 issue of *Sojourners.*

J. Dana Trent was a graduate of Duke Divinity School, professor of World Religions, and author of *Dessert First: Preparing for Death While Savoring Life* when the article "Sabbath as Resistance" appeared in the June 2018 issue of *Sojourners.*

Sandi Villarreal was editor-in-chief of *Sojourners* when the article "Rest Is Holy, Not a Reward for the Productive" appeared on sojo.net on July 29, 2021.

Isaac S. Villegas was pastor of Chapel Hill (N.C.) Mennonite Fellowship and president of the governing board of the North Carolina Council of Churches when the article "Mutual Aid's Radical Christian Roots" appeared in the May 2022 issue of *Sojourners.*

Jim Wallis, a founding member of Sojourners, was editor-in-chief of *Sojourners* when the article "Longing for Incarnation" appeared in the December 1992 issue.

Rabbi Arthur Waskow, a leader of the movement for Jewish renewal and founder of The Shalom Center (theshalomcenter.org) in Philadelphia, traveled widely with his wife, Phyllis Berman, to speak, lead religious services, and offer Bible-based storytelling. The article

"Holy Economics" appeared in the September-October 1997 issue of *Sojourners.*

Valerie Weaver-Zercher was a contributing editor to *Sojourners* and editor of the thirtieth-anniversary edition of *Living More with Less* (Herald Press, 2010) when the article "Simple Living Becomes Sexy" appeared in the December 2010 issue of *Sojourners.*

Jonathan Wilson-Hartgrove, a preacher, author, and community cultivator, was the author most recently of *Strangers At My Door: A True Story of Finding Jesus in Unexpected Guests* (Convergent) when the article "Is a Contemplative Life Still Possible?" appeared on sojo.net on December 11, 2017.

Rabbi Dr. Shmuly Yanklowitz was the president and dean of the Valley Beit Midrash, the founder and president of Uri L'Tzedek, the founder and CEO of The Shamayim V'Aretz Institute, and the author of fourteen books on Jewish ethics when the article "The Sabbath" appeared on sojo.net on January 3, 2017.

Faith-Marie Zamblé, an artist and writer, was a MFA candidate in dramaturgy and dramatic criticism at the Yale School of Drama when the article "What Minimalism Lacks" appeared in the July 2018 issue of *Sojourners.*